ME DE TAFILET
Tafilet
Prov^ce de Touet
ou de Tuath
BARIE
de Sara
les Hadet
les ... Arabes
Lac au tour du quel il n'y a aucune habitation
les Esgue Arabes
ou PAYS
les Sobair Arabes
Puits
R. de Ticarte
ou de Tecort
Guargala ou Huerguela
Gadamis
ou Teorregu
Chaté ou Faisan
Desert de Nesisa
Desert d'Ighide
Arabes
On y trouve une grande quantité d'excellentes dates et du Sené.
LES LUMPTUNES
ou LES LEMTA
d'ou sont sortis les Morabitins nommez Almoravides par les Historiens.
Roudan Majalat
Desert de Hair ou
il y a des Puits de bonne eau
ou DESERT DE BARBARIE
Arcan
IGA, ZUENZIGA
DE SOUDAN
LES TERGA dont le pays est fort tempere et produit beaucoup d'herbes
Pays de Caour
les Hembrun Arabes
Desert des Lemptunes habité par une nation superbe et brutale
les Vahaye Arabes
s de Gogden
ait quelque fois 8. journées sans trouver de l'eau
Desert d'Azarud
par les eaux de pluie
Desert d'Agades
Desert de Canum
ou l'on recueille quantite de manne que l'on vend en cette Ville
de Ghir
Agdes ou Agades nommee par les Arabes Andegast
Canum ou Alkanem
ROYAUME DE CANUM ou d'ALKANEM
M. de Tauton ou il y a de bonnes mines de fer
Sahra Nisar
ROY^ME D'AGDES ou D'AGADES ou il vient de tres bon Sené
Deserts et passages dangereux et pleins de voleurs
MBUT
UCTOU
et de bon
Guguere
Desert de Tasar tres rude et tres Sec
Deghir
Seemara
NIGRITIE
Cabra
Ilayma
R^E DE CASSENA
ROYAUME DE ZEGZEG
R. DE ZANFARA
Lasara
Zanfara ou DE PHARAN
Germa
Berissa
Lac de Guarde
ou R^E DE GHANA
Alura
Semegda
Lac de Sigismis
les 2 Villes de Ghana
Niger fl.
Tirca
Ouangara ou Ghanara
R^E D'OUANGARA d'ou l'on tire de l'Or du Sene et des esclaves
YAUME GAGO
Timbu ou Tamby
R^E DE GUBER
Plaines Sablonneuses
Guber
Pays de Lamlem
Malel
Dau
Gago
ROYAUME DE BITO dont les habitans sont riches
ROYAU^ME DE TEMIAN dont les habitans sont a ce qu'on dit Antropophages
Desert de Zeu
R^E D'ULCAMI ou d'ULCUMA
ROYAUME DU GR. ARDRE
ROYAU^ME D'ISAGO
ROYAU^ME DE GABOU d'ou il vient du Jaspe et des esclaves
ROYAUME DE DAUMA
R. de Volte
Tafou
Joio
Bo
R^e de Jabou
Jabou
Oudobo
Ousoubou
OU
R^E DE JUDA
GUINEE proprement dite
le Gr^d Benin
R. Formosa
Corfo
ROYAUME DE BENIN
Xabier
Fort Anglois
Fort François
Quahou
Gr^d Popo R^e
AMBOU R^E
Aboura
Lampi R^e
Petit Popo R^e
Rade de Juda
Atambane
Agaton
Boudedou
Ouvere
R. Forcados
I. Forcados
Coloma
R^E D'OUVERE
Pays de Calbary
Rio del Rey
les Calbongos Peuples mechans et trompeurs ennemis des autres Calbongos leurs voisins
les Calbongos
Jamoer ou la Grande Riv. de los Camarones
R. de Volte
Christiansbourg
Petit Acara
Moco
Andoni
Krike
R. Ramos
C. Formosa
Fokke
R. Calbary ou R. Real
R. Calbary
Haute Terre d'Amboizes
Moniba
R. Moneba ou Tandagat
R. Barba ou Boura
Nassau
Corse
de la Mine
OLFE DE GUINÉE
les Isles d'Amboizes
Fort Portugais
I. de Fernand Po
Rio do Campo
DE S^T. THOMAS
Village
I. Branca
les 7. Montagnes
R. d'Angre ou Danger

GHANA

The Autobiography of Kwame Nkrumah

"WHOEVER you are holding me now in hand,
Without one thing all will be useless,
I give you fair warning before you attempt me further,
I am not what you supposed, but far different.

Who is he that would become my follower?
Who would sign himself a candidate for my affections?

The way is suspicious, the result uncertain, perhaps destructive,
You would have to give up all else, I alone would expect to be your sole and exclusive standard,
Your novitiate would even be long and exhausting,
The whole past theory of your life and all conformity to the lives around you would have to be abandon'd,

. . . . .

For it is not for what I have put into it that I have written this book,
Nor is it by reading it you will acquire it,
Nor do those know me best who admire me and vauntingly praise me,

. . . . .

For all is useless without that which you may guess at many times and not hit, that which I hinted at;
Therefore release me and depart on your way."

WALT WHITMAN

The Autobiography of Kwame Nkrumah

THOMAS NELSON & SONS

Edinburgh NEW YORK *Toronto*

SECOND PRINTING, OCTOBER, 1957

Library of Congress Catalog Card Number: 57–8425

Manufactured in the United States of America

To my mother

Acknowledgment

MY GRATEFUL THANKS are due to Erica Powell, my Personal Secretary to whom I dictated most of this book, for the many hours of her spare time she devoted to the compilation of the manuscript. Without her constant effort to persuade me to set aside a few minutes, whenever possible, for the writing of this book, and without her patience and industry the book would never have been completed for publication in so short a time.

List of Illustrations

LIST OF ILLUSTRATIONS

Contents

Preface

IN 1934 WHEN I APPLIED to the Dean for admission to Lincoln University, I quoted from Tennyson's *In Memoriam:*

So many worlds, so much to do,
So little done, such things to be.

This was to me then, as it still is today, an inspiration and a spur. It fired within me a determination to equip myself for the service of my country.

When I wrote that letter, however, I little knew that it would take ten years in America and two-and-a-half years in England, living almost as an exile, to prepare for the struggle that has so far engaged me and which, after nearly eight years, has almost been won.

Those years in America and England were years of sorrow and loneliness, poverty and hard work. But I have never regretted them because the background that they provided has helped me to formulate my philosophy of life and politics. At the end of my student days in America I was offered lectureships in several Negro universities, including Lincoln. This was certainly tempting; it promised an end to my struggle for existence, a pleasurable life without worry in an atmosphere that I had long felt to be a part of me. But I could not dismiss from my mind, in a matter of a few days, the flame of nationalism that had been fanned and kept alight for over ten years.

Independence for the Gold Coast was my aim. It was a colony and I have always regarded colonialism as the policy by which a foreign power binds territories to herself by political ties with the primary object of promoting her own economic advantage. No one need be surprised if this system has led to disturbances and political tension in many territories. There are few people who would not rid themselves of such domination if they could.

At this time I devoted much energy to the study of revolutionaries and their methods. Those who interested me most were Hannibal, Cromwell,

Napoleon, Lenin, Mazzini, Gandhi, Mussolini and Hitler. I found much of value to be gleaned and many ideas that were useful to me later in my own campaign against imperialism.

At first I could not understand how Gandhi's philosophy of non-violence could possibly be effective. It seemed to me to be utterly feeble and without hope of success. The solution of the colonial problem, as I saw it at that time, lay in armed rebellion. How is it possible, I asked my-self, for a revolution to succeed without arms and ammunition? After months of studying Gandhi's policy and watching the effect it had, I began to see that, when backed by a strong political organization it could be the solution to the colonial problem. In Jawaharlal Nehru's rise to power I recognized the success of one who, pledged to Socialism, was able to in-terpret Gandhi's philosophy in practical terms.

The Gold Coast revolt against colonialism is not a new thing. Its roots are deep. There was the Confederation of 1868 when certain chiefs came together to defend themselves not only against their tribal kin the Ashantis, but also against political encroachments from abroad. After the bond of 1844 which gave Britain trading rights the Gold Coast had come increas-ingly under her control.

The next great move of political cohesion and conscience was the for-mation of the Aborigines Rights Protection Society by chiefs and literate Africans with the object of defending Gold Coast land. When this col-lapsed because of an ever-widening rift between the chiefs and the edu-cated people, the latter, binding themselves together and supported by their educated brothers in other West African territories, established the National Congress of British West Africa. This was the first indication of West African nationalism. However, because it lacked the support of the masses, it disintegrated in 1930.

The vacuum that this left in Gold Coast politics was eventually filled by the formation of the United Gold Coast Convention by the merchant and lawyer class of the country. It was when I realized that this move-ment was doomed to failure because it ignored the interests of the masses, that I broke away in 1949 and formed the Convention People's Party.

I saw that the whole solution to this problem lay in political freedom for our people, for it is only when a people are politically free that other races can give them the respect that is due to them. It is impossible to talk of equality of races in any other terms. No people without a government of their own can expect to be treated on the same level as peoples of in-dependent sovereign states. It is far better to be free to govern or mis-govern yourself than to be governed by anybody else.

The formation of the C.P.P. coincided with a political reawakening among the workers and young people of the country. Ex-servicemen who had taken part in the Second World War returned to the Gold Coast dissatisfied with their position after having been given the chance of comparing their lot with that of other peoples, and they were prepared to take any line which would better their conditions. There was a general dissatisfaction with the British colonial policy that had been adopted until that time, especially the policy of indirect rule which so encouraged tribal feudalism. Again, the Russian revolution and its aftermath had left its mark by spreading ideas of workers' solidarity, trade union movements, freedom and independence. Events in Asia also added a glow to the political awakening.

The C.P.P. was not merely a mass movement. Mass movements are well and good but they cannot act with purpose unless they are led and guided by a vanguard political party. And when the time comes for a ruling power to accord self-government it will do so more willingly if it can hand over to a properly constituted political party with a majority backing rather than to a revolutionary nationalist movement. Rallying round me all those who genuinely wished for progress I resisted both the opportunist element and the reactionary forces and sought to establish the C.P.P. as the democratic instrument of the people's will and aspirations. We were freely elected to power in 1951. Three years later, and again in 1956, the same confidence was shown by the country.

The first objective then is political independence, for which I believe the organization itself must take two forms. First there is the period of "positive action"—a combination of non-violent methods with effective and disciplined political action. At this stage open conflict with the existing colonial regime is inevitable and this is a test of strength for the organization. Since it is marked by non-violence and since the forces of might are on the side of colonial power, there is little chance of complete success in this period.

The second stage is one of "tactical action," a sort of contest of wits. From now on the movement must make its ideology clear and convincing. The ideology of my Party may be formulated as follows: no race, no people, no nation can exist freely and be respected at home and abroad without political freedom.

Once this freedom is gained, a greater task comes into view. All dependent territories are backward in education, in science, in agriculture, and in industry. The economic independence that should follow and maintain political independence demands every effort from the people, a total mobilization of brain and manpower resources. What other countries have taken three hundred years or more to achieve, a once dependent territory must try to accomplish in a generation if it is to survive. Unless it is, as it were, "jet-propelled," it will lag behind and thus risk everything for which it has fought.

Capitalism is too complicated a system for a newly independent nation. Hence the need for a socialistic society. But even a system based on social justice and a democratic constitution may need backing up, during the period following independence, by emergency measures of a totalitarian kind. Without discipline true freedom can not survive. In any event the basis must be a loyal, honest, hard-working and responsible civil service on which the party in power can rely. Armed forces must also be consolidated for defense.

In this way self-government was won for the Gold Coast. Its independence will be incomplete, however, unless it is linked up with the liberation of other territories in Africa. Ghana now joins the independent states of Egypt, Ethiopia, Liberia, Libya, Morocco and Tunisia. Elsewhere the continent is ruled by no less than six European powers.

Our example must inspire and strengthen those who are still under foreign domination. In this belief I have written the story of my life so far. If in any way it helps the cause of freedom it will have served its purpose.

KWAME NKRUMAH

Accra, October 1956

GHANA

The Autobiography of Kwame Nkrumah

Birth and Early Childhood

THE ONLY CERTAIN FACTS ABOUT MY BIRTH APPEAR TO BE THAT I was born in the village of Nkroful in Nzima around midday on a Saturday in mid-September.

Nzima lies in the extreme southwest of the Gold Coast and covers an area of about a thousand square miles stretching from the river Ankobra on the east to the river Tano and its lagoons on the west. It has a population of about 100,000 people, and was known to Europeans for many years as Apollonia because it was on the feast day of St. Apollo that the white man first set foot in Nzima Land.

In the outlying areas of the Gold Coast nobody bothered to record the dates of births, marriages and deaths, as is the custom of the western world. Such happenings were remarkable only because they provided a cause for celebration. By tribal custom it was enough for a mother to assess the age of her child by calculating the number of national festivals that had been celebrated since its birth. In most cases, however, even this was unknown as nobody was concerned very much with age: time did not count in those peaceful communities.

The national festival of Nzima is called Kuntum. According to my mother's calculations, forty-four Kuntums have taken place since I was born, which makes the year of my birth 1912.

On the other hand, the priest who later baptized me into the Roman Catholic Church recorded my birth date as the 21st September, 1909. Although this was a mere guess on his part, I have always used this date on official documents, not so much because I believed in its accuracy, but in so far as officialdom was concerned, it was the line of least resistance. It was not until recently that I came to realize how near the mark this guess must have been.

For recently, I spent a short holiday in Nzima and had the opportunity to revisit some of my childhood haunts and to recapture the past. As I sat with some friends on the sea shore at Half Assini our eyes were drawn to the rusty bulk of the *Bakana,* a cargo boat owned by the British and African Steam Navigation Company, which had been wrecked in 1913 and had come to rest on the sea shore.

The *Bakana* had been a landmark to me for so long that I had never realized how significant a part it could play in throwing light on my age. One of my friends asked what had happened and whether I could remember it. Although I was certainly no older than three or four years at the time, I can well remember being told the story of this disaster.

On the night of the August 27, 1913, the *Bakana,* on her way back from Nigeria to the United Kingdom with a cargo of oil, got into difficulties in a particularly heavy surf between Dixcove and Half Assini. In spite of the efforts of the captain to turn the ship seawards, the *Bakana* was dragged by a strong current nearer and nearer towards the shallow water until she got her propeller embedded into about five feet of sand. Two ships, the *Ebani* and the *Warri* arrived the following day and endeavored to pull her out to sea, but the *Bakana* refused to be moved. The master, Captain Richard Williams, then gave orders to abandon ship and the crew and a few passengers were safely lowered into surf boats and taken ashore. The surf boat which was carrying the captain to one of the other ships capsized and he was drowned. His body was recovered from the sea and he was buried in the center of Half Assini where, although the gravestone has suffered by erosion, it is still possible to read most of the inscription: "Captain Richard Williams, who perished in the surf, August 28th 1913, aged 40 years. . . . Day dawns and the shadows flee away."

I remember more vividly, however, the stories that circulated about the cause of the shipwreck, how the god of the river Ama Azule, wishing to visit his goddess of the neighboring river Awianialuanu, had planned this disaster in order that he should have a boat at his command. The superstition surrounding this was strengthened by the fact that the *Bakana* was actually dragged nearer and nearer to the mouth of the river until eventually she reached its mouth where she lies today, firmly embedded in the sand, a huge rusty shell, deserted by all but the surf that destroyed her, but majestic still in spite of her torn and broken masts and her gaping hull.

In fact the people of Half Assini still say that they see the lights of a ship—believed to be the *Bakana*—as she sets out to sea at night and ploughs her way to Awianialuanu.

My mother confirms the fact that I was a small boy at the time and that the event occurred some little time after she had brought me from Nkroful to live with my father in Half Assini. Assuming, therefore, that the year of my birth was 1909, the Saturday nearest to the middle of September in that year was the 18th. It seems likely, therefore, that I was born on Saturday, September 18, 1909.

On the day I was born there was much celebration and beating of drums in the village of Nkroful, not, I may say, in honor of my birth, but in connection with the funeral rites of my father's mother who had died a short while before. As far as the Akan tribe (of which the Nzimas form a part) is concerned, funerals receive far greater honors than do births and marriages. The ceremonial rites performed for the dead presuppose the existence of a supernatural world and, in order that they should not be deprived of comfort there, they are buried with gold, clothes and other necessities of life. Continuous wailing is carried out by relatives and friends of the deceased person, and this goes on throughout the first few days. During the third week following the death a ceremony of remembrance of all the deceased members of the clan is held, commencing with the offering of libations to the spirits and ending in the small hours of the morning with games, dancing and feasting.

And so, on that particular day in Nkroful, my birth was of very little interest to the villagers. I am told, however, that there was a good deal of commotion going on where I was, for I apparently took so long to show any signs of life that my mother had given up all interest in me as she believed me to be dead. This is not as heartless as it may sound for it is a strong belief among the Akans that if a mother mourns the death of her child she will become sterile, and this, to an African woman, is the worst thing that can befall her.

But my female relatives, having dragged themselves away from the funeral celebrations, would not give in so easily. They were determined to put life into me and proceeded to make as much noise as they could with cymbals and other instruments, at the same time jolting me about—and even stuffing a banana into my mouth in an effort to make me cough and so draw breath. They finally succeeded in arousing my interest and, their job completed, handed me back to my anxious mother, a yelling and kicking Saturday's child.

Great importance is attached by the Akans to the day of the week on which a child is born for this determines his Platonic soul. They believe that a man is possessed of three souls: the blood soul (or *moyga*) transmitted by the female and considered synonymous with the clan, the *ntoro* which is transmitted by the male, and the *okra,* or Platonic soul. In order that there should be no mistake about the *okra,* a specific name is given to the child according to the day of the week on which he was born. A male child born on Sunday is called Kwesi; if born on Monday he receives the name Kojo. And so on. For a boy born on Saturday the name is Kwame. There are other superstitions surrounding a child's birth. For instance, the first child is supposed to be less bright, the third child to be precocious and incorrigible, the ninth child to bring good luck and the tenth child to bring misfortune. Sometimes the fear of bad luck at the birth of a tenth child is so strong that the infant may be smothered at birth or during early infancy.

Whilst I can claim to fall into the pattern of things by being born on a Saturday and bearing the name of Kwame, it is surely disheartening that I was the first and only child of my mother and am therefore, according to tradition, less bright than average!

Nkroful is a typical West African village composed of mud and wattle houses and bamboo compounds. The ground is high and stony leading down via a steep escarpment to a stream on one side and to a swampy lake on the other. I lived there with my mother until I was nearly three years old when we left to join my father who was a goldsmith in Half Assini.

Half Assini is about fifty miles from Nkroful and is on the borders of the French Ivory Coast and the Gold Coast. It is unfortunate for Nzimas that the Tano river and the Ayi Lagoon into which it drains were taken to form the boundary between the two countries, for the people had set up fishing villages all round the lake and are now divided. This has caused much discontent because of customs authorities, language and other barriers, which they encounter when crossing from one side to the other.

Many of them still travel on foot the longer way round by the sea shore. Every day, even today, it is a common sight to see women with the heaviest of loads on their heads set off at a trotting pace on their seven-hour journey. And when they arrive at their destination they are still trotting! In these days it is also quite a common thing to see trucks travelling by this route, but this can only be done when the tide is low.

There were no trucks in the days of my childhood, indeed there were not even proper roads, and when I left Nkroful with my mother it was necessary to make the journey to Half Assini on foot, travelling through Esiama and along the sea shore. This took nearly three days and we had to spend two nights in the villages en route. At other times when we used to journey into the bush together and we could not complete our journey in one day, we would sleep out in the open forest. I remember helping my mother to collect pieces of wood and dead leaves in order to make a fire to keep wild animals away. I had no fears of such things myself; like all small children I had complete confidence in my mother.

And she was a most worthy and vigilant protector. Although she allowed me a lot of freedom and I never felt myself tied to her apron strings, she was always at hand when I needed her and she had a knack of knowing my wants without either of us speaking a word. She never seemed to use her voice to command; there was something about her presence, her quiet, decisive movements, that placed her above most people and gave her a natural leadership.

My father was a man of strong character, extremely kind and very proud of his children. Although I was probably one of the most willful and naughtiest of children, I can never remember his lifting a finger against me. As a matter of fact I can only remember my mother beating me really hard on one occasion. That was when, because I couldn't get my own way about something, I spat into a pan of stew that was being prepared for the family meal.

We were a large family, for, although I was the only child of my mother and father, my father had quite a number of children by other wives whom he married by native custom. Polygamy was quite legal and even today it is quite in order for a man to have as many wives as he can afford. In fact, the more wives a man can keep the greater is his social position. However unconventional and unsatisfactory this way of life may appear to those who are confirmed monogamists, and without in any way trying to defend my own sex, it is a frequently accepted fact that man is naturally polygamous. All the African has done is to recognize this fact and to legalize, or to make socially acceptable, a thing which has been done and will doubtless continue to be done by man as long as he exists. It is interesting to note that divorce in this polygamous community is negligible compared with countries practising monogamy, especially when divorce can be obtained to much more easily than in a monogamous society. For a marriage can be brought to an end for any of the following reasons: adultery, barrenness or impotency, as the case may be, drunkenness, sexual incompatibility, the quarrelsome nature of the woman, unharmonious relationship with a mother-in-law, and discovery of marriage within one's own clan.

All members of a clan are considered to be blood relations and if a marriage takes place between two of the members, it is believed that the whole clan will be visited by the wrath of the gods. In my parent's case, for instance, both were of the same tribe, but my father was of the Asona clan and my mother was from the Anonas. As heredity is governed by the matrilineal line, I belong not to my father's clan, as would be the case in Western marriages, but to my mother's. My father's line decends through the eldest son of his sister, a member of the Asona clan.

Apart from our immediate family, which consisted of about fourteen people in all, there always seemed to be relatives staying with us and our little compound was usually full of people. It is a custom among Africans that any relative, however distant the relationship may be, can at any time arrive at your home and remain under your roof as long as he wants. Nobody questions his arrival, how long he intends staying, or his eventual departure. This hospitality is sometimes very much abused, for if one member of the family does well for himself he usually finds his compound filled to capacity with men and women, all claiming some distant kinship, and all prepared to live at his expense until the money runs out.

My family lived together very peaceably and I can remember very few quarrels. The women of the house used to take turns each week to cook the meals and look after my father and at the same time they either worked in the fields or did some petty trading in order to supplement the family income. It was a wonderful life for us children with nothing to do but play around all day. Our playground was vast and varied, for we had the sea, the lagoon and the thrill of unexplored bush all within easy reach.

But we had no toys. I remember one of our playmates, whose father had some money, one day produced a child's bicycle and was to be found daily pedaling it up and down the beach. We were extremely envious of him and longed to be allowed to ride it, but he was very possessive and rarely let the thing out of his sight. Today, however, it is he who may be envious of other people, for his father died and left the family not only penniless, but also quite unequipped to make livings for themselves.

It was probably this bicycle that inspired my half-brothers to build one of a sort out of two iron hoops that they found. What I remember most about that incident is the way they treated me almost as a mascot and something rather sacred. Although they all wanted to sit on the contraption and be the first to try it out, it was me they placed on the seat, holding me firmly in case I should come to harm.

Looking back on the kindness and consideration with which they always treated me, I sometimes wonder whether they did not in their heart of hearts regard me as a spoilt little brat. Probably they were so afraid that I would run home screaming to my mother, whom they held in high rgard, that they were careful to give me no cause for complaint. Certainly my mother rarely denied me anything and doubtless I took advantage of this, but I believe that she tried to make her affection too obvious because whenever she was serving our meals, she always gave me mine last. I insisted on sleeping in her bed until, of my own free will, I decided to join my half-brothers, and I remember how I used to be angry when my father came to sleep in our bed and I insisted on sleeping between them. Several times he tried to explain to me that he was married to my mother, but I told him that I also was married to her and that it was my job to protect her.

Unlike most growing children, I was very rarely ready for my food. In fact my mother used to get worried because of the trouble she had in forcing me to eat. She discovered that I would sometimes wake up hungry in the night and so she formed the habit of putting some baked plantain under my pillow so that if I woke at any time through hunger, I could eat this and go back to sleep. I very rarely ate a meal during the day and only returned from my games in the evening to eat the food that had been prepared. My parents never complained about this and once they realized that I was flourishing in spite of my small and irregular meals, they ceased to worry.

Although there were plenty of children with whom I could play, my happiest hours were spent alone. I used to wander off on my own for hours on end quietly observing the birds and the lesser animals of the forest and listening to their numerous and varied calls. Sometimes, however, I was not content merely to sit and watch them; I wanted to touch and caress them. It was not long, therefore, before I devised a means of trapping them—not to kill but to bring home as pets. Many times I returned with a squirrel, a bird, a rat or a land crab. On one occasion I remember refusing to go with my mother on a journey unless she allowed me to take a pet bird along with me. Clutching the small cage against my body I suppose I either smothered the poor thing or else killed it with fright. Anyhow, we had not gone more than five miles when I suddenly discovered that my precious bird was dead. This caused me so much distress that my mother was unable to console me and there was no alternative but to return home.

I had heard many stories about ghosts, for such things are a very real part of tribal society. Instead of being afraid of these tales, however, I remember sitting and wishing that I could die simply because I should then rank among those privileged souls who could pass through walls and closed doors, sit among groups of people unobserved and make a general nuisance of themselves!

I do not know whether this longing for things supernatural indicated psychic power, but my mother has many times related the following incident which occurred one day, when, strapped to her back in the normal manner of a young African child, I was travelling with her on one of our frequent journeys together. It happened that she had to wade through a stream on the way and, as we neared the center, I suddenly cried out in excitement that I was standing on a fish. Although startled by my sudden and noisy outburst, my mother was even more surprised when she discovered to her utter amazement that she had actually trapped a fish with one of her feet. It ended happily, for she managed to catch it and we had it for dinner that evening.

To strangers I must have appeared a strange and difficult child. Few would have believed that the small boy who kept himself in the background with his finger in his mouth or who would make himself scarce for hours on end, could, when roused, spit fire like a machine gun and use every limb and finger nail in defending his idea of justice. Two men in particular ran away from me in horror.

The first was a policeman who, in the course of his duty, reprimanded one of my half-brothers for doing some kind of mischief on the beach. As he grabbed hold of my brother's arm I was indignant and began to pound him with sand at such a rate and with such force that he let his victim go and ran away. He reported the matter to my father and I received a severe telling off, but I was sure I could detect a twinkle of amusement in my father's eyes.

The second man was in love with one of my half-sisters and came to our compound to ask her hand in marriage. At first I did not understand who he was or what he had come for until in the general excitement someone explained to me that he had come to take my sister away in marriage. I yelled and screamed like one possessed and kicked at the poor love-sick man until he was forced to run from the compound!

I soon learned, however, that life for a growing boy was not all play; at least, not for boys with parents like mine. Although my mother had never had the benefit of formal education herself, she was determined that I should be sent to school at the earliest opportunity. My father, probably due to my mother's persuasive power, was strongly in favor of this also. Even though I could often get around my father, I knew that once my mother's mind had been made up there was nothing I could do about it.

I found my first day at school so disappointing that I ran away determined never to return. But my mother turned a deaf ear to my raging protests and quietly but determinedly dragged me by the arm each morning and deposited me in the schoolroom. Eventually I realized that I had lost the battle and decided that as I was going to be forced to stay there, I might as well get to like it and do what I could to learn something. To my surprise I soon found that I enjoyed my lessons and looked forward to going to school, even though we lived in fear and trembling of the teacher because of his firm and active belief in the adage "Spare the rod and spoil the child." I disliked being forced to do things against my will, for I had not been accustomed to it, and I used to think what a wonderful paradise school would be if we were left in peace to do our studies without the presence of the schoolmaster.

All the various grades were housed in one room and the master used to teach a class at a time. It must have been a hard job for him, and we did nothing to ease his lot. Luckily I was keen on learning, so keen, in fact, that soon my only dread was that my father might one day be unable to afford the school fees, which at that time amounted to threepence a month. Because of this I started rearing a few chickens which I sold for sixpence each. By this means I could not only help to meet the school fees, but I had money to buy books as well. In addition, any fears about my father's poverty were guite unfounded because I can never remember him denying any of us anything we asked and he was particularly generous where I was concerned.

One thing in particular stands out in my mind during my early schooldays, probably because it was my first lesson in discipline. We were not fond of the teacher because of his frequent use of the stick, often we thought without just cause. One day we learned that an inspector was coming to the school and immediately saw our chance of getting our revenge on the master. We got together and decided to play truant for the whole day during the inspector's visit. My one regret was that I was not able to see the expression on the inspector's face when he found an empty classroom or, better still, the look of horror and amazement on the face of the teacher. It must certainly have caused him much embarrassment, but the following morning he got the last laugh, for, as soon as we showed our faces, he was waiting for us with his stick. We were each stripped naked and given twenty-four lashes on our bare bottoms. This hurt so much that for the next three days I was quite unable to sit down at my school desk. But whatever injury this caused to my body and my pride, I knew well enough that I had deserved it. And from that day I have always learnt to accept punishment that I feel I have justly earned, however humiliating this may be.

At about this time I came under the influence of a Roman Catholic priest, a German called George Fischer. This large and well disciplined man seemed to take a liking to me and he did much to help me in my studies. In fact he became almost my guardian during my early school days and so relieved my parents of most of the responsibility with regard to my primary education. My father was not at all religious but my mother was converted to the Catholic faith and it was through her and Father Fischer that I was also baptized into the Roman Catholic Church.

In those days I took my religion seriously and was very often to be found serving at Mass. As I grew older, however, the strict discipline of Roman Catholicism stifled me. It was not that I became any less religious but rather that I sought freedom in the worship of and communion with my God, for my God is a very personal God and can only be reached direct. I do not find the need of, in fact I resent, the intervention of a third party in such a personal matter. Today I am a nondenominational Christian and a Marxist socialist and I have not found any contradiction between the two.

Probably it was the same fear that my aspirations might be held in check by the Roman Catholic Church that made me also afraid of getting myself tied up with women. In those days my fear of women was beyond all understanding. I remember there used to be a young girl who lived a short way from my home and she used to wait for hours in a little lane dividing our compound from the next one. If I happened to come out into the lane she used to approach me and try to start a conversation with me. When she saw that I simply stared at her like a frightened animal, she probably thought I was shy and so she bravely whispered to me that she loved me. I was horrified and abused her as if she had hurt me. I rushed in and told my mother of the wickedness of the girl. My mother laughed and said, "You should be flattered, my boy. What is wrong with somebody being fond of you?"

The girl was persistent in her advances and she started bringing tempting dishes of food which she gave to my mother for me to eat. As soon as I knew that this girl had provided the food, I refused to eat any of it; it was days before my mother could persuade me to eat anything.

I have never outgrown that feeling towards women. It is not fear today, but something deeper. Perhaps it is a dread of being trapped, of having my freedom taken away, or being in some way overpowered. And I have the same feelings about money and organized and obligatory religion. All three of them represent to my mind something that should play a very minor part in a man's life, for once any of them get the upper hand, man becomes a slave and his personality is crushed.

Perhaps if I had heeded the passionate words of the girl in the lane I would have been content to spend the rest of my days with her in Half Assini, teaching at the local school or following in my father's trade. But things didn't work out that way.

Achimota and Teaching Days

AFTER EIGHT YEARS AT THE ELEMENTARY SCHOOL, I BECAME A pupil-teacher for one year at Half Assini. I suppose I must have been about seventeen at the time; anyhow, I was not very big because I can well remember having to stand on a box in order to write on the blackboard.

In 1926 the Principal of the Government Training College in Accra visited the school where I was teaching and, when he saw the work I was doing, he was sufficiently impressed to recommend that I should go to his college to train as a teacher.

This marks a turning point in my life for in the following year I came to his college, a raw youth bewildered at first by city life and, like most boys who leave home for boarding school, thoroughly homesick. Half Assini, with its roads of sand like tracks in the desert, seemed far preferable to the traffic, the crowded streets and the noise of Accra.

There was also the usual ragging and bullying of freshmen to be gone through. This seemed to last a long time until one day, when I was wondering whether education was really worth the misery of it all, one of my persecutors began to talk to me as if I was one of them. I had apparently passed the test. After that I was dragged in to rag my successors and realized that my initiation was complete.

This year brought sadness when I received a message that my father had died. He had developed a large sore on one of his feet which became steadily worse. My mother, in search of a cure, took him away to a nearby village, but after about two months blood poisoning set in and within a very short time he was dead.

I got permission from the Principal of the college to go home and left immediately. But the roads were not as they are now and the journey took several days, so that by the time I arrived my father was already buried.

The death of my father was a great tragedy to me. Apart from the void that it left in our family circle, it also broke up the home. According to our custom, when a man dies his wife and children become the responsibility of his successor and they automatically move to the house of the deceased man's next of kin. And so my mother left Half Assini and went to live with my uncle at the mouth of the Ankobra river.

About this time the Prince of Wales College at Achimota was officially opened by the Governor, Sir Gordon Guggisberg, before a large and colorful gathering of chiefs and government officials. Among the chiefs was the Kumasihene, the notorious ruler of Ashanti who had earlier been deported to the Seychelles by the Governor because of alleged participation in human sacrifices.

But the figure to whom all Africans looked that day was Dr. Kwegyir Aggrey, assistant vice-principal and the first African member of the staff. To me he seemed the most remarkable man that I had ever met and I had the deepest affection for him. He possessed intense vitality and enthusiasm and a most infectious laugh that seemed to bubble up from his heart, and he was a very great orator. It was through him that my nationalism was first aroused. He was extremely proud of his color but was strongly opposed to racial segregation in any form and, although he could understand Marcus Garvey's principle of "Africa for the Africans," he never hesitated to attack this principle. He believed conditions should be such that the black and white races should work together. Co-operation between the black and white peoples was the key note of his message and the essence of his mission, and he used to expound this by saying: "You can play a tune of sorts on the white keys, and you can play a tune of sorts on the black keys, but for harmony you must use both the black and the white."

But I could not, even at that time, accept this idea of Aggrey's as

Aggrey House, 1929. I am seated first on the left in the middle row

The Nzima Literature Society

As a teacher at Axim

As a student in America

On the eve of my departure from London
for the Gold Coast in October, 1947

With my mother and Ackah Watson soon after my return to the Gold Coast

Showing how I used to parcel up the sheets of toilet paper to get them out of prison to Gbedemah

IMPortant

Dear Kob.

I have read the draft of the Manifesto. It is a good ~~work~~ done and much labour has been ~~put~~ expended on it. You and Lamptey deserve my congratulation for such comprehensive document.

However, it is too elaborate to serve as a Manifesto for an election Campaign; that of an election campaign should be short, brief, simple direct, popular and

Photostatic copy of a message I sent to Gbedemah from prison, written on a sheet of toilet paper

My release from prison

My journey from prison

The day I came out of jail, *l.* to *r.* Komla Gbedemah, Kojo Botsio, myself and Tommy Hutton-Mills—all "ex-prison graduates"

The 1951–54 Cabinet (*l.* to *r.*) T. Hutton-Mills, K. A. Gbedemah, J. A. Braimah, R. Saloway, K. Botsio, His Excellency the Governor, myself, R. Armitage, A. Casely-Hayford, P. Branigan, Ansah Koi

Members of the 1951–54 Legislative Assembly

Part of the Academic Procession at Lincoln University Commencement Day, June 5, 1951, when I received the Honorary Degree of Doctor of Laws. (*l.* to *r.*) Kojo Botsio, myself, Dr. W. H. Johnson, and Dr. Horace M. Bond, President of Lincoln

President Horace Mann Bond, of Lincoln University, confers the Honorary Degree of Doctor of Laws on the Prime Minister, June 5, 1951

Receiving my Seal of Office as Prime Minister from His Excellency the Governor, Sir Charles Arden-Clarke, in 1952

being practicable, for I maintained that such harmony can only exist when the black race is treated as equal with the white race; that only a free and independent people—a people with a government of their own—can claim equality, racial or otherwise, with another people.

At the beginning of the rainy season, in April or May, the training college closed down for vacations. I had been so busy adjusting myself to my new life that I had not been able to look around for a means of earning any money. On account of this I could not go home to Half Assini but had to stay on in the college and do what I could to earn my living until term began again. In the evening after the college had broken up, I was standing in the deserted art auditorium talking with two other students, who had also been forced to stay behind, when Aggrey suddenly walked in. He was brimming over with life and excited about his leave which he was spending in England and America. He stayed and joked with us for a time and then, just as he was about to leave us, his mood became serious as he said, "Brothers, pray for me. So far I have been able to make you hungry but I have not been able to satisfy your hunger. Pray for me that when I come back I may satisfy your hunger." But he never came back to us and those were the last words we ever heard him utter. After visiting England he went to New York where he became suddenly ill. A week later the news flashed to Accra that Aggrey was dead.

The sudden shock of this news, followed by the gradual realization that I had lost for ever the guidance of this great man, sapped everything from me and I was quite unable to eat for at least three days. But it was during this period that I made the discovery that even on an empty stomach I seemed to have more than enough energy to carry on with my studies. This realization proved invaluable in later years in America and England when, through poverty, I had to carry on without food—to carry on not only with my studies, but also with the work which I had to do in vacations in order to earn money for my university fees.

It was because of my great admiration for Aggrey, both as a man and a scholar, that I first formed the idea of furthering my studies in the United States of America. My plan was to finish the teacher training course, return to teaching for five years and endeavor to save the necessary passage money.

The Accra Training College became part of the Prince of Wales College in 1928. The principal was the Reverend A. G. Fraser, who, with Guggisberg and Aggrey, had played a major role in establishing the college. As a first year student I did not come under his direct teaching, but all of us drew much inspiration and encouragement from his Sunday evening sermons. He is the only one of that great triumvirate who is still alive.

We were the first batch of students to be trained at Achimota as teachers. I thought myself very fortunate because as teacher-trainees we lived side by side with the secondary school students and we were therefore able to exchange ideas and learn from one another. In return for being able to pick up a little Latin and higher mathematics in the hope of being able to sit for the London matriculation examination later on, I endeavored to impress the secondary students with my knowledge of educational psychology and other subjects outside their curriculum.

Although I was desperately keen on learning as much as could be crammed into my head, I never became a swot or a bookworm. Friendships came easily and I was keen on sports. We had a Cingalese sports trainer who was not only an excellent trainer, but also a charming man, and under his guidance I trained religiously over short distances and ran in the intercollegiate sports in the 100, 220 and 440 yards. I discovered that sportsmanship was a vital part in a man's character, which led me to realize the importance of encouraging sport in the development of a nation.

But I could not bring myself to say the same for drill. How I hated having to get up at five-thirty in the morning and turn out on the courtyard for a route march! I used to arrive feeling, and no doubt looking, half asleep. But this didn't last long. Soon we were shaken to attention by loud roars from a massive figure which must have weighed all of three hundred pounds—our drill master. I could never keep in step, a thing which used to annoy the man beyond measure, and my legs were constantly being jolted into position by the shocks and tremors of his thunderous voice. The only light relief to this hour of torture was to watch him giving orders as we stood at ease. His stomach was so large that every time he bellowed it moved up and down with the vibrations. This tickled me so much that I had a hard job to prevent myself laughing aloud.

It was my housemaster who probably had the most to contend with as far as I was concerned and it was not surprising that he labelled me "an impossible chap." To such a keen disciplinarian, I must have been a hard person to bear. It was not so much that I was unwilling to abide by the rules and regulations, in fact I tried desperately hard to do so, but throughout my life I have always found it most difficult to detach myself from anything in which I have become engrossed. A most annoying restriction was the roll call at six each Sunday evening which was followed by a service in chapel. It was essential that every student should be present for roll call or have a pretty good reason for absenting himself.

In Aggrey House our housemaster was just about as strict as it was possible to be and the words with which he slated us were like whiplashes. It was because of my fear of having to come up face to face with him and endure these cutting remarks that I would move heaven and earth in order not to be late for roll call. But once it didn't work out. I had borrowed somebody's bicycle to go to Accra and was on the way back at breakneck speed, when a small girl rushed out into the road in front of me. I braked and swerved and threw myself off the machine. The child had fallen in a heap in the road and was screaming with fright, but I had luckily avoided hurting her. However, I couldn't leave her in the road screaming, so I took her to her mother and left my last two shillings with her as a peace offering.

I found that I was badly bruised and my knee was grazed and bleeding, but, remembering the all-important roll call, I hobbled to my bicycle, remounted with some difficulty and rode on as fast as my raw and aching limbs would allow me. Of course it was well after six o'clock when I arrived at Achimota and, as everyone was then in chapel, I rushed up to my bed and got into it as quickly as possible, my ears keenly tuned for footsteps and my heart banging like a door knocker.

Immediately chapel was over, the housemaster lost no time in making his way to my dormitory. I told him I felt ill and tried my best to look it, but he was not easy to convince. He went away and fetched the doctor who, after finding that my temperature was normal, was about to pronounce me as bogus, when I displayed my cuts and bruises. Grudgingly they allowed me to stay where I was and I got away with a few scathing remarks from the housemaster and a large plot of ground to weed.

I spent a lot of my spare time at Achimota weeding and gardening. In fact I and my contemporaries were for the most part responsible for the appearance of the grounds as they are today. In those days the ground was covered with virgin bush and it took many hours of real work to clear it. Some of us used to do this during vacations also, when we were given a shilling a day for our labors. It was the only way I could remain on the college site.

During my third year at Achimota I became interested in amateur dramatics and played the title role in a house play called "Kofi Goes Abroad." This was the story of a student who went to England to study medicine, and the difficulties he encountered with the witch doctors when he returned to his country to practice. The rivalry between them came to the test when a witch doctor failed to cure a man who was sick with a fever. They sent for the young Kofi to see whether he would have any better luck. Of course he cured the man to the delight of everyone and proved to the people that his scientific knowledge could outwit superstition and witchcraft.

I took a great interest in tribal drumming and Asafu dancing, both of which I enjoyed and carried out with reasonable skill. The Fanti and Nzima elements at the college got together and formed the Asafu Company and we spent many evenings entertaining ourselves and anybody else who cared to watch us.

In spite of a full and active life, we did not neglect religion. By the time I arrived at Achimota, however, I was already forming my own ideas on this subject as against those set down by the Roman Catholic Church. I believed strongly that churchgoing should be a matter of conscience and should not be obligatory and I very soon began to cut the regular church services. It caused the usual repercussions among those who were supervising our religious lives, and I was very promptly summoned before the Bishop, who warned me against my unorthodox ways. I told him quite honestly that those were my convictions but that I would give the matter deeper thought. So, even though I was rarely to be found at Mass, I observed a regular silent hour in the dormitory and thus exasperated my friends because during those periods I would neither talk nor listen to what they were saying.

In spite of my bad example both as a man of discipline and as a man of religion, I was made a prefect during my senior year. I found no difficulty in carrying out the various tasks that this promotion called for, because I had never had trouble in dealing with people and found that they were invariably co-operative and ready to do as I asked. By this time, however, I was becoming increasingly interested in speech-making. This began soon after Aggrey died when a few of us got together and formed the Aggrey Students' Society in his memory. The Society acted as a forum for speech-making and members used to prepare lectures and deliver them to the other members of the Society. Eventually this became a debating society. I thoroughly enjoyed these debates and could never resist taking the side of the minority group, whether I agreed with their view or not, because it prolonged the debate and gave me a chance to express views that I would otherwise never have thought of. I discovered that at whatever disadvantage I began, I usually ended up winning the day, frequently converting many of my opponents to the point of view that I had conveniently supported. Although this was only a kind of game with me then, it turned out to be my most valuable discovery. Without this "gift of the gab," my battle would have been lost from the very beginning and my whole struggle would have been in vain.

Perhaps I carried my love of debating outside the confines of the Aggrey Students' Society and into the classrooms, for I can remember on more than one occasion being reminded by my Method teacher, Mr. Herbert (now Lord Hemingford), that I was at Achimota "to be taught and not to teach." Twenty years later when I had occasion to address the University College students at Achimota, I was surprised to find that Mr. Herbert had returned, after years of absence, to resume his teaching there. When I had concluded my talk (which was entitled "The Political Philosophy of Plato"), he came to congratulate me but added, with a touch of humor, that although he had to admit that he had taught me and that what he had just heard was no doubt the result of the foundation he had given me, he wanted to make it quite clear that he was in no way responsible for the political ideas which I had expressed!

Looking back on Achimota days I realize that they were among my happiest, probably because they were the last days of leisure I have ever enjoyed—days when I could read, without fear of being disturbed, the book that interested me most; have long discussions with my friends on an endless variety of topics; or wander through the woods surrounding the college, alone with my thoughts.

I graduated in 1930 and the time came for me to leave Achimota. With the lines of our farewell hymn, "Forty Days And Forty Nights," still on my lips, I sadly left the college walls. My student days were over, for the time being at any rate, and the struggle to further my education and somehow to earn the means with which to do this lay immediately ahead. I was determined and confident, but my heart was heavy and as I looked towards the college it seemed as though a large stone was lodged in my throat.

I pulled myself together. This was not the time for sentiment. There was much work to be done and I had to maintain myself at the same time.

In spite of disagreement with the Bishop when at the college, I was given a job as primary school teacher at the Roman Catholic Junior School at Elmina where I taught Lower Class One. Although I had been trained in kindergarten teaching, this was my first experience of teaching children for any length of time, and I was surprised and touched to discover how attached they became to me. After school was over they were never keen to leave me and I usually found myself with two or three of them curled up in my bed at night. At first their mothers used to come round, worried and wondering where they had gone, but as soon as they knew they were with me, they were quite pleased to leave them.

In the hope of bettering the lot of the teacher, I used much of my spare time at Elmina to help found the Teachers' Association there. I felt that if such an association were formed it would be the first step towards improving their status as teachers, supplying them with the means of airing some of their grievances and getting them remedied by the authorities.

A year later I was promoted head teacher of the Roman Catholic

Junior School at Axim. While I was there I took a private course to prepare myself for the London Matriculation, but later failed the examinations in Latin and mathematics. Nevertheless it was good experience and stood me in good stead when I had to pass through the freshmen year at Lincoln. When I was not studying, my spare time was devoted to forming the Nzima Literature Association, which is still functioning today, and also a number of literary societies in the Axim area. It was through this work that I met Mr. S. R. Wood who was then Secretary of the National Congress of British West Africa. This rare character first introduced me to politics. He knew more about Gold Coast political history than any other person I have ever met and we had many long conversations together. I told him I was determined to get to America. He supported the idea wholeheartedly and wrote me a testimonial, which I still possess, to help me gain admission to Lincoln University in Pennsylvania.

After two years in Axim, I went to teach at the Roman Catholic Seminary at Amissano near Elmina. This was a new institution and it was the first time that the Roman Catholic Church had established such a place in this country to train its own clergy. It was an honor to be the first teacher of the Gold Coast appointed to train these young men in their preliminary studies for the great vocation. Certainly, I thought, I must have been forgiven my religious waywardness at Achimota. Maybe it was felt that here was the surest way of attracting a straying sheep back to the fold, and in a way it was right. For, as a teacher of these young novices, I too had to observe the strict rules of the seminary and my life at Amissano was quiet and lonely. But, unlike the discipline that I had always kicked against, I subjected myself to this so readily that it became almost enjoyable. It may have been the effect of living closely confined in such a religious atmosphere that changed my feelings, but it was certainly during this period at the seminary that I regained the religious fervor to such an extent that I seriously formed the idea of taking the vocation of priesthood myself. I wanted to be a member of the Jesuit Order and the idea lingered with me for a whole year. Eventually, however, the old desire to be up and doing, to further my education, and to proceed to America in order to do this, got the better of me and I felt that the walls of the seminary would enclose me for life if I didn't soon take action.

My nationalism was also revived at about that time through the writings in his own newspaper, the *African Morning Post,* of Nnamdi Azikiwe, a Nigerian from Onitsha. Azikiwe, who later became the first Prime Minister of Eastern Nigeria, was himself a graduate from an American university, and when I had first met him after he had addressed a meeting of the Gold Coast Teachers' Association some years earlier in Accra, I had been greatly impressed by him and had been more determined than ever to go to America.

While Azikiwe was busy championing the cause of the new nationalism in the country, Wallace Johnson, a Sierra Leonean, established himself as the first labor organizer in West Africa by forming the Youth League. Unfortunately the two of them became involved in a sedition case over an article written by Johnson and published by Azikiwe in the *African Morning Post* in 1936 called "Has the African a God?" They appealed to the West African Court of Appeal and later to the Privy Council, but when both appeals were dismissed, they returned to their respective countries. The words contained in this article which formed the basis of the charge for sedition were as follows:

"Personally, I believe the European has a god in whom he believes and whom he is representing in his churches all over Africa. He believes in the god whose name is spelt Deceit. He believes in the god whose law is 'Ye strong, you must weaken the weak. Ye "civilised" Europeans, you must civilise the barbarous Africans with machine guns. Ye Christian Europeans, you must "Christianise" the pagan Africans with bombs, poison gases etc!'

"In the Colonies the Europeans believe in the god that commands 'Ye Administrators, make Sedition Bill to keep the African gagged, make Deportation Ordinance to send the Africans to exile whenever they dare to question your authority.'

" 'Make an Ordinance to grab his money so that he cannot stand economically. Make Levy Bill to force him to pay taxes for the importation of unemployed Europeans to serve as Stool Treasurers. Send detectives to stay around the house of any African who is nationally conscious and who is agitating for national independence and if possible round him up in "criminal frame up" so that he could be kept behind the bars.' "

Although the article was seditious under Gold Coast law, it was at least an attempt to arouse the nationalism of the Gold Coast people at that time, and what is of greater importance, it made the Europeans aware that the Africans were not blind to all that was going on; it was the first warning puff of smoke that a fire had been lit, a fire that would prove impossible to extinguish.

America

Early in 1935 I realized that more decisive efforts would be needed if I was ever to get to the United States. Although I saved every penny I could lay hands on there was still not enough to pay for a passage. Then I thought of a relative who might help, a man who had moved years ago to Lagos in Nigeria.

To Lagos I went. Rather than dip into my precious savings to meet the cost of transport, I decided to stow away on a boat which was leaving Axim for Lagos. Mingling with the crew, I slipped on board and stayed down with the firemen for the whole of the voyage, sharing their food and the extreme discomfort and heat of the boiler room. It was my first experience at sea and I was violently sick the whole time. Consequently when I arrived in Lagos I looked like nothing on earth. Unwashed, unshaven and with tattered clothing I certainly looked as if I had worked my passage, and no questions were asked when I got off the boat at Lagos.

It would have been unthinkable to visit anyone in such a filthy condition. There was nothing for it but to go to the market and buy a new pair of flannels and a shirt. Hiding behind the mass of clothing on the market stall, I hurriedly changed and emerged looking a more respectable being. It was not until I arrived at my relative's house, however, that I was able to wash and shave.

I spent several days here, for my host had many questions to ask about our relations and friends. When the time came for me to leave he kindly gave me money to supplement my savings, and also paid my passage back to Axim. I thanked him in high spirits; my trip to America was at last becoming a reality.

Some months before, I had successfully applied to Lincoln University for admission, but only one or two close friends, with whom I stayed, knew of my plans. Now I strove to complete my arrangements. As there was no American Consul in the Gold Coast at the time I should have to travel first to the United Kingdom to obtain a U.S. visa. Thanks to my kinsman's generosity I had one hundred pounds. To this the Chief of Nsaeum, another relative, added fifty pounds, out of which I paid for a third-class passage from Takoradi to Liverpool. Within a month of my return from Lagos everything was in order and I waited impatiently for the day of departure.

My joy was overshadowed, however, by the thought of having to break the news to my mother. I knew how much I meant to her and how deeply she would grieve over my going. Accordingly I went home and stayed with her for a few days but it was not until the night before I was due to leave that I had the courage to tell her. She was obviously very shocked but showed no sign of grief and we sat up talking the whole night through. I cannot recall all we discussed during those hours, but I remember very clearly my mother listing carefully all that I should do and all that I should avoid whilst I was away. She also related in detail the history of my ancestors, of the chief Aduku Addaie, the first of my forebears to settle in Nzima centuries ago, whose sister Nwia gave birth to my matrilineal line. She also told me of my claim to two stools or chieftaincies in the country, those of Nsaeum in Wassaw Fiase and Dadieso in Aowin. I took notes of all that she told me and always carried them with me until one day I lost them in a New York subway.

The following morning I packed my few possessions into the canoe which was to take me across the Ankobra river on the first stage of my journey to Takoradi. As I looked upriver where the swirling muddy waters disappeared among a mass of jungly growth, I saw the women and children of the village standing knee-deep in the water unconcernedly bathing or washing clothes. At this peaceful picture of African rural life, I felt my first pang of homesickness. I took a deep breath and forced myself to smile as I came back up the bank to say a final goodbye to my mother. Then I saw that she was in tears. In spite of trying so hard to hide her feelings this final parting proved to be too much. With tears in my own eyes I told her that if she would rather I stayed behind she had only to say so. She stood and looked at me for a few minutes. "It cannot be helped," she said, "may God and your ancestors guide you."

And so, with very heavy hearts, we waved goodbye, little knowing that it would be twelve years before we saw each other again.

I boarded the motor vessel *Apapa* at Takoradi and was shown into a third-class cabin. In these strange surroundings I felt desperately alone and sat on my bunk close to tears. But as providence would have it, looking suddenly on the bed I saw a telegram. When I opened the envelope I found it was from Nnamdi Azikiwe and read: "Goodbye. Remember to trust in God and in yourself." These few words, so well timed, at once cheered me. I began to count my blessings and to remind myself that this, after all, was the beginning of all that I had planned and saved for.

The journey was uneventful except for one quite unforgettable experience. I had struck up an acquaintance with an Indian passenger, and when we arrived at the Canary Islands he invited me to go ashore and take a look at Las Palmas, the capital. I accepted gladly and together we went into the town. Not knowing anything of life outside my native country I followed him in all innocence into a building which looked like a hotel. We sat down at a table and, although I only wanted a glass of water—which was all I ever drank—he insisted on ordering beer from an old woman who was hovering about in the shadows. The beer arrived and was immediately followed by two elegant Spanish girls in negligees. I kept my eyes glued to the table legs and prayed that they would hurry up with their business and vanish as quickly as they had come. But to my utter horror and embarrassment one of them came over, planted herself on my knee and began stroking my hair and generally enveloping me with her limbs. I had only seen white women from a distance and the fact that one of them should approach me at such uncomfortably close quarters completely unnerved me. I uttered a cry, jumped up, spilling both the woman and the beer on to the floor and ran as fast as my trembling legs would carry me back to the ship. My Indian friend found this so amusing that he never ceased to laugh about it for the rest of the trip.

On arrival in Liverpool I was met by the agent of George Grant, a Nzima timber merchant. I stayed in a hotel for the first week then I travelled up to London in order to have my passport visaed for the United States. Bewildered and very much out of my depth I began to wonder if it would not be better to give the whole thing up and return home. But just as I was feeling particularly depressed about the future, I heard an excited newspaper boy shouting something unintelligible as he grabbed a bundle of the latest editions from a truck, and on the placard I read: "MUSSOLINI INVADES ETHIOPIA." That was all I needed. At that moment it was almost as if the whole of London had suddenly declared war on me personally. For the next few minutes I could do nothing but glare at each impassive face wondering if those people could possibly realize the wickedness of colonialism, and praying that the day might come when I could play my part in bringing about the downfall of such a system. My nationalism surged to the fore; I was ready and willing to go through hell itself, if need be, in order to achieve my object.

When I returned to Liverpool the timber agent invited me to stay with him and his wife, and they were both so hospitable and welcoming, that I began to feel less bitter. I was also learning that the ways of the Western World were very different from those of my country. One evening as we were talking over a meal the woman said to her husband: "Oh, don't be silly!" My eyebrows shot up in surprise and I waited, anxious and embarrassed, for the man's rebuke. But he took not the slightest offense and carried on talking. In Africa I dread to think what would have happened to the woman who told her husband not to be silly. Such a statement could have been used at that time as grounds for divorce. Today, of course, with the influence of the West, our women say pretty well what they are thinking without reserve and their husbands have had to resign themselves to it.

After a fortnight's stay in Liverpool, I set sail for the United States in one of the boats of the Cunard White Star Line. This trip was very much better than my previous one from Takoradi to Liverpool because I made several friends. One of them, a young Dutchman, who was going out to finish his theological studies at

Harvard Divinity School, remained a good friend of mine the whole time that he was in America. Once we went to a service at the Abyssinian Church in New York, one of the biggest Negro churches that I have ever known. On that Sunday the church was so packed with people that we could not get inside and we had to go to an annex adjoining the main building where another Negro minister was preaching. Acting in a most dramatic fashion he began to tell us the story of how Jesus carried the cross to Calvary. After some time the women in the congregation were completely overawed and began to weep and to shout: "It is Jesus! Have mercy! Hallelujah!" There must have been as much noise in that church as from the crowds in Jerusalem centuries before.

It was very embarrassing. Here was a European witnessing a most undignified Negro service. As we left the church I tried to apologize but he seemed surprised at this and said, with all sincerity, that it was the most beautiful thing he had seen so far in any church. If other denominations introduced something like it, he added, they might have a greater following. It was my turn to be astonished and I believe it was this young man who got me interested in theology.

I arrived in New York towards the end of October. London and Liverpool had prepared me for America, otherwise I think the shock of New York after the peace and quiet of my native land would have finished me. I stood openmouthed at what I saw. There was so much going on that it was a job to focus my eyes on anything for long enough to find out what it was. I was conscious of being hemmed in by the most gigantic buildings, so high that surely they must pierce the heavens; of being jostled about by the never-ending crowd; of being hooted at by what seemed like a hundred impatient drivers every time I thought about crossing the road. But somehow I felt neither lonely nor afraid, for there was an air of suspense, of excitement and gaiety and I felt rather as if I had wandered on to the stage during the performance of some revue.

I knew nobody in New York but had been corresponding with a Sierra Leonean who had graduated from Lincoln University. He was not expecting me so I called a taxi and directed the driver to the address in Harlem that he had given me in his last letter. Luckily he was in and he made me very welcome. I felt immediately at home in Harlem and found it difficult to believe that this was not Accra. I would have been very happy to stay there longer but two days was all that I could spare. I was already nearly two months behind schedule, the school year had begun and I was in a hurry to get to Lincoln and begin my studies. I had written to the Dean, both from the Gold Coast and again from Liverpool, explaining the delays but I could not feel secure until I presented myself and was admitted.

Lincoln University, founded in 1854, was the first institution in the United States to give highter education to Negroes and to train these students for service and leadership within the Negro population of the States. The idea and its achievements were the direct result of the inspired efforts of the Reverend John Miller Dickey, a Presbyterian minister, and his Quaker wife, Sarah Cresson Dickey.

When I arrived at Lincoln I had only the equivalent of forty pounds in my pocket, a second-class teacher's certificate and a letter of introduction from Mr. S. R. Wood. I went to the Dean and explained my financial difficulties, that forty pounds was all the money I possessed but that I was prepared to work my way through College. He did not take readily to this—no doubt he had heard the same tale too many times before—but as the only alternative was to ship me back to the Gold Coast and as he was too kindhearted to resort to such a measure, he accepted me.

I was put on probation, on the understanding that if I did well in the forthcoming examination I would be allowed to enter the Freshman Class. It was a challenge because I was two months behind the rest of the students but after much hard work I sat for the examination and was awarded a scholarship. Lincoln was small; competition for places was severe and it was made very clear to us all that there was no room for slackers. There was accommodation for only about two hundred students and so, if anyone dropped consistently much below the second grade, he was asked to leave in order to make room for the next and possibly more conscientious applicant on the waiting list. When a student was classified as Grade One or Grade Two he was awarded a scholarship which meant that each semester a certain amount of money was allowed him by the university for his fees. Luckily I always made the first or second grade and so, during the whole of my time at Lincoln, I was helped by scholarship money.

Although this paid only part of my expenses, it was of vital importance to me.

There were two opportunities of earning money which were open to scholarship holders only. We could act as library assistants and also wait in the dining hall. As it happened the work in the library was a great pleasure to me, but in any case there was not a job, however distasteful, that I would not have attempted at that time.

I found another profitable occupation later on when our sociology and economics lecturer gave us a lot of private reading to do from which we had to make reports. Many of the students made very heavy weather of these reports and grudged having to spend their spare time writing them up. So, ever on the lookout for means to line my pockets, I undertook to write the reports for them at a dollar a time. In this way I raised quite a few dollars towards my out-of-pocket expenses.

I was still very interested in speech-making and during my first year took part in the Freshman oratorical contest where I gained second place and won a gold medal. Unfortunately this medal was later taken from me as a souvenir by one of the many girls whom I knew but with whom I could spend very little time. Another girl relieved me of my fraternity pin. This was a mark of membership of the Phi Beta Sigma Fraternity of Lincoln, the motto of which is "Culture for Service and Service for Humanity." It was a source of wonder to me that, after the gruelling initiation ceremony, members were not left with more permanent marks of membership. I remember it as one long period of torture and humiliation, the most memorable moments being when my trousers were ripped off in front of everyone, when I was chased like a fox by the hounds across fields, captured, beaten and then pushed blindfolded through a hedge. I must admit that the ordeal nearly got the better of me. I suppose there is nothing like suffering and hardship to bind people together, for once you had made the grade it was a great fraternity to belong to. I also became a Freemason of the thirty second degree for as long as I was in the United States.

I had never experienced any difficulty in getting along with my fellow students but I was very touched and highly honored when they voted me as being the "most interesting" among them, recording this in the Class Year Book of 1939.

I graduated from Lincoln in 1939, a Bachelor of Arts with a major in economics and sociology, but could not get my degree straight away as I still owed the University some money. My original intention on leaving Lincoln was to enter the Columbia University School of Journalism, but I was so financially crippled that this was quite out of the question, for the time being at any rate. I was again very despondent, but just when my prospects seemed at their blackest I received a letter from the Professor of Theology and Philosophy at Lincoln, Dr. Johnson, inviting me to return there as an assistant lecturer in philosophy. This was quite an honor but not what I had planned for myself. However, I really had little option, for the nature of my passport as a student was such that I was not allowed to stay "out of school" during the winter months. I sat and thought about it. The offer had certainly arrived at a most opportune moment. I was desperately broke. Maybe it was the hand of fate. In the end I accepted and so, in the autumn of that year, returned to Lincoln as a philosophy assistant.

I thoroughly enjoyed it as it turned out. But I was not fully occupied. To my way of thinking, unless I was busy pretty well the whole of the twenty-four hours of each day I was wasting my time. I spent my spare moments reading every book on modern philosophy that I could lay my hands on. After acquainting myself with the works of Kant, Hegel, Descartes, Schopenhauer, Nietzsche, Freud and others, I appreciated the truth in the saying that law, medicine, and the arts are the arms and legs of learning but philosophy is the brain.

Later in the same year I gained admission to the Lincoln Theological Seminary and at the same time arranged to continue my studies in philosophy and education at the University of Pennsylvania in order to get my Master's degree. The previous July I learnt that I had been awarded a scholarship of one hundred dollars by the Presbytery of Washington. This was really wonderful news and it could not have come at a better time, for with this money I was able to pay for some of the courses at Pennsylvania.

I graduated from the seminary at Lincoln with a Bachelor of Theology degree in 1942 at the head of my class. As was the custom, the duty fell to me to deliver the seminary graduation oration that year. The subject I chose was "Ethiopia shall stretch forth her hands unto God . . ." It was delivered extempore and I was a little dubious as to its success. However, when professors and past students rushed forward at the end to shake my hand enthusiastically, I knew that they had appreciated it.

In the same year I received my Master of Science degree in Education from the University of Pennsylvania. By this time I had also become a full instructor in philosophy, first year Greek and Negro history. Negro history was a most popular subject and the classroom was always packed to capacity. I think I enjoyed lecturing on this subject as much as my audience appeared to enjoy listening. Another course which I liked was social philosophy; this also attracted a lot of students to my class. However, I never considered myself to be anything more than a novice and it was consequently a very pleasant surprise to me when in 1945—the year I left America—I was honoured by the *Lincolnian* (the magazine of Lincoln University) which voted me "the most outstanding professor of the year."

In February, 1943, I received the Master of Arts degree in Philosophy from the University of Pennsylvania and began to prepare myself for the Doctorate of Philosophy examinations. In spite of the fact that, apart from teaching and studying, I was having to travel backwards and forwards three times a week from Lincoln University to the University of Pennsylvania, a distance of well over fifty miles, I managed within two years to complete the courses and the preliminary examinations for the doctorate. All that remained before the degree could be conferred on me was the writing of the thesis.

But at that time there were other demands on my energy. In order to keep body and soul together, I got a job as a counter in the Sun Shipbuilding Yard at Chester where I worked in all weathers from twelve midnight until eight the following morning. It froze so hard on several occasions that my hands almost stuck to the steel and although I put on all the clothes that I possessed, I was chilled to the marrow. At 8 A.M. I used to return to my lodgings, have breakfast, sleep for a few hours and then begin research for the writing of my thesis.

One morning when I arrived home I had my breakfast as usual then went to sleep and did not wake up until four the following morning—a sleep of about eighteen hours. When some of my friends called for me to go to work at the shipyard my landlady, receiving no reply to her knocks on my door, assumed that I had already left. Without doubt I was getting to the end of my tether and it was soon after this that I caught pneumonia.

It was a bitterly cold night and I was shivering more violently than usual. At about four in the morning I began to feel very ill and simply did not know how to carry on. I went to the company's doctor to ask if I could be excused further duty. I felt that if only I could get home to bed all would be well. When he took my temperature, however, he immediately summoned the ambulance and rushed me off to Chester hospital where I was put into an oxygen tent in a supposedly critical condition. In spite of this, I was fully conscious and my mind was perfectly calm and clear. As I lay in bed I had time at last to view my life in reasonable perspective. It semed folly to struggle on as I had been doing, trying to use all the twenty-four hours of each day. Coupled with this, probably because I realized how close I had been to death, I longed to see my mother again more than anything else in the world. By the time I was able to get out of bed I had made up my mind that I would leave America and return home as soon as ever this could be arranged.

Hard Times

MY TEN YEARS IN AMERICA HAD BEEN HAPPY AND EVENTFUL, but at the same time they had been remarkably strenuous. Life would have been so much easier if I could have devoted all my time to study. As things were, however, I was always in need of money and had to work out ways and means of earning my livelihood.

When the first summer vacation came round at Lincoln I was at a loss to know what to do because it was a rule that no student could remain on the campus after term had ended. I went to New York and stayed with a Sierra Leonean friend in Harlem. He was in no better straits than I was and so we immediately set about planning how to get a job. We thought we had a brainwave and went to the fish and poultry market early each morning, bought fish at wholesale prices and spent the rest of the day trying to sell it on a street corner. This job was particularly uncomfortable for me as I seemed to have some kind of an allergy towards fish. Although both my arms and eventually my body became covered in the most irritating rash, I would willingly have stuck it out if the job had shown the least bit of profit. After two weeks of this, however, it was clear that I was losing what little money I had and so I decided to give it up. This caused a row between the two of us, which was a pity for it meant that I was not only without a job but also without a place to stay.

I was wandering down Seventh Avenue in Harlem wondering where I could turn next when I suddenly ran into a fellow student from Lincoln who came from Demerara in British Guiana. I told him of my difficulties: no money, no job and nowhere to go. "Don't worry, old chap," he said encouragingly, "I think I can solve the accommodation problem as a start." He explained that he knew a West Indian family who were extremely kind and sympathetic and that if he went along and put my case before them, he felt they might help me out. Sure enough, by the time I had told my story tears were in the eyes of the womenfolk who offered me their small spare room, and added that I was not to worry about the payment until I managed to find a job.

It was through a doctor friend of this family that I was introduced to my first girl friend in America. This was Edith, a nurse in Harlem hospital. I must have been a great disappointment to her. I was quite penniless so, apart from taking her for walks and gazing into shop windows, I could not offer her much in the way of entertainment. And I must have been a bit of a bore because my favorite amusement at that time was to stand and listen to the soapbox orators at the street corners. I was quite happy to spend my evenings there either quietly listening or, as was more often the case, provoking arguments with them. Poor Edith! She was crazy about dancing, the movies and the gayer things of life. It was not surprising, therefore, that she slowly drifted away from me.

It was round about this time that I found a job in a soap factory. I had imagined that I would leave work each day exuding the scent of roses or honeysuckle but this was far from the case. It turned out to be by far the filthiest and most unsavory job that I ever had. All the rotting entrails and lumps of fat of animals were dumped by lorries into a yard. Armed with a fork I had to load this reeking and utterly repulsive cargo into a wheelbarrow and then transport it, load after load, to the processing plant. As the days went by, instead of being steadily toughened, I had the greatest difficulty in trying not to vomit the whole time.

At the end of two weeks I was almost fit to be transformed into a bar of soap myself. My limbs ached so much at the day's end that I had to rub myself nightly with liniment before I could hope to get any sleep and build up enough energy to tackle the next day. A doctor friend of mine advised me strongly to leave the job. If I did not, he said, I would certainly never complete my education in America.

Taking his advice I began to look for other work. Job hunting in America at that time was most difficult because the country was just emerging from the depression. Life was so hard on some people that sometimes I would see men and women picking scraps of food from out of the dustbins. In fact, had it not been for the generosity of my landlady, I should have been doing the same thing.

As I seemed to have no luck in finding a job I decided to go to sea. In order to do this I became a member of the National Maritime Union, a body affiliated to the Congress of Industrial Organizations, which was at that time one of the most active trade union organizations in the United States. As the competition for employment was so great in New York, I went to Philadelphia where the demand was less. There I was lucky in getting a job aboard the *Shawnee,* a ship of the Clyde Millory Line plying between New York and Vera Cruz in Mexico.

Every summer thereafter, until the outbreak of the Second World War in September, 1939, I managed to get employment at sea. When I first applied for a job, the official of the shipping line asked me brusquely, "Can you wait, boy?" At first I thought he was asking me to postpone my application and when I hesitated, he raised his voice and said: "Well, come on! Can you wait at table?" Terrified of being turned down, I assured him that I could wait. So I was sent to sea as a waiter.

I was dressed up smartly in clothes to suit my new position and the time for the first meal approached. The dining room started to fill up and the head waiter told me to "Get along, then!" I felt like a frightened rabbit as I looked helplessly around the kitchen for somebody to give me a lead. And I had said I could wait! The head waiter glared at me and shouted: "Well, take in the soup!" I mumbled "the soup," as I looked round for it. When I found it I betrayed myself completely by pouring it into—or rather onto—a flat plate which was not discovered until I had carried it carefully into the dining room and placed what little there was left of it before the first passenger I saw with nothing in front of him. I was in too much of a hurry to get back to the kitchen and crawl in with the next plate to notice the strange looks that were appearing on the faces of the passengers. When I got into the kitchen, however, I found the head waiter almost ready to throw a fit. He got hold of my collar and started to shake me. How dare I say that I could wait! he demanded. When I could get my breath back I apologized profusely and pleaded with him not to be too hard on me because I was so desperately in need of the job. Luckily, underneath his stiffly starched exterior he had a very soft heart. He hastily put another man into my uniform and told me that I could wash pots for the rest of the trip. This was a soul-destroying job, but at least it did not require experience. Later I was promoted to dish washing. I was extremely careful with the dishes but one day as I was taking them out of the huge steam contraption through which they passed, one broke and cut my hand so deeply that I still have the scar today.

For the next trip, having learnt a little about dining room routine and the names of various foods, I was promoted to Mess Room Waiter. The officers were not quite so tricky as the passengers and after being chivvied around a bit, I soon got into the way of things. Eventually I managed to get the cream of jobs, that of bellhop. This was most sought after as the tips were good and a smart uniform was provided complete with a pillbox hat. It had embarrassing moments, however. One day a bell rang from one of the cabins. I knocked on the door and a lady's voice told me to enter. The next moment I beheld a most attractive woman reclining on her bunk almost completely naked. I was so taken aback that I rushed out again before she had time to speak. The bell went again and, with cheeks aflame under my dark skin, I once again knocked on the door. The voice, full of laughter, called out that I could come in, that all was safe and I had no need to worry. I went in with my eyes respectfully on the ground and took her order. When I looked at her, at her request, she was quite covered up.

This kind of life was a new experience to me. I had no knowledge of the ways of sailors and I was sometimes pretty shocked at their topics of conversation and the pornographic literature that used to be handed round among them. They used to try to persuade me to go ashore in the various South American ports where we docked. Sometimes I would join them, just for the fun of it and because I didn't want to be thought of as something unusual, but after my experience in Las Palmas, I was always a little wary of such pastimes. I did meet a French woman, however, who seemed to be of a rather better sort and I used to visit her every time the boat went to Mexico. But somehow or other she got the idea that I had promised to marry her. Perhaps it was the language difficulty—anyhow, rather than argue the point, I said that I would be back the following trip to stay. I had not lived with sailors for nothing!

I was really sorry when war broke out and my sailor days came to an end for, apart from the lighter side of it, the pay was reasonably good and we were always assured of three good meals a day.

On the other hand, except for the camaraderie which existed among the crew boys, there was always a most haunting feeling of loneliness, loneliness not in the sense of being without companions, but of being nobody's concern. Many times as I walked in the streets of Vera Cruz or in other foreign ports the thought struck me that anybody could have set upon and killed me and nobody would have missed me unduly. I don't suppose any steps would have been taken to discover even my identity.

I learned, too, that to sleep under the stars in my native Africa was, in spite of the raiding mosquitoes, a far happier prospect than sleeping out in the cities of America. When I first visited Philadelphia with a fellow student neither of us had any money for lodgings and, as we had nowhere else to go, we walked back to the railway station and sat on one of the benches intending to pass the night there. We had not reckoned on the ubiquitous American police. At about midnight we were rudely shaken out of our doze and greeted by a firm but not unkind voice saying: "Move on, chums, you can't sleep here."

With aching limbs and eyes almost blind for want of sleep, we felt that it was the most cruel thing that had yet been done to us. We shuffled out of the station and wandered into the nearby park. Luckily, unlike the London parks, the gates were not locked against us, and we managed to find a couple of benches where we thought we could spend the rest of the night undisturbed. Again fate was unkind for no sooner had we closed our eyes than the rain started. It came down so heavily that we were forced to abandon our makeshift beds and spent the remaining few hours of darkness standing about in doorways with other tramps, trying to keep dry.

For wet nights thereafter I devised another plan. The idea came to me in New York one night after I had been ejected from my room and had nothing in my pockets except twenty-five cents. During the day the problem of shelter had not seemed so acute, but when night came and I found that the streets had been taken over by stray cats and down-and-outs like myself, it was a very different picture altogether. Suddenly I got an idea. For a nickle I bought a subway ticket and boarded a train plying between Harlem and Brooklyn. With this ticket I travelled backwards and forwards on the train the whole night, getting what sleep I could. It was, of course, a very disturbed night for every time the subway reached its destination I got out and changed coaches in case the guard became curious about me being in the same coach for so long.

Poverty and need drive one to surprising ends. For want of something better to do and because it provided me with an evening's free entertainment, I used to go round quite a lot to various Negro religious gatherings and revivalist meetings. The only one that I gave much attention to was a movement headed by Father Divine, and then only because of the privileges attached to membership. By being a follower of Father Divine I discovered that it was possible to obtain a good chicken meal for half a dollar, instead of the usual two or three dollars charged at other restaurants, and also a haircut at a certain barber's shop for only ten cents instead of a dollar. To an impoverished student this was quite enough to attract him to any sort of movement and as long as I could be fed and shorn at cut prices by merely raising my arm above my head and whispering "Peace," I fear I did not concern myself with the motives of Father Divine's group.

One thought did cross my mind though. It was a condition of membership that no one should be married because they were married to the church. If a couple were legally married before they entered Father Divine's mission, then the union was in name only. I wondered whether this was not a movement backed financially by some white Americans to exterminate the Negroes, for, apart from the marriage ban, as far as I could see nobody ever paid anything towards the movement and yet it never lacked funds. Anyhow, I was truly grateful at the time for the benevolence of Father Divine.

While I was studying theology at Lincoln Seminary I spent much of my free time preaching in Negro churches. Almost every Sunday I was booked to preach at some church or other and I really enjoyed doing it. I had made many friends for the Negro churches play the part of community centers more than most places of worship. It was after I had been preaching in a Baptist Church in Philadelphia that I was introduced to Portia and her sister Romana. They invited me back to their house for dinner and from that time on a strong friendship existed among the three of us. It was Portia, however, who became my special friend. She was extremely generous and many times provided me with pocket money when I was out of funds. It was she who taught me the meaning of a "Dutch treat" when we shared the expenses on an outing. I was really not worthy of such a devoted girl friend for, as usual, I neglected her shamefully. I was always pleased to see her but I never wanted anything permanent to develop from our friendship. It often amazed me how Portia stuck by me so long. Probably she believed that with patience even the most stubborn of men will give in in the end. I remember one day thinking that she must be psychic. I had struck up a mild friendship with some girl or other and the second time I saw her I had to go on to Portia's house for dinner. When I arrived looking, as I hoped, innocent and composed, Portia took one look at me and accused me of "two-timing" her, as she put it. I denied it but she insisted and she said that she would go as far as to say that that very night I had embraced another girl. I felt it was impossible to hold out against anybody with second sight and I confessed that some girl had in fact kissed me but that there was nothing in it—which there hadn't been. Then she said smugly, "It might be a good idea if you washed the lipstick off your collar before you do anything else."

Unfortunately, the fact that I enjoy women's company has led to a great deal of misunderstanding from those who look at my life from outside. I have never wanted to become too entangled with a woman because I know that I would never be able to devote enough attention to her, that sooner or later whether she were married to me or not, she would begin to wander away from me. I was afraid, too, that if I allowed a woman to play too important a part in my life I would gradually lose sight of my goal. Few people have been able to understand this attitude of mine and I have been described by various people as a Don Juan, an impotent man, and even a eunuch! Those who know me, however, regard me as a very normal man with probably more than average self-discipline.

When I was in Philadelphia I carried out an intensive survey of the Negro from a religious, social, and economic standpoint. This work, which was given to me by the Presbyterian Church, took me to over six hundred Negro homes in Philadelphia alone as well as many others in Germantown and Reading. I enjoyed the work immensely and it was certainly an eye-opener to the racial problem in the United States which, particularly in the Southern part, was acute. When I compared this racial segregation with the modernity and advancement of the country it made my heart sink.

I well remember my first experience of active racialism below the Mason-Dixon line. I was travelling by bus on one of my lecture tours from Philadephia to Washington and the bus stopped en route at Baltimore for the passengers to refresh themselves. I was parched from thirst and I entered the refreshment room at the terminal and asked the white American waiter if I could have a drink of water. He frowned and looked down his nose at me as if I was something unclean. "The place for you, my man, is the spittoon outside," he declared, as he dismissed me from his sight. I was so shocked that I could not move. I just stood and stared at him for I could not bring myself to believe that anyone could refuse a man a drink of water because his skin happened to be a different color. I had already experienced racial segregation in the buses and in restaurants and other public places, but this seemed to me to be stretching it rather far. However, I said nothing but merely bowed my head and walked out in as dignified a manner as I knew how.

While at the University of Pennsylvania I helped to set up an African Studies Section there. It was there also that I began to organize the African Students' Association of America and Canada. This was actually the beginning of my political activities in the United States. When I first arrived this Association was only a small gathering of African students who used to meet occasionally but who, because of lack of organization, were not strong enough to achieve anything effective. I arranged things so that the organization took in not only the students but also Africans engaged in other types of work in the country. By this means I was able to bring them all together. At the first conference I was elected president, a position I held until the day I left for England.

With the assistance of fellow African students, in particular Ako Adjei (now Minister of the Interior in my Government) and Jones Quartey (now in the Institute of Extra-Mural Studies of the University College at Achimota), I arranged for the publication of the Association's official newspaper which was called the *African Interpreter*. Through the medium of this newspaper we tried to revive a spirit of nationalism.

It was not easy going by any means for we were continually coming up against internal conflict between the Nigerian and Gold Coast elements. The Nigerians claimed that there was no question of considering African or West African unity at the existing stage of colonial dependency and insisted that we should leave these colonial territories to struggle for themselves, each one working out its own salvation as best it could, without any link or co-operation with the other territories. I and the Gold Coast students, on the other hand, felt strongly that the question of territorial solidarity—that is to say, each territory mapping out and planning its own liberation—could not hope for ultimate sucess until it was linked up with the other movements in West Africa. We believed that unless territorial freedom was ultimately linked up with the Pan-African movement for the liberation of the whole African continent, there would be no hope of freedom and equality for the African and for people of African descent in any part of the world.

The idea of West African unity, which, of course, I strongly supported, became the accepted philosophy of the African Students' Association and we directed the students that when they returned to their respective territories they should work hard politically to organize these particular areas, but that in so doing they should maintain close contact with the political activities of their territories. By this means they would maintain not only unity within their own territories, but would pave the way for unity among all the territories in West Africa.

At that time I was interested in two sociological schools of thought in the United States, one represented by the Howard Sociologists led by Professor Fraser, and the other led by Dr. M. J. Herskovits, Professor of Anthropology at Northwestern University. The Howard school of thought maintained that the Negro in America had now completely lost his cultural contact with Africa and the other school, represented by Herskovits, maintained that there were still African survivals in the United States and that the Negro of America had in no way lost his cultural contact with the African continent. I supported, and still support, the latter view and I went on one occasion to Howard University to defend it.

Apart from all my academic work and the various activities that I have mentioned, I made time to acquaint myself with as many political organizations in the United States as I could. These included the Republicans, the Democrats, the Communists and the Trotskyites. It was in connection with the latter movement that I met one of its leading members, Mr. C. L. R. James, and through him I learned how an underground movement worked. I was also brought into contact with organizations such as the Council on African Affairs, the Committee on Africa, the Committee on War and Peace Aims, the Committee on African Students, the Special Research Council of the National Association for the Advancement of Colored People and the Urban League. My aim was to learn the technique of organization. I knew that when I eventually returned to the Gold Coast I was going to be faced with this problem. I knew that, whatever the programme for the solution of the colonial question might be, success would depend upon the organization adopted. I concentrated on finding a formula by which the whole colonial question and the problem of imperialism could be solved. I read Hegel, Karl Marx, Engels, Lenin and Mazzini. The writings of these men did much to influence me in my revolutionary ideas and activities, and Karl Marx and Lenin particularly impressed me as I felt sure that their philosophy was capable of solving these problems. But I think that of all the literature that I studied, the book that did more than any other to fire my enthusiasm was *The Philosophy and Opinions of Marcus Garvey* published by his wife. Garvey, with his philosophy of "Africa for the Africans" and his "Back to Africa" movement, did much to inspire the Negroes of America in the 1920's. It is somewhat ironical that the white Americans in the

South supported Garvey in these movements of his. They did this not because they were interested in the emancipation of the Negro as such, but because they wanted to get rid of the black man in the South and felt that this would solve the Negro problem. It was unfortunate that I was never able to meet Garvey as he had been deported from the country before I arrived, in connection with some kind of alleged fraud that he had got involved in. He eventually went to England where he died in 1940.

In an attempt to put into writing some of the experiences and philosophies I had gained from my association with the various organizations and how these could be best employed in dealing with the colonial question, I started writing the pamphlet which was later entitled *Towards Colonial Freedom*. Although the first draft was completed in the United States, it was not until I was in London that I managed to scrape up enough money to publish it.

In a short preface I stated my point of view as "an uncompromising opposition to all colonial policies" and put forward supporting arguments of which the following is a brief summary:

> Existence for the colonial peoples under imperialist rule means their economic and political exploitation. The imperialist powers need the raw materials and cheap native labour of the colonies for their own capitalist industries. Through their system of monopolist control they eliminate native competition, and use the colonies as dumping grounds for their surplus mass-produced goods. In attempting to legitimize their presence they claim to be improving the welfare of the native population. Such claims are merely a camouflage for their real purpose of exploitation to which they are driven by economic necessity. It is from this that the African peoples must constantly strive to free themselves.
>
> The whole policy of the colonizer is to keep the native in his primitive state and make him economically dependent. To ensure increased efficiency in the local handling of the colonies' resources, the colonizer grants loans and invests capital in improving internal communications,

social and welfare services, ostensibly to better the native. The big trade combines exert a rigid monopolist control which effectively prevents the native from sharing in the capitalist profits, but without native labour such profits would never be made. The history of the colonies shows throughout that they have been mere pawns in the hands of the imperialist powers, who have vied with each other in their race to acquire untapped resources. This has reduced the native population to economic slavery and degradation from which it must free itself.

Whether the dependent territory is administered as a colony, protectorate, or mandate, it is all part of an imperialist plan to perpetuate its economic exploitation. The colonies gain no advantages whatsoever from being dependent; socially and technologically their progress is hindered; they pay for a nominal protection against aggression by providing troops for the mother country in time of war and their political freedom will never be automatically granted but won by their own endeavors. Britain may claim that she holds the colonies under trusteeship until they are capable of self-government, but it is not in her interests to relinquish her strangle hold. The African, however, was perfectly capable of governing himself before the advent of the white man and should be allowed to do so again.

The problem of land ownership in the colonies has arisen because the colonial powers have legally or illegally seized valuable mining and plantation rights. The British are more careful than other imperialists to legitimize this seizure, but even their semi-legal methods do not disguise the fact that they have no right to rob the native of his birthright.

The national liberation movement in the African colonies has arisen because of the continuous economic and political exploitation by foreign oppressors. The aim of the movement is to win freedom and independence. This can only be achieved by the political education and organiza-

> tion of the colonial masses. Hence workers and professional classes alike must unite on a common front to further the economic progress and indigenous enterprise of the people which is at present being stifled.

Re-reading the pamphlet today with the events in the Gold Coast of 1948–51 in mind I am not surprised that my views remain the same. Consider this:

> "The idea that Britain, France or any other colonial power is holding colonies under 'trusteeship' until, in their opinion, the colonies become 'capable' of self-government is erroneous and misconceived. Colonial powers cannot afford to expropriate themselves. And then to imagine that these colonial powers will hand freedom and independence to their colonies on a silver platter without compulsion is the height of folly."

Few subject territories have so far been able to take up the challenge implied in these words. But it is worth noting that those which have built up a political organization against colonialism have quickly been successful.

London Days

IN MAY, 1945, I LEFT NEW YORK FOR LONDON. SEVERAL OF MY friends came to wave me off at the quayside. I couldn't believe that I was really leaving them, that I was leaving the country that had been my home for ten long years. I was too stunned for emotions to play much part in the leave-taking and it was not until the boat sailed out from the harbor and I saw the Statue of Liberty with her arm raised as if in a personal farewell to me that a mist covered my eyes. "You have opened my eyes to the true meaning of liberty," I thought. "I shall never rest until I have carried your message to Africa."

Five days later we docked in Liverpool. I was no longer the ardent youth setting out on a strange venture, inexperienced and easily shocked by the ways of the Western World. Ten years in America had seen to that.

There was still a lot to learn, however. While waiting at Lime Street station for the London train, I decided to buy a newspaper. I went to a newsboy and handed him the penny or twopence, whatever the price was, and he told me to help myself. I picked up what I took to be a single copy and as I was walking away the boy started running madly after me shouting "Hi, there! Stop!" I looked round wondering whatever could be wrong with him. Then, examining my purchase, I discovered that I had taken about ten copies of the newspaper by mistake. I had been so used to the bulky American papers that I never gave it a thought. I had forgotten the restriction of newsprint in England since the war. I explained this to the boy but

I don't suppose he could believe it as he had probably never set eyes on any daily paper boasting more than ten or twelve pages.

Incidents like this apart, I quickly felt at home in England. And the longer I stayed there, the more I felt how easily my roots could take a hold. Nobody bothered about what you were doing and there was nothing to stop you getting on your feet and denouncing the whole of the British Empire. In fact one of my pleasures in London was to buy a copy of the *Daily Worker*, the only paper I really enjoyed reading, and push my way into the underground with the business men. There, surrounded by copies of *The Times*, the *Telegraph* and the *Manchester Guardian*, I used to unfold my *Daily Worker* as ostentatiously as I could and then watch as pairs of eyes were suddenly focused on me. But the gaze of these bowler-hatted gentlemen was not in any way hostile and the atmosphere was always one of mild amusement.

The only person I knew of in England was George Padmore, a West Indian journalist who lived in London and who had written several articles which had aroused my interest and sympathy. I was so impressed by his writings that I wrote a letter to him from the States introducing myself and asking whether he would be able to meet me at Euston Station when I arrived. I heard nothing from him because I had left America too soon for a reply to have reached me, so I had no idea whether he would be at the station or not. I got out of the train and searched anxiously up and down the platform. We saw each other at about the same moment and from the first moment I liked him. He did much to help me during my early days in London and the more I knew him and talked with him, the more I respected his integrity and his knowledge of the colonial question.

He took me first to the West African Students' Union Hostel where I managed to get a room. But immediately I went into the place I knew it would not answer my purpose for long. The atmosphere was chilly and formal and I knew my irregular hours would never be allowed there. So I at once set about looking for somewhere else to live. This was far more difficult than it might sound, for accommodation was extremely scare in London after the war. And of course many landladies objected to taking in colored lodgers. As one of them explained to me in an effort to apologize: "It isn't as if it was me, dearie, but I've got me other gentlemen to consider." She at least had the decency to speak her mind but I remember walking up a street once and seeing a large notice in a front room window saying "Vacancies." With aching feet I hopefully walked up the small front path and rang the doorbell. Nothing happened for a few minutes and then the door was opened just wide enough for a pair of eyes to make themselves visible. Before I could even get a word out, the door was slammed in my face. Thinking that there might be some mistake, I rang the bell again, but this time not even the eyes appeared.

One day I decided to sport a bus ride. I had walked so many miles on the London pavements that my shoes were almost worn out and in my mind I had been working out whether it was cheaper to buy a bus ticket or to pay for my shoe repairs. At all events, it was a lucky chance that directed me to the bus that morning because as soon as I boarded it the first person I saw was Ako Adjei, my co-worker on the *African Interpreter* of American days. We were both immensely pleased to run up against each other again. He told me he was busy studying law and I told him my depressing stories about London landladies. But soon I was able to forget these dragons and lose myself in animated discussion of our mutual experiences in America and about our plans for the future. Ako kindly agreed to help me look for lodgings. I dreaded to think what the peeping eyes would have done had they seen *two* black faces outside the door, but in any case room-hunting was certainly a far more pleasant task with a companion. No doubt the search was all the more difficult because I had to have something cheap. Otherwise I suppose London landladies are as flexible as most human beings when they have a few pound notes waved in front of their faces.

One day we trekked round the Tufnell Park area and as we were walking down Burleigh Road, we decided to try our luck at Number Sixty. We knocked at the door without much hope and fully prepared for it to be slammed in our faces. It was opened by a young woman who enquired very civilly what we wanted. She listened attentively to what we had to say and then she said she couldn't promise us anything definite until she had consulted her husband, but that we should return the same afternoon. We went back wondering whether this was really going to be the end of my long search. And it was. We were shown in and I was taken to see a little room about ten feet square which I was told could be all mine for thirty shillings a week without meals. I felt so happy about getting anything at all that I would have accepted it even if there had been no furniture. And this little room became my home for the whole of my stay in London from June, 1945 until November, 1947. The family proved extremely kind and took a great interest in my well-being. I was very rarely in before midnight as I used to work until all hours. But whatever time I came in, I always knew that I would find something to eat left for me in the oven. In return for all their kindness, I insisted that my landlady leave all the dirty dishes for me to wash. This I did regularly before I went to bed.

My purpose in going to London was to study law and, at the same time, to complete my thesis for a doctorate in philosophy. As soon as I arrived in London, therefore, I enrolled at Gray's Inn and arranged to attend lectures at the London School of Economics. It was here that I met Professor Laski when he lectured there on political science, a subject in which I was keenly interested. Later on I registered at University College as well in order to read philosophy. I abandoned the research work that I had been doing in ethno-philosophy, which was the subject of my original thesis, and decided instead to work on another thesis on what was then a new theory of knowledge, Logical Positivism. I began this study under Professor Ayer.

In spite of this, it was only a matter of weeks before I got myself tangled up with political activities in London.

As in my American days, I associated myself with all political movements, and also with all parties, and I felt that the Communist Party in England was fortunate in having among its leaders personalities such as Mr. Emil Burns, Mr. Palme Dutt and Mr. Harry Pollitt.

The first move was to become a member of the West African Students' Union, of which I later became vice-president. After much organization, the Union became an effective body both in taking care of new students (especially in finding accommodation and arranging for their registration at the various Inns of Court or Colleges) and also in agitating for better conditions in West Africa by petitions to the Colonial Office. Sometimes students got into difficulties with the payment of fees and the Union would either write to their families asking for financial assistance or, if this was fruitless, endeavor to find a means of helping them out from its meager funds. Sometimes there would be disputes with landladies whom, because of their scarcity value, we had to cherish; occasionally someone would end in trouble with a girl picked up in Piccadilly or the Tottenham Court Road. There was never a dull moment and I thoroughly enjoyed the work.

About a month after I arrived in London I found myself busily engaged with George Padmore, T. R. Mackonnen (a gifted speaker) and Peter Abrahams (the colored South African writer) in making hurried preparations for the Fifth Pan-African Congress which it was planned to hold in the Town Hall at Manchester in October that year. George Padmore and I became joint secretaries of the Organization Committee and we worked night and day in George's flat. We used to sit in his small kitchen, the wooden table completely covered by papers, a pot of tea which we always forgot until it had been made two or three hours, and George typing at his small typewriter so fast that the papers were churned out as though they were being rolled off a printing press. We dispatched hundreds of letters to the various organizations throughout Africa and the West Indies explaining the aims of the Congress and the political tactics that should be adopted to achieve liberation in the colonies.

The Congress took place as planned in October under the joint chairmanship of Dr. W. E. B. DuBois an Afro-American scholar and one of the founders of the National Association for the Advancement of Colored Peoples, and Dr. Peter Milliard, a Negro physician from British Guiana, practising in Manchester. The Congress was a tremendous success and was attended by over 200 delegates from all over the world. We listened to reports of conditions in the colonial territories and both capitalist and reformist solutions to the African colonial problem were rejected. Instead, the Congress unanimously endorsed the doctrine of African socialism based upon the tactics of positive action without violence. It also endorsed the principles enunciated in the Declaration of Human Rights and advised Africans and those of African descent, wherever they might be, to organize themselves into political parties, trade unions, co-operative societies and farmers' organizations in support of their struggle to political freedom and economic advancement.

The important declarations addressed to the imperialist powers of the world were adopted by the Congress, one written by Dr. DuBois and the other written by myself. These declarations asserted the determination of colonial peoples to be free and condemned the monopoly of capital and the use of private wealth and industry for personal profits alone. They made a stand for economic democracy as being the only real democracy and appealed to colonial people everywhere—the intellectuals, professional classes, and the workers—to awaken to their responsibilities in freeing themselves and saving the world from the clutches of imperialism.

Although this conference was the fifth of its kind that had taken place, it was quite distinct and different in tone, outlook, and ideology from the four that had preceded it. While the four previous conferences were both promoted and supported mainly by middle-class intellectuals and bourgeois Negro reformists, this fifth Pan-African Congress was attended by workers, trade unionists, farmers, co-operative societies, and by African and other colored students. As the preponderance of members attending the Congress were African, its ideology became African nationalism—a revolt by African nationalism against colonialism, racialism and imperialism in Africa—and it adopted Marxist socialism as its philosophy.

But the main reason why it achieved so much was that for the first time the delegates who attended it were practical men and men of action and not, as was the case of the four previous conferences, merely idealists contenting themselves with writing theses but quite unable or unwilling to take any active part in dealing with the African problem. Like Garveyism, the first four conferences were not born of indigenous African consciousness. Garvey's ideology was concerned with *black* nationalism as opposed to *African* nationalism. And it was this Fifth Pan-African Congress that provided the outlet for African nationalism and brought about the awakening of African political consciousness. It became, in fact, a mass movement of Africa for the Africans.

I had little to do with the speakers themselves at this Congress, for

I was kept far too busy supervising the organization. But I remember one evening Makonnen came to see me behind the scenes in a state of great agitation. Could I possibly see a Dr. Raphael Armattoe, he said. Dr. Armattoe, a native of Togoland who had been invited to speak at the conference, came in and declared that he had lost his suitcase in which he had several things of value. He felt that since we had been responsible for his attendance at the conference, we should make good the loss he had sustained. He proceeded there and then to list the items and assess their value and presented me with the account. The Congress was already very much in debt but I decided it was better to pay the man and get over it the best way we could. Later, through a Mr. Ashie Nikoe, who was leading a delegation of farmers to protest against the setting up of the Gold Coast Cocoa Marketing Board, we received fifty pounds from the president of the Aborigines Rights Protection Society in the Gold Coast.

Having formulated the program for Pan-African Nationalism, the Congress came to an end. Padmore, Abrahams and I then left for London, while Makonnen, Jomo Kenyatta (who was later held responsible for the Mau Mau movement in Kenya) and Dr. Milliard remained in Manchester to organize the Pan-African Federation there.

A Working Committee was set up as a result of the Congress, with the object of giving effect to the program that was drawn up. Dr. DuBois presided over this and I was appointed general secretary. At a meeting of the Committee held in London soon after the Congress had come to an end, it was decided that the headquarters of the Pan-African Congress should be established in London to act as a kind of clearing house for the various political movements that would take shape in the colonies. We started looking for an office in which to set up these headquarters, but because of financial difficulties we could not succeed.

It was at this juncture that Ashie Nikoe, Wallace Johnson, Bankole Akpata, Awooner Renner, and Kojo Botsio approached me and suggested that we should set up a West African National Secretariat in order to put into action the new Pan-African nationalism, with particular reference to West Africa and with the object of calling a West African National Congress and of directing the program of self-government for the West African colonies, British as well as French.

I was offered and accepted the secretaryship of the West African National Secretariat and, because of the demand of the West African delegates for a center in London from which they could effectively direct their program, I set about looking for an office. Before long I found one—a small room at 94 Gray's Inn Road which was at that time the office of a Gold Coast barrister, Koi Larbi. This little room became our headquarters and it must have been the busiest little place of its size in the whole of London. It was rarely empty for, as soon as word went round of its whereabouts, it became the rendezvous of all African and West Indian students and their friends. It was there that we used to assemble to discuss our plans, to voice our opinions, and air our grievances.

As general secretary, all the organizing of the Secretariat rested on my shoulders, and as we never had any money this was no easy task. One of our main difficulties was the acute shortage of coal. As we were invariably in the office until well after midnight, in all weathers and seasons, coal was a necessity in winter. However enthusiastic and loyal a person may be to a cause, it is almost impossible to give of your best with icicles forming at the end of your nose, with feet and hands swollen with frostbite, and with the electric light bulbs dimmed by the constant fog of human breath. So, much of our time during the winter months was spent walking miles and miles around London in search of lumps of coal, preferably those bits surrounding a coal hole after the merchant had refilled it or the bits that fell off coal trucks—if we were lucky enough to be first on the scene.

But even if we had difficulty in warming our bodies round a fire, our hearts were constantly warmed by the ever ready offer of help by several English girls. These girls—most of them of good class families—used to come and type for hours on end in the evenings and they never asked a single penny for their work. The best we could do for them was either to put them in a taxi and pay their fare if we happened to be in funds or, and this was more often the case, to accompany them to the tube station and wave them goodbye. I did one day go to the cinema with one of them, however. I remember as we were about to go in an Englishman made some scathing remark about the girl being in the company of a black man (only that was not the expression he used). The next thing I knew was that the girl had given him a resounding slap on the face and told him to mind his own business and not to use such offensive language. Being the cause of it all, I suggested to her that I take her home and leave her, but she insisted that we carry on.

We were therefore very impressed by English women. There was a warmth of sincerity and sympathy surrounding them; their hearts were big and what they did for us they did in a quiet and unassuming way and expected neither thanks nor reward.

Within a few months of starting the West African National Secretariat, letters began to pour in from all quarters of the globe. As the volume of work increased I realized the necessity of a newspaper as an official organ of the Secretariat in order to spread some of the ideas that we were then formulating. And so I started to make plans for the publication of a monthly paper to be called *The New African.* I managed to collect fifty pounds which I deposited with the publishers who undertook to print three thousand copies for the first month. In March, 1946, the first issue appeared, subtitled "The Voice of the Awakened African" and with the motto "For Unity and Absolute Independence." Within a few hours of its appearance, the paper was completely sold out at threepence a copy. With the able assistance of a Nigerian student, Bankole Akpata, I preached through its editorial columns African unity and nationism and attacked imperialism and the unjust laws in the colonies.

While the *New African* became in London the voice of the West African National Secretariat, a magazine called *Pan Africa* was established by Makonnen and Kenyatta in Manchester to serve as the organ of the Pan-African Federation. After a short time, however, we were forced to stop publication of the *New African* owing to lack of funds. In fact the balance of one hundred and fifty pounds which we owed the printers was settled by me only after I had returned to the Gold Coast.

Before the paper collapsed, we were able to use it in order to call the first West African Conference in London. It was in this connection, in an effort to include in the conference Africans from the

French territories of West Africa, that I paid a visit to Paris. It was my first trip to the Continent. I had heard much of Paris and was expecting something quite out of the ordinary. I found the city disappointing. Of course, I had not gone there with a view to enjoying myself; I had no money and time was too precious to waste on frivolities. I went to meet the African members of the French National Assembly—Messieurs Apithy, Leopold Senghor, Lamine Gueye, Houphouet-Boighy and others. We had long discussions and planned, among other things, a movement for the Union of West African Socialist Republics. As a result of my visit, Apithy and Senghor came to London to represent the French West Africans at the West African Conference. Two such conferences were held at which it was decided to endeavor to drive home as forcibly as possible the idea of West African unity and nationalism among the students and other Africans who were then studying in Europe and America.

By this time the political conscience of African students was aroused, particularly in London, and whenever they met they talked of little else but nationalist politics and colonial liberation movements. Not long after my arrival in 1945, the Labor Party won its victory over the Conservatives in the first post-war general election. The West African Students' Union did what they could to bring about a Labor victory because they felt that this Party was the most understanding and the most sympathetic towards the colonial problem. They arranged for various Labor members to give talks to the students and through these I met several prominent Socialists, among them Mr. Creech Jones (later Secretary of State for the Colonies) and Dr. Rita Hinden, Secretary of the Fabian Society Colonial Bureau. But I regret that our hopes in the Labor Party were completely dashed to pieces; in fact we saw little difference between Labor colonial policy and that of the Tories. Consequently, at a Labor Party Meeting, Mr. Creech Jones was exposed to much heckling by colonial students who made a point of being present.

Perhaps the most difficult part of the work of the West African National Secretariat was the formation of the Colored Workers' Association of Great Britain. When I arrived in London it was to find that the Africans and colored workers were divided into two groups, the students on one side and the non-students on the other. The non-students were composed mainly of seamen who had come from various African territories before and during the war and had stayed on for various reasons thereafter. They were for the most part unemployed and almost destitute. Our aim was to help them find a job or, failing that, to find ways and means of getting them repatriated. The work connected with these colored workers led me on fairly regular visits to Liverpool, Manchester, and Cardiff, and one of the duties that devolved on me was to look into the living conditions of Africans in Britain. Sometimes these were so appalling that they defied description. In the East End of London, particularly, the meanest kind of African mud hut would have been a palace compared to the slum that had become their lot. However clean they tried to be, for the African is probably the most particular of any race about his cleanliness, it was impossible to eradicate the lice, the rats and the stench of bad drainage exaggerated by the filthy living of their neighbours.

Through living in such conditions they had in many cases given up trying to lead a decent life. I used to sit and listen to their problems; sometimes they had got into trouble with English girls or they had got on the wrong side of the law for petty thieving. Several times I had to visit men who had been imprisoned in Wormwood Scrubs. The prison cells were certainly a vast improvement on what some of them had to put up with, but it was not so good to have their freedom taken away from them.

It was a saddening experience, but by establishing the Colored Worker's Association, an effort had been made to get something done for them. Consequently they felt more hopeful and began to improve their conditions. And meeting them regularly, discussing with them their difficulties, and trying to offer a solution, went a long way to alleviate their misery. I also found that by intervening in time it was often possible to keep disputes out of court. There were, of course, many cases of racial antagonism where, after a few drinks had been taken on both sides, fights would begin. But I usually found that each party, after I had talked the matter over with him, was sorry for what had occurred and was ready to shake hands and forget.

If such a case had been left for the police to deal with by fines or imprisonment, the bitterness would have been intensified.

There was so much to be done for the colored workers that the West African National Secretariat became centered more or less on their organization, and the West African Students' Union focused its attention on the students. But both were always to some extent a political clearing house for African affairs.

It was after a mass meeting of the students' and workers' organizations in Britain, held in Holborn Hall, that I again visited Paris. This time a proposal was made at a meeting with the African Deputies of the French Assembly to hold a West African National Conference in Lagos in October, 1948, to which all political organizations and popular movements in the whole of Africa should be invited. It was proposed that I should be responsible for the convening of this conference and the plans that I laid before them for carrying this out were immediately approved.

As soon as I returned to London I set to work to get the wheels in motion. We held demonstrations and meetings in Trafalgar Square and Hyde Park. A socialist Member of Parliament who was very often to be seen speaking for us on such occasions was Fenner Brockway. We used to collect a crowd of people who were always sympathetic, but I am convinced that they thought we were exaggerating. It was quite obvious that the average man in the street in Britain had no idea whatever of the conditions prevailing in his country's colonies.

By this time I had ceased my law studies, primarily because I had no money but also because I had become so deeply engrossed in socio-political activities that I had no time to do any serious study. My thesis, too, second destined to be an unfinished work, but at that time such matters seemed trivial compared with the need for arousing African nationalism, for only by prompt and concerted action could we ever hope to achieve even a small part of the program we had set ourselves.

Indeed I was poor! I used to frequent the lower class restaurants in Camden Town and Tottenham Court Road, buying a cup of tea and, if finances allowed, a bun or a bread roll, and spend hours discussing politics with the various men who used to gather there.

The cafe proprietors were on the whole a very decent lot, for I never remember being asked to move on. One day Padmore and I were sitting in one of these cafes discussing some problem or other. All of a sudden I became conscious that we were being carefully scrutinized. I raised my eyes and there, peering at us with most profound interest, was a small girl. Suddenly she screamed with excitement as she said: "Mummy! *It talks!*" The poor mother was crimson with shame as she came across and tried to snatch her awkward child away. But we laughed and told her not to mind.

The students who supported the West African National Secretariat organized themselves into student groups and met regularly for discussions at the headquarters. One of these groups, of which I was the chairman, became the vanguard group and we called ourselves "The Circle." Membership cost seven guineas and only those who were believed or known to be genuinely working for West Africa unity and the destruction of colonialism were admitted. The document that we drew up giving the aims and purpose of this organization, the oath of allegience, and duties of "Circle" members, is reproduced as Appendix B of this book.

Members of "The Circle" began to train themselves in order to be able to commence revolutionary work in any part of the African continent. They were like a special service group of the Secretariat and it was they who directed the program and activities of the National Headquarters and took the lead in calling meetings and conferences and arranging lectures and discussions.

One day I received a letter from Ako Adjei, who was then back in the Gold Coast, asking me if I would return and take on the job of general secretary of the United Gold Coast Convention. He explained that the U.G.C.C. was being faced with the problem of how to reconcile the leadership of the intelligentsia with the broad masses of the people and, knowing of my political activities in both the United States and in England, he had recommended to the Executive Committee that I should be invited to become general secretary. He added that the Executive Committee had offered to pay me one hundred pounds a month and to provide me with a car. The money and the car didn't interest me so much. The job of general secretary, however, most certainly did. I saw the opportunity that I had been waiting for, the chance to return home and actively help my people by the experience I had gained in party organization abroad.

It seemed too good to be true, and I decided it might be better to be a little cautious and to try and find out more about what was going on in the Gold Coast. In order to play for time until I could find out something of the real spirit, motive and aims of those who had started this movement, I replied to Ako Adjei that I was considering the proposition. In any case I was so actively engaged at that time in preparing for the West African National Conference (which, in fact, never took place), that I was hesitant about rushing off leaving so many strings untied.

It so happened that Tony Maclean, a member of the Extra-Mural Department of the University College at Achimota was on leave in England at the time and it was through him that I found out the exact political situation obtaining in the Gold Coast. He knew personally the promoters of the U.G.C.C. and gave me his honest opinion of each one of them. From what he told me, I concluded that the sponsors of the movement were men whose political philosophy was contrary to the political aspirations of the people of Gold Coast. He told me, however, that one among them, namely William Ofori Atta, appeared to him to have some idea of the political, social, and economic needs of the country.

This assessment of the situation forced me to the conclusion that it was quite useless to associate myself with a movement backed almost entirely by reactionaries, middle-class lawyers and merchants, for my revolutionary background and ideas would make it impossible for me to work with them.

Then I received a letter from Dr. J. B. Danquah, one of the promoters of the movement, in which he urged me to take on the job. I asked several people for their opinions, but they all seemed unwilling to persuade me one way or the other, for it was a tricky period. It might be our beginning, but it could also be the end. Still unable to decide what to do, I called a meeting of the West African National Secretariat and put the matter before them. After much serious discussion they decided that it was perhaps best for me to accept the offer. It was rather like the dawn of action at the end of a long and intensive training. However well equipped you may feel to meet any emergency during the training period, when you are faced with the prospect of the real thing, you suddenly feel like a raw recruit again. But I was very sure of the policy that I would pursue and fully prepared to come to loggerheads with the executives of the U.G.C.C. if I found that they were following a reactionary course.

Now that the matter had been decided I wrote and accepted the post. I also wrote another letter to Danquah explaining that I was without funds and that I would need about a hundred pounds to cover my passage and travelling expenses. This sum was sent to me by return mail by George Grant, the president of the U.G.C.C., and I immediately started making preparations for my departure.

I had not yet completed the arrangements for the convening of the West African National Conference and I decided that on my journey back to the Gold Coast I would stop off at Freetown and Monrovia in order to make personal contacts in an effort to pave the way for this conference which was scheduled to take place in Lagos in October of the following year.

I called a meeting of the students and the colored workers in order to put my plan before them and to say goodbye. There were many protests against my departure, especially from the members of the Colored Workers' Association. However, I explained to them that the time had come to start putting into practice the things that we had been planning for, that this was the chance for which we had been waiting, and that I would neither forget them nor let them down.

On the 14th of November, 1947, Kojo Botsio and I left London for Liverpool. At Liverpool I unexpectedly encountered difficulties with the authorities at the docks for, unknown to me, the police had collected quite a file of information about my political activities in London. They were not at all happy about my presence at communist meetings. In the end, after lengthy questioning they grudgingly stamped my passport and I was allowed to embark. I had the feeling that while they were happy to see the back of me, they were a little worried as to what I was going to be up to in the Gold Coast. I could have told them then, but they would never have understood.

Botsio and I stood on the deck of the motor vessel *Accra* and silently watched the shores of England recede farther and farther away from us. It was not a happy parting for me. I had thoroughly enjoyed my stay there and had become extraordinarily attached both to the country and the people. But much was to happen before I saw England again.

Return to the Gold Coast

IN THE ENTHUSIASM FOR MY PLAN OF CALLING AT EVERY POSSIBLE port along the West African coast I had overlooked the fact that the boat I was on and the others that I would later join were on their normal runs and were hardly likely to accommodate one third-class passenger by cruising leisurely along the coast in order that he could disembark to sow the seed of Pan Africanism. It was with immense chagrin, therefore, that I found we were not scheduled to call at Gambia and that the first port of call was Freetown, Sierra Leone.

When the boat docked at Freetown I disembarked, taking with me only a small suitcase. I waved goodbye to Kojo Botsio who, as a schoolmaster returning to take up a teaching post at Akim Abuakwa State College in the Gold Coast, had kindly offered to include my luggage (mostly books) with his. By this time Wallace Johnson had returned to Freetown, and as he had so little room himself, he arranged for me to stay with a friend of his. There was quite a lot of disagreement in the country over Wallace Johnson who was chairman of the West African Youth League. I realized that the first important step was to endeavor to sort out this difference of political opinion and to get concerted action. I therefore asked for a private meeting with all the political leaders and, after much discussion and airing of views, we managed to come to some sort of agreement as to how the leaders in Sierra Leone could form a united front and work together for West African unity.

During my two weeks' stay in the country I addressed a large audience at the Wilberforce Memorial Hall, several mass meetings both in Freetown and in the Protectorate, and also the students at Fourah Bay College. I made some important political contacts and felt that my visit had been a success.

From Freetown I journeyed to Monrovia, the capital of the Republic of Liberia. Here the political atmosphere was different. I began to wonder whether Liberia, an independent country, would think seriously about a West African Conference. I had already met Messrs. Edwin Barclay and William Tubman when, as President and President-Elect respectively, they visited the United States. That was the first time I had ever seen Africans who were heads of state, and I was greatly impressed and encouraged. In those days we looked upon Liberia as the symbol of African redemption, as it was the only independent state, in spite of the fact that nobody ever said anything good about the country. To be like Liberia, in fact, was then considered to be the worst thing that could befall any country. I must say that in 1947 I could see the foundation for such sayings. I was not impressed at all with what I saw of Monrovia. However, when I visited the country again five years later the place had changed so greatly that I could hardly recognize it. President Tubman had certainly lost no time in introducing many long overdue administrative, economic, and social reforms, all of which have contributed to the advancement of the Republic.

Unfortunately, when I landed in Monrovia in 1947, Mr. Tubman, who was then President, was away on trek and because my boat was due to sail after only a two night's stop, I could not wait for him to return. I was disappointed but I managed to see several politicians with whom I discussed my mission. The general impression seemed to be that, since Liberia was an independent state, it might be difficult for her to send a delegate to a conference composed solely of representatives of territories of colonial status. She might, however, send an observer.

I then set sail for Takoradi in the Gold Coast, this being the next port of call on the scheduled run. I travelled as a deck passenger and incognito. I had enough experience of the efficiency of the British police to know that notice of my embarkation at Liverpool would have been sent to the port authorities at Takoradi, together with a dossier of unsavory facts about my alleged communist associations in London and I did not believe in meeting trouble half way. The less my fellow passengers and the crew knew about me, therefore, the better it might be. Without disclosing my name I mixed freely with the other passengers and the crew boys and we had a most enjoyable trip.

At Takoradi, the immigration officers had to be faced. Hesitantly I approached one of them, an African, and with downcast eyes handed him my telltale passport. The name written in the little white docket at the top suddenly seemed to me to have assumed the most enormous proportions. As the officer held the passport in his hand for so long without opening it, I raised my eyes, prepared to meet the worst. He was looking at me in amazement, his eyes protruding from his head. Then his mouth moved slowly and he whispered softly: "So *you* are Kwame Nkrumah!" I nodded. The game, I felt, was up. He beckoned me to follow him and I did so. As soon as we had gone out of earshot of the other passengers and officials, his whole manner changed. He shook my hand enthusiastically and told me how they—the Africans—had heard so much about me, that I was coming back to my country to help them, and how they had been waiting anxiously for my arrival day after day. He told me to go on my way and that he would see to my papers and other formalities and return the passport to me in due course.

It was wonderful to be standing once again on my native soil. I telephoned Mr. R. S. Blay, an Nzima lawyer living in Sekondi and a member of the United Gold Coast Convention, who came at once to collect me in his car and take me straight away to his residence in Sekondi. The following day I left for Tarkwa to stay at the house of my good friend Ackah Watson.

Ackah Watson had been looking after my mother during my absence, and I had written to him from London asking him to fetch my mother from Nkroful to Tarkwa, as I felt that if I went to Nkroful to see her word was sure to get round that I was back. I badly wanted some time with my mother and a short rest.

I think both my mother and I received a shock when we first saw each other again after twelve years of separation. At least I did when I realized that her sight was failing and when I noticed with sadness that she had gone quite grey and that with age she had lost much of her former beauty. She seemed smaller than I ever remembered her, perhaps because she had become frail.

The first shock she had was when I smiled at her and she noticed my teeth. When I left her my two top front teeth were divided by a fairly wide gap. In the United States I found this a handicap because whenever I made public speeches, it affected my delivery, especially where the "s's" were concerned. I therefore decided to have them removed and replaced by two false ones. The idea that one could have teeth removed and others put in their place was quite foreign to my mother and when she missed the gap between my two front teeth, she began to wonder whether I was really her son. Then, to assure herself, she examined my hands, for she always said that she would know me anywhere by my hands. I suppose one would say that they are somewhat delicately made for a man and the fingers are rather unusual in that they are the same thickness all the way up. This makes it impossible for me to keep a ring on them.

As soon as she had convinced herself that this was her prodigal son, her hitherto wonderfully controlled emotions broke through the barrier and, as she clutched me to her, I felt her body vibrate with deep sobs. And then, like an English April day, the sun suddenly took over and we both laughed with joy. We drew up two wooden stools and lost no more time in filling in a twelve year gap by recounting to each other all that had taken place in our respective worlds. She never asked me, and I never told her, the reason for my sudden return, nor did I discuss with her my political ideas for the future.

During that fortnight at Tarkwa I was able to rest and to take stock of affairs. It was undoubtedly a period of political ferment throughout the world. The colonial liberation movement was having its effect in China, Burma, India, Ceylon, Palestine, Indo-China, Indonesia and the Philippines and it was also having its effect in West Africa and on the African students abroad. Even though there were no overt signs of political unrest in Africa, the several territories were seething under the surface. The Gold Coast, for instance, was at that time considered to be a model colony, well behaved and well conducted. Little did the world realize then that this peaceful country was shortly to become the spearhead of African regeneration and renaissance.

In the Gold Coast the gap between the African intelligentsia on the one hand, and the Governor and the colonial government on the other, had widened. During Guggisberg's administration, the nomination of chiefs to the Legislative Council and the setting up of the Provincial Council of Chiefs provoked the remnants of the Aborigines' Rights Protection Society who strongly opposed these measures.

Between the administration of Guggisberg (1919–27) and that of Sir Alan Burns (1941–47), a great political awakening took place in the country. The system of indirect rule, that is, the government by officials through the chiefs, accentuated by the depression of the 1930's, was having its repercussion and the Gold Coast African was beginning to think seriously about the political and economic problems facing his country.

With this dawning of political consciousness Burns, like Guggisberg before him, started to introduce various political reforms that he believed to be necessary. He appointed Africans to the Executive Council. Although this was generally welcomed, a section of the intelligentsia was opposed to it because they declared that those who were appointed to the Executive Council were either chiefs or people who were generally known to be favorable to the Administration. A constitutional memorandum was drafted by the dissenting intelligentsia, endorsed by the Joint Provincial Council of Chiefs and forwarded to the Secretary of State. Burns, however, refused to accept this memorandum and in October, 1944, he announced to the Legislative Council that the Colonial Office had approved the new constitution which he had prepared in consultation with the chiefs and other African members of the Legislative Council. This was known as the Burns Constitution and although it was hailed by some as being a big step forward towards self government, the politically awakened section of the community soon became disillusioned and set about agitating for its abolition.

The intelligentsia, having been successful in creating opposition to the Burns Constitution, now began to plan the launching of a political movement which could upset it. The idea of a political party as such never occured to them and the party system was alien to them. In fact one of my numerous so-called crimes, according to my political opponents, is that I have introduced the party system into the country.

It was at this juncture that the United Gold Coast Convention was born at Saltpond on December 29, 1947, "to ensure that by all legitimate and constitutional means the control and direction of Government shall within the shortest time possible pass into the hands of the people and their Chiefs."

It is of interest to note here that Dr. Danquah, one of the Vice Presidents of the U.G.C.C., supported the Burns Constitution so strongly at first that he allowed himself to be nominated by the Joint Provincial Council of Chiefs as their representative in the Burns Legislative Council. Soon after that, however, the Kibi "ritual" murder took place. When paramount chief Nana Sir Ofori Atta I died, his son, Akyea Mensah, was brutally murdered in cold blood. It was alleged that other members of the family wanted to get rid of him so that they could avail themselves of the property of the chief. This act was wrongly interpreted as a ritual murder—a stupid custom which used to be observed on the death of chiefs when a number of innocent men were slaughtered in order to pacify the departed spirit of the chief. The trial of this murder case resulted in the sentencing to death or to life imprisonment of sons and relatives of the late Nana Sir Ofori Atta who were supposed to have been implicated in the crime. This led to an acute difference between Burns and Danquah, who was a half brother to Nana Ofori Atta, and thereafterwards he withdrew his support from the Burns Constitution and started agitating for a new one.

Because the U.G.C.C. at the beginning lacked the support of the masses and of some of the chiefs, it is not difficult to see why it failed to make much impression. It was in an effort to make it appear a popular movement that I was invited to become its general secretary.

Just before I left Tarkwa I held my first public meeting in the Gold Coast in the Roman Catholic schoolroom there. I spoke for some time and told the people of my experiences abroad and the reasons why I had returned to the Gold Coast as general secretary of the U.G.C.C. The room was packed and it was the first time that I had addressed an audience since my return to the country. From their absorbed interest and their acclamation I sensed that they, a representative gathering of the working class of the country, were indeed ready to support any cause that would better their conditions.

From Tarkwa I journeyed to Saltpond in order to meet the Working Committee of the United Gold Coast Convention. The members received me enthusiastically and made many speeches of welcome before we finally settled down to the business in hand. The first item on the agenda was my appointment as general secretary. This, it was agreed by everybody, should be confirmed forthwith. When the question of salary arose, however, there was diversity of opinion. The hundred pounds a month and the car had obviously, I realized, been used only as a bait for I soon discovered that the Convention (which itself lacked any kind of program or mass organization) had no funds at all and had not even attempted to open a banking account. As the payment of a hundred pounds was quite out of the question, they compromised by offering me twenty-five a month instead. I realized that even this sum was going to be difficult for them to find and I proposed that I would work for nothing so long as they would take care of my board and lodging expenses. The whole roomful of them turned to look at me in astonishment. As each one was making an income of around two to three thousand a year, they must have thought I was either a pretty queer character or that in some shrewd way I was trying something too clever for them to see. Later on, when they knew me better, it became a standing joke with one of the members in particular that I was quite indifferent to money and never understood the value of it. At that time, however, they couldn't make me out. They obviously intended taking no chances for they would not agree to my proposal and insisted on paying me twenty-five pounds a month. It mattered little to me, one way or the other, and I accepted their offer. In January of the next year, therefore, I began my official duties as general secretary of the U.G.C.C. I was made to understand that every effort was going to be made by the Convention to abolish the Burns Constitution, but I was not told what kind of a constitution they had planned to replace it.

The following two weeks I spent in organizing an office. Once more I set out on a room hunt and eventually managed to hire an old office of the United Africa Company, the biggest firm in West Africa. I managed to secure the services of a typist and in a few days got the office fairly well set up. The first thing I did was to call a meeting of the Working Committee of the Convention on January 20, 1948. At this meeting I laid before the members for their consideration the program which I had drawn up for the organization of the Movement. This included the following points:

"*Shadow Cabinet:—*

The formation of a Shadow Cabinet should engage the serious attention of the Working Committee as early as possible. Membership is to be composed of individuals selected *ad hoc* to study the jobs of the various ministries that would be decided upon in advance for the country when we achieve our independence. This Cabinet will forestall any unpreparedness on our part in the exigency of Self-Government being thrust upon us before the expected time.

"*Organizational Work:—*

The organizational work of implementing the platform of the Convention will fall into three periods:

First Period:

(a) Co-ordination of all the various organizations under United Gold Coast Convention: i.e. apart from individual Membership of the various Political, Social, Educational, Farmers and Women's Organizations as well as Native Societies, Trade Unions, Co-operative Societies, etc., should be asked to affiliate to the Convention.

(b) The consolidation of branches already formed and the establishment of branches in every town and village of the country will form another major field of action during the first period.

(c) Convention Branches should be set up in each town and village throughout the Colony, Ashanti, the Northern Territories and Togoland. The chief or Odikro of each town or village should be persuaded to become the Patron of the Branch.

(d) Vigorous Convention weekend schools should be opened wherever there is a branch of the Convention. The political mass education of the country for Self-Government should begin at these weekend schools.

Second Period:

To be marked by constant demonstrations throughout the country to test our organizational strength—making use of political crises.

Third Period:

(a) The convening of a Constitutional Assembly of the Gold Coast people to draw up the Constitution for Self-Government or National Independence.

(b) Organized demonstration, boycott and strike—our only weapons to support our pressure for Self-Government."

This was approved in principle—although there was a later denial by the members before the Watson Commission—and I was asked to get the organization going in full swing.

When I first read through the draft constitution of the United Gold Coast Convention I was struck by the fact that the Working Committee only intended concerning themselves with the Colony proper and, to a lesser degree, with Ashanti. The Northern Territories and Trans-Volta Togoland did not feature in their program at all.

I felt most strongly, however, that a united movement should embrace the whole country, and I was pleasantly surprised when my recommendations, including as they did plans for the organization of each of the four regions, the Northern Territories, Ashanti, the Colony and Trans-Volta Togoland, were accepted without comment. They probably felt that although I could not hope to succeed, there was no harm in trying.

At a subsequent meeting we discussed the colors for the Convention and a suitable design for its flag. The lawyers present argued that it was an offense in law to fly a party flag. They went to great lengths in an endeavor to prove their point by quoting sections of the statute on the subject. I disagreed wholeheartedly and asked them, if in other dependent territories this was allowed, what the objection would be in our particular case? I supported my case with facts, quoting the names of parties in other countries and, as nobody could find any form of defense to put up against this, I won the day. We decided without much difficulty that the party colors should be red, white and gold. I then suggested that the emblem might be a soaring eagle representing the emergent Ghana. As this was not acceptable to Danquah and his two relatives, William Ofori Atta and Akufo Addo, I asked them to suggest an alternative. At the following meeting Danquah produced his design for an emblem for the new state of Ghana. I was completely taken aback when I saw it for he had depicted an animal with two heads and one stomach which, according to the African, symbolizes selfishness, lack of interest in others and, in short, was hardly in keeping with what I imagined the U.G.C.C. had been formed for. Fortunately there was a division of opinion and they failed to come to an agreement, so the hideous monstrosity was never adopted.

When I took up my appointment as general secretary I found, on going through the minutes book, that only thirteen branches had been formed throughout the country. On looking further into the matter, however, I discovered that this was entirely incorrect. In actual fact just a couple of branches had been established and these were inactive. I saw at once the urgent need for a country-wide tour with the object of setting up branches of the U.G.C.C. in every part of the country. The results of this were most successful for, within six months, I had established 500 branches in the Colony alone. I issued membership cards, collected dues and started raising funds in one way and another for the organization, and in a short while I was able to open a banking account on behalf of the Working Committee.

The organization and building up of a political movement in the Gold Coast at that time was no easy task. It called for much intensive travelling and the roads in many cases were just bumpy tracks. Things might have been a bit better if I had had a more reliable car, but the ancient model that was supplied to me rarely finished a journey. It usually meant that I had to leave it with the driver while I continued my trek on foot. Sometimes if a "mammy" truck happened to be rattling past I managed to get a lift, but I was not always lucky in this respect. Most times I managed to arrange things so that I spent the night in one of the villages but on several occasions, when I had got stuck too far out in the bush by nightfall, I was obliged to sleep on the roadside.

During those days all my worldly goods—two suits, two pairs of shoes, and a few underclothes—could be easily stored in one small suitcase. This considerably facilitated my movements, especially as most of the time I had to carry my case myself. I travelled extensively to every corner of the country, holding rallies, making contacts and delivering hundreds of speeches.

I was not surprised to find a feeling of discontent and unrest among the people, for while I was editing the *New African* in London I came across many African soldiers who had served during the war in Burma and the Middle East. They had become fully conscious of their inferior standard of living and when they returned to the Gold Coast they lost no time in seeking better conditions. This, together with a feeling of political frustration among the educated Africans, who saw no way of ever experiencing political power under the existing colonial regime, made fertile ground for Nationalist agitation. It was consciousness of political and economic hardships and the social unrest after the war that led to the crisis in February and March, 1948.

It was while I was staying with my mother at Tarkwa that the news reached me that a certain sub-chief of the Ga State, Nii Kwabena Bonne, had organized a country-wide boycott of European and Syrian merchants in order to force the foreign shopkeepers to reduce the exorbitant prices of their goods. This movement, which was supported by many chiefs in the country, was intended as an anti-inflationary method by the common people. A meeting was held at Tarkwa at which Nii Bonne spoke. I was not able to attend the meeting myself but I received a full report of what took place. My first reaction was that, in spite of the weakness of the organization in its planning and methods, here at least was an attempt to give voice to the dominant political wishes of the people. The boycott soon spread to other towns in the Colony and in Ashanti. It lasted for about a month and was conducted peacefully without any violence or disruption. It was then called off.

When Nii Bonne first launched this campaign, I had only just returned to the country and had not even taken up my appointment as general secretary of the U.G.C.C. During the month that followed I was so preoccupied with setting up an office in Saltpond and organizing the various branches of the Convention, that I had no time to take part in the boycott, sympathetic though I was. However, my arrival in the country, my almost immediate appointment as general secretary of the U.G.C.C. and this boycotting campaign were so synchronized that, although the events were coincidental, it was easy to understand why the British Government and my political opponents readily associated me with the campaign. It was generally believed, in fact, that I was its instigator.

Nii Bonne and his supporters in this boycott had never been members of the United Gold Coast Convention and I was therefore quite certain that the campaign had nothing whatever to do with the U.G.C.C. But in all fairness it must be said that the U.G.C.C., in our agitation for self-government, would not have been against taking advantage of any grievance that presented itself if by so doing we could further our political purpose.

On February 20, 1948, I delivered my maiden speech in Accra where I addressed a large meeting in the Palladium. I had to drive there from Saltpond and, as usual, my decrepit car broke down. Luckily, after a time, we managed to get it going and it delivered me safely—though long after the scheduled time—to the Palladium Cinema which was often used for rallies and meetings. I was a little anxious, as I thought that the people might have got the idea that I was not coming and that they might have left the place already, but there they were, waiting patiently in their thousands, curious and expectant. I addressed them on "The Ideological Battles of Our Time." After I had finished I realized more fully than ever before, from the reaction of the crowd, that the political consciousness of the people of the Gold Coast had awakened to a point where the time had come for them to unite and strike out for their freedom and independence. It was at that meeting that Danquah, in supporting my speech, told the crowd that "if all the leaders of the U.G.C.C. failed them, Kwame Nkrumah would never fail them."

On the same day that the boycott was called off—on February 28, 1948—it so happened that there was also a peaceful demonstration of the Ex-Servicemen's Union. These two events were entirely unconnected and it was mere coincidence that they should have happened on the same day. I was certainly aware of the general dissatisfaction of the ex-servicemen and I was acquainted with their union through my job as general secretary of the U.G.C.C. As a matter of fact it had been my intention to organize them in due course as an arm of our movement. I was fully aware that they intended to make a peaceful demonstration in order to bring their grievances before the Governor but neither I nor anybody else could have possibly foreseen that this demonstration would have such tragic results.

The trouble began as the contingent of ex-servicemen approached the crossroads at Christiansborg just before they branched off to Christiansborg Castle, the official residence of the Governor. They had by now left the route prescribed and when they arrived at the crossroads they were commanded to halt by the police. They refused to do so on the grounds that it was a peaceful demonstration. This brought about a clash between them during which the European police officer in command ordered his men to open fire. As a result of this two ex-servicemen were killed on the spot and five other Africans were wounded.

When the news of this shooting reached the business center of Accra, where hundreds of Africans were out shopping for the first time since the lifting of the boycott, the people were quite naturally inflamed. In a matter of minutes the whole town was in a commotion. Africans started assaulting European and Syrian shopkeepers for failing to reduce their prices, as had been announced earlier as a part of the terms for calling off the boycott, and rioting and looting followed and continued for days.

The news of these disturbances in Accra reached me the same day that I was addressing a party rally in Saltpond. A meeting of the Executive Committee was called immediately and it was decided that I should proceed at once to Accra. Arriving there I convened a meeting of the leading members of the Accra branch of the U.G.-C.C. and afterwards went round the town to see for myself what was happening. The reports that I had believed to be exaggerated were, in fact, an underestimation of the turmoil and damage that had been done. The looting and rioting seemed to be quite out of hand and many buildings, including the large stores of the United Africa Company and the Union Trading Company, were on fire. As a result of this disorder 29 people lost their lives and about 237 were injured.

Realizing that the situation was critical, I summoned a meeting of the Executive Committee in order to discuss the draft of a telegram which we had decided should be sent to the Secretary of State for the Colonies, who was then Mr. A. Creech Jones. I felt that a simply worded telegram to the point was all that was necessary to convey what we wished to say, but Danquah thought otherwise. In the end two telegrams were dispatched, a long one drafted by Danquah and a short one drafted by myself. In these telegrams we asked on behalf of the people and the chiefs that a special commissioner be sent out immediately to hand over the administration to an interim government of the chiefs and people and to witness the immediate calling of a constituent assembly. Although I realized that by this telegram alone we could not expect to destroy British imperialism in the Gold Coast, at the same time I considered it an opportunity not to be missed.

While I was in Accra a rumor reached me that the police were searching for the six leaders of the U.G.C.C. Luckily two women supporters offered to give me shelter until such time as I could leave Accra. They were untiring in their day and night watch and in the way they looked after me. I stayed with them for several days with my small typewriter, and it was actually while in hiding in that house that most of the plans were laid which were later embodied in the program of the Convention People's Party.

After a while, however, I realized that if I remained long in the house I might endanger the lives of these women and so, after an emergency had been declared by the Governor and after the telegrams had been safely dispatched to the Secretary of State, I left Accra for Saltpond.

Arrest and Detention

ON ARRIVAL BACK IN SALTPOND I WAS GREETED WITH THE NEWS that the United Africa Company had ordered us out of the office we had rented from them. I never discovered for certain who was behind this sudden eviction order, but it seemed pretty certain to me, having regard to the coincidence of events, that the Administration had had a hand in it, believing, as they did, that I was connected with the disturbance in Accra.

The following day, therefore, I moved to Cape Coast and managed to get a suitable place there on Prospect Hill. During the following week, while I was busy reorganizing the new office, news again reached me that an attempt was being made to round up and arrest the six members of the U.G.C.C. The "Big Six," as we came to be known, referred to Danquah, Ofori Atta, Akufo Addo, Ako Adjei, Obetsebi Lamptey and myself.

That same night I was suddenly awakened by two European police officers and two plain-clothes men who ordered me roughly to get up and go along with them. Still in a daze at this nocturnal interruption, I was meticulously searched. They found two things that appeared to satisfy their suspicions about me, judging by the interest they took in them and the pleasurable grunt that was made by the one who took them off me. These were an unsigned Communist Party card that I had been given in London and that I had long since forgotten about, and the document known as "The Circle." Both these were confiscated. They demanded to know what I was doing with the Communist Party card in my pocket. Was I, in fact, a member of the British Communist Party then? they asked. I told them in all honesty that the card was of no consequence and explained to them where I had got it and that when I was in England I had associated myself with all parties ranging from the extreme right to the extreme left wings in order to gain as much knowledge as I could to help me in organizing my own nationalist party on the best possible lines when I eventually returned to my country. They made no reply to this but told me to get my hat. "I never wear a hat," I told them. When they made signs for me to follow them, I stood where I was and asked them on what authority they were arresting me. Of course I had little doubt that everything was in order as far as they were concerned, but in spite of this I made a cursory examination of the wretched looking document that was produced for me entitled "The Removal (F. N. K. Nkrumah) Order, 1948." Dated March 12, 1948, and signed by the then Governor, Sir Gerald Creasy, this read as follows:

> "WHEREAS I am satisfied with respect to FRANCIS NWIA KOFIE NKRUMAH, alias F. N. KWAME NKRUMAH, that it is expedient for securing the public safety and the maintenance of public order to make a Removal Order against him under the provisions of regulation 29 of the Emergency (General) Regulations, 1948 inserted in such Regulations by the Emergency (General) (Amendment) (No. 2) Regulations, 1948:
>
> Now in exercise of the powers conferred upon me by the said regulation 29 of the above Regulations, and in pursuance of such regulation, I DO HEREBY MAKE THIS ORDER, and direct that the said FRANCIS NWIA KOFIE NKRUMAH, alias F. N. KWAME NKRUMAH shall be apprehended and detailed and that he shall be removed in custody, as soon as may be, to such place in the Gold Coast as I shall hereafter appoint by directions under my hand.
>
> AND I DO HEREBY FURTHER ORDER and require that the said FRANCIS NWIA KOFIE NKRUMAH, alias F. N. KWAME NKRUMAH, from the time of his removal to the

place to be so appointed by me, and so long as this Order continues in operation, shall at all times—

(a) remain and live in, and not leave or be absent from, the place to be so appointed by me;

(b) comply in all respects with such directions and requirements as I may issue at any time.

This Order may be cited as the Removal (F. N. K. NKRUMAH) Order, 1948, and shall come into operation on the 12th day of March, 1948."

It seemed to be pretty well in order and so, as I realized that there was no alternative but to accompany them to wherever it was they intended I should go, I proceeded downstairs followed closely by the four police officers.

Fortunately for me, I made no resistance whatever, because when I reached the bottom of the stairs I suddenly found myself face to face with a squad of uniformed police each pointing a gun at me. The shock this gave me was so great that I instinctively pulled back a few paces. Believing that I was probably about to be made the target of a firing squad, I turned to one among them and asked him what they intended doing with me. While he playfully tossed two hand grenades in the air as if they might have been rubber balls, he commenced to abuse me in such a way and with such language that I felt utterly disgusted. He said, among many other things, that if I thought I could become Governor of the Gold Coast they would be very glad to show me what they did with such people. During a brief pause while he was obviously searching frantically in his brain for something fresh to say, I said quietly: "Have you quite finished? If so, let's go." I was thereupon pushed into a police van and, seated between two police officers, driven away to an unknown destination. Once or twice I wondered anxiously whether the van would be halted at some quiet and out-of-the-way place where not even my last words would be heard. I was annoyed at being dragged out of bed at such an hour and I began to doze.

After what seemed to be hours of travelling, the van came to a halt. I was dragged out and discovered that I was at Accra airport.

There I was joined by my five companions which cheered me somewhat, for until then I had believed that I was the only one being hounded to earth. Before long we were put into a plane and flown up to Kumasi in Ashanti where we spent three days in the prison, in safe custody.

It all happened so suddenly that it seemed like a nightmare and, apart from the initial feeling of fright, my senses were rather dulled and numb. As the key turned on us in Kumasi jail, our spirits sank and Danquah began to sob noisily and declared that he "would never forgive them for this."

While we were in the prison we held several meetings among ourselves to discuss the problem that might face us if a commission of enquiry were appointed to look into the causes for the recent disturbances. We even went so far as to draw up plans for a shadow cabinet and a future constitution for the Gold Coast, if and when the Burns constitution was thrown overboard.

It was during this period when we were thrown together in such close proximity that I got the first indication of disagreement between myself and the other five members. I became painfully aware that they were losing interest in me because whenever we entered into a discussion, the five of them would always make a point of supporting the opposite point of view to mine and nothing I proposed was acceptable to them. There appeared to be a general belief among them that the whole tragedy of our arrest and suffering was my fault and they began to make it plain that they regretted the day they had ever invited me to take up the secretaryship of the U.G.C.C. Not satisfied with that, they even began to blame Ako Adjei for his part in recommending me to them.

This disagreement, which ultimately resulted in the breach between myself and the Working Committee, was bad enough, but the thing which increased its severity a hundredfold, as far as I was concerned, was when I suddenly discovered to my horror and grief that there was a reason for the formation of the U.G.C.C. which I had never suspected. Some of the most prominent persons in the movement had been affected in one way and another by the result of the Kibi "ritual" murder trial and this was what had influenced them to join the U.G.C.C.

In the early hours of the morning of our third day in custody, we were suddenly awakened and told to pack at once and to be ready to leave by 3 A.M. It was only later that I discovered the reason for this sudden removal. Apparently, when the youth of Ashanti heard that we had been detained in Kumasi prison, they planned, under the fearless leadership of Krobo Edusei, now a Minister without Portfolio, to attack the prison and release us. However serious this threat may have been, it certainly had an effect on the prison authorities who wasted no time in getting us quietly out of the way.

We left Kumasi by bus and arrived in Tamale, the capital of the Northern Territories, about eight hours later. The news of our plight and our journey northwards had already reached Tamale by the time we arrived, and crowds of people had assembled to see us. But it was a sad crowd and both men and women were weeping. It seemed almost as if we were on our last journey to the scaffold. Beyond anything else, however, the very sight of us must have aroused sympathy for, owing to excessive dust on the road, we were completely covered by a film of dirt, so much so that it was impossible to distinguish one from the other of us.

We were taken to a bungalow on the outskirts of the town where we were left under guard for three days. Then we were split up and taken individually to various places in the Northern Territories, none of us knowing at the time where we were going. My destination was Lawra. Here I was put in a small hut and kept under police guard night and day. It was a very lonely existence but surprisingly enough I enjoyed it. It was the first time in thirteen years that I had been able to remain quietly and undisturbed in one place for any length of time and also, after the recent bickerings of my five companions in this plight, I was really thankful to be away from them. At least I could be left with my private thoughts and whatever plans I evolved could not be immediately squashed by a majority. I was allowed to read books but these, as well as any letters that came, had first to be censored by the District Commissioner. Newspapers were forbidden.

To say that I was completely alone throughout this period of detention is not entirely true, for each night I was paid regular visits by a mongoose. This peculiar little creature used to appear at dusk and stay with me throughout the night. Sometimes I would wake up and find the poor thing sleeping by my side. I was touched by its friendliness and attachment for me and I used to look forward to seeing it scuffling in as soon as it began to get dark. I discovered later that it belonged to a doctor who had trained it as a pet and who was then on leave, so obviously the creature was as lonely as I was.

After about six weeks of this more or less solitary confinement, the District Commissioner came into my hut one evening and asked me to have my things packed ready to leave for Accra the following morning. The next morning a truck came for me and, after picking up the other five at their various outposts, we arrived in Tamale where we boarded a plane for Accra. On arrival at Accra we were put in the annex of the Lisbon Hotel, situated at the airport. We then discovered that the other members of the Executive Committee who had not been arrested had secured the services of a British lawyer, Mr. Dingle Foot, K. C., to present our case before the Commission of Enquiry which had been set up by the Governor under the chairmanship of Mr. Aiken Watson, K.C. The other members of the Commission were Dr. Keith Murray (now Sir Keith Murray) at that time rector of Lincoln College, Oxford, Mr. Andrew Dalgleish a well-known authority on trade unionism, and Mr. E. G. Hanrott of the Colonial Office, who acted as secretary. They arrived in April, 1948, and were appointed "to enquire into and report on the recent disturbances in the Gold Coast and the underlying causes, and to make recommendations on any matter arising from their enquiries."

The first thing the Commission did was to ask for our release so that we could appear before them. This was arranged and for the first time in about eight weeks we breathed again the air of freedom.

Each one of us was called individually before the Commission to give evidence and answer questions. I remember well Mr. Watson asking me what I had been studying in America and London. When I told him he raised his eyebrows and turning to the other members of the Commission he remarked: "Gentlemen, I fear we are in danger of getting into deep waters here."

The most interesting thing was that, with the exception of one man, Mr. S. E. Ackah, every member of the Executive Committee of the United Gold Coast Convention completely disowned the recommendations that I had put before them in connection with the organization of the U.G.C.C. Several of them, upon being cross-examined, did admit that I had submitted these recommendations to the Executive but added that they had never associated themselves with it. The general idea that they were trying to put over was that I was merely an employee of the Convention and that as such they could not be entirely responsible for all my actions. And so I was left holding the baby.

The Commission completed its work and issued its report in June of that year. In their report they stated that with regard to the political situation, they had come to the conclusion that the Burns Constitution of 1946 was outmoded and they recommended its replacement by a more democratic constitution which was to be drafted by the Africans themselves. They agreed that the people must be allowed to taste some political power as a means of satisfying their rational aspirations and they recommended that a committee should be set up to consider the drafting of a new constitution.

As far as the observations which the Commission made about myself are concerned, it is as well to let the Report speak for itself:

> "From the internal evidence of the Minute Book of the Working Committee, the Convention did not really get down to business until the arrival of Mr. Kwame Nkrumah on 16th December, 1947, and his assumption of the post as Secretary.
>
> "Mr. Nkrumah has had a varied career. He had a very diversified education in the United States and Great Britain and in both countries appears to have taken a prominent part in all political institutions designed to promote a forward African policy. Although somewhat modest in his admissions, he appears while in Britain to have had Communist affiliations and to have become imbued with Communist ideology which only political expedience has blurred. In London he was identified particularly with the West African National Secretariat, a body which had for its objects the union of all West African Colonies and which still exists. It appears to be the precursor of a Union of West African Soviet Socialist Republics.
>
> "Mr. Nkrumah appears to be a mass orator among Africans of no mean attainments. Nevertheless he appeared before us as

a 'humble and obedient servant of the Convention,' who had subordinated his private political convictions to those publicly expressed by his employers. From the internal evidence we are unable to accept this modest assessment of his position. As appears from the Minute Book, the warmth of his welcome is reflected in the enthusiastic invitation from one member of the Working Committee to Mr. Nkrumah to 'use the organisation as his own.' From this it is clear that, for the time being at all events, he was occupying the role held by all party secretaries in totalitarian institutions, the real position of power.

"There was found among Mr. Nkrumah's papers a document purporting to be the constitution of a secret organisation called 'The Circle.' Members of this body were required to swear personal loyalty to Mr. Nkrumah with disquieting threats in the event of infidelity.

"In a working programme circulated just before the disturbances we have been inquiring into, Mr. Nkrumah boldly proposes a programme which is all too familiar to those who have studied the technique of countries which have fallen the victims of Communist enslavement. We cannot accept the naive statement of the members of the Working Committee, that although this had been circulated, they did not read it. We are willing to believe that they did. On the other hand we feel that the Working Committee, fired by Mr. Nkrumah's enthusiasm and drive, were eager to seize political power and for the time being were indifferent to the means adopted to attain it.

"It is significant that, although from his evidence it must be plain that Mr. Nkrumah has not really departed one jot from his avowed aim for a Union of West African Soviet Socialist Republics, the Convention has not so far taken any steps to dissociate themselves from him.

"Mr. Kwame Nkrumah has never abandoned his aims for a Union of West African Soviet Socialist Republics and has not abandoned his foreign affiliations connected with these aims."

It is important to note that the inclusion of the word "Soviet" by the authorities was entirely a product of their imagination. It was never included by me in the document called "The Circle." No doubt the authorities were so bent on labelling me as a "man to be watched," that they thought the introduction of the word "Soviet," in itself was all that was needed to imply a threat of communism in its most extreme form to the Gold Coast and to Africa as a whole.

In December, 1948, as a result of the Watson Commission, a committee was appointed by the Governor. This committee, which later became known as the Coussey Constitutional Committee, was under the chairmanship of Mr. Justice (now Sir Henley) Coussey and consisted of forty members, each of whom had been nominated by the Governor. A most important section of the community, however, had been entirely excluded from the Committee. These were the workers—the farmers, the miners, the petty traders—and the trades union movement. It was little wonder that dissatisfaction set in among a large section of the community who felt that, as the radical elements had been left out, the true political aspirations of the people could never be satisfied. This dissatisfaction became so acute that in the following November I felt obliged to convene the Ghana Peoples Representative Assembly in protest.

The Widening of the Gap

WHEN I RETURNED TO SALTPOND, WHERE I HAD SUCCEEDED IN renting fresh premises, I found that things were not going at all well as regards the office management. I therefore approached the Working Committee and asked if they would appoint a committee from among them to come and investigate matters and submit their recommendations as to what improvements could be made in the running of the office. They appeared to be very keen to help me in this and at once appointed a two-man committee composed of Obetsebi Lamptey and William Ofori Atta.

They timed their visit to Saltpond when I was away on a party rally. On my return I was met by an extremely agitated chief clerk who related to me all that happened. It appeared that office management was the last thing that these two men were interested in. They made straight for the files and scrutinized all the correspondence that had taken place, impatiently turning over pages until they found something of interest. My chief clerk looked on horrified as they took possession of whatever they fancied, especially when they grabbed and confiscated certain letters that he had typed for my signature. These letters were quite harmless but because I had used the word "comrade" in several cases, they presumably jumped on them as proof positive in their minds that I was a Communist.

Another letter which they impounded and which caused quite a stir among them was from one of our members, in which he told me that he knew of a way whereby the Convention could be vested with supernatural powers and that if I would contact him on this subject, he would be prepared to use his influence to achieve this. My reply to this gentleman was that if he possessed such powers, I felt that the best thing would be for him to appear personally before the Working Committee of the U.G.C.C. and put his case before them.

In due course I was faced with various charges by the Working Committee. As I expected, they were fearfully excited about the word "comrade." To them the word was obviously synonymous with communism!

"Is this not proof that you are a Communist?" they asked me. Astounded at such ignorance, I said nothing, but waited to hear what else they had got to say.

They expressed their objection to my reply to the second letter concerning *ju-ju* on the grounds that I should have submitted the man's letter to them first—that I had, in fact, acted outside my authority. Then they brought up the matter of my secretary, Saki Scheck, accusing me of paying him his salary of four pounds a month out of the coffers of the Convention. It became obvious that they were determined to rid themselves of me at all costs.

The limit of my patience was exceeded when they drew their final grievance out of the bag. They strongly objected, they said, to my founding the Ghana College, because by so doing I had acted outside my authority by not consulting them beforehand on the matter—and the formation of such a school was in any case outside the regulations of the Education Department.

I was flabbergasted.

"Are you trying to tell me that you were not consulted on this matter? Are you also inferring that the formation of the Ghana College was not in the interests of most of you personally and of the U.G.C.C. as a whole?" I proceeded to refresh their memories on the subject.

When I and my five colleagues were detained in the Northern Territories a number of students from various colleges and secondary schools went on strike in sympathy with us. As a result of this they were expelled. When I was released and returned to Saltpond the parents of these expelled students came to me in desperation beseeching me to do something for their children.

I reminded the Working Committee that, after putting the matter before them, they set up a committee, of which I was a member, to look into the matter. This committee drew up a memorandum which we submitted to the Working Committee recommending that either a school should be established to accommodate these unfortunate students, or that a way should be found to admit them to existing secondary schools throughout the country.

"By your indifference to those recommendations," I continued, "you demonstrated very clearly that you had little interest in what became of these students. You had conveniently forgotten that it was on account of the injustice that was being meted out to you that these boys, by expressing active sympathy, are in their present predicament."

I told them that it was purely to protect the good name of the U.G.C.C., which had been endangered by their actions, that I took it upon myself to take action.

"And don't go away with the mistaken idea that I did this for personal gain. On the contrary, the project cost me much in money, time and energy."

Now that I had got them where I wanted, I decided to acquaint them with further facts about the establishing of this college.

I managed to hire the Oddfellows Hall on M'Carthy Hill in Cape Coast for eight shillings a month. Here the students were housed. I then arranged for three teachers, who had also been expelled from their posts for the same reason, to come and teach the boys. Owing to lack of funds, these men agreed to work without pay until such time as the finances of the school were established. From my salary of twenty-five pounds a month I spent ten pounds on kerosene tins, packing cases, and boards to serve as seats and desks for the first batch of ten students, who ranged in standard from Grades One to Six.

"It is a pity," I told the members of the Working Committee, "that you were not present at the opening ceremony. You would have been deeply touched. Only Charles Dickens could have aptly described the scene. But one did not notice the bare boards, the kerosene tins and the packing cases. The sun was shining too brightly on the faces of those grateful students and tutors. Take my word for it, they will succeed and the college will expand, for it has firm foundations of courage and determination."

How well I remember that scene on the morning of July 20, 1948. I spoke without notes for about twenty minutes. In fact most of my speeches at that time were extemporaneous. It was, as I remarked in the opening words of my speech, an informal opening on very modest lines. Apart from a few friends of the masters and some of the parents of the students who had got wind of the ceremony, nobody had been invited. "When the formal opening of the college takes place," I encouraged them, "that will be the occasion to invite the public to witness the launching of an educational enterprise which may prove a significant landmark when the history of our hectic times comes to be written." I explained that it was the task of the Ghana National College to liberate the minds of our youth so that they should be ready to tackle the many problems of our time.

"Throughout history," I went on, "great things have often had small beginnings." I quoted as an example the founding by Booker T. Washington of the Tuskegee Institute and its growth from one pupil to thousands.

"In establishing the Ghana National College, we have taken upon ourselves a grave responsibility," I continued. "The times are changing and we must change with them. In doing so we must combine the best in Western culture with the best in African culture. The magic story of human achievement gives irrefutable proof that as soon as an awakened intelligentsia emerges among so-called subject people, it becomes the vanguard of the struggle against alien rule. It provides the nucleus of the dominant wish and aspiration—the desire to be free to breathe the air of freedom which is theirs to breathe. If we cannot find breadth of outlook and lofty patriotism in our schools and colleges, where else, in the name of humanity, can we find them?

"The African today is conscious of his capabilities. Educational and cultural backwardness is the result of historic conditions." I then urged all present and future students—both boys and girls (for I hoped that the College would become co-educational)—to consider laziness as a crime. "Think! Study hard! Work with sustained effort!" I said. "As never before we want thinkers—thinkers of great thoughts. We want doers—doers of great deeds. Of what use is your education if you cannot help your country in her hour of need?

"In spite of the humble conditions under which we have started," I said, "I bring you a message of hope and inspiration. I bid you shake hands with yourselves and your teachers over your study tables and over the blackboards. I look forward to the time when there will be a chain of Ghana Colleges in all the four territories which make up the Gold Coast—leading up to the founding of the University of Ghana.

"In the name of the people of the Gold Coast," I concluded, "in the name of Humanity and in the name of Almighty God, I bid you go forward till we realize a free United Gold Coast in a United West Africa!"

Sure enough, the Ghana College thrived. A year later the number of students had increased to two hundred and thirty and there were over a thousand names on the waiting list. Following on the success of this college I later founded over a dozen Ghana national secondary schools and colleges throughout the country.

But the Working Committee were not at all grateful for what I had achieved in the name of the Convention. They continued to complain bitterly about the whole thing.

Still nursing their grievances, they suggested to me that I should resign my post as general secretary and that I should be given a hundred pounds to buy a one-way ticket to the United Kingdom and carry on there where I left off.

I challenged this and once more denied their charges, which I told them I considered to be cooked up. It had some effect, and certain members of the Committee began to waver. They feared that my removal from the U.G.C.C. might cause the complete breakdown of the movement. They could not blind themselves to the fact that I had a strong personal following and they were beginning to consider me a key man in the survival of the movement. They therefore proposed that instead of my removal, I should be offered the post of treasurer. I accepted this for it suited my purpose well enough, and, more important, it completely defeated the purpose of the Working Committee. As far as the rank and file of the U.G.C.C. were concerned, the intentions of the Working Committee appeared highly illogical. They felt that if I was considered to be unworthy of the job of general secretary and incapable of managing the affairs of the Convention, how was it that I was considered to be suitable to undertake the job of treasurer? And coupled with this, the words of Danquah were still fresh in their minds: "If all of us fail you, Kwame Nkrumah will never fail you." They argued that if Danquah could be bold enough to assert this at two mass rallies in Sekondi and Accra, how then could he denounce the same Kwame Nkrumah in the very next breath? Moreover, to the embarrassment of the Working Committee, they made their protests manifest by the hundreds of letters and telegrams that poured into the office of the U.G.C.C.

The Working Committee had many headaches as far as I was concerned, and it was no doubt because they feared the truth of certain suspicions that they had about me that they acted so hastily and made such a fiasco of their attempt to dismiss me. For instance, they would certainly have heard some kind of rumor about the birth of my newspaper.

For the whole time that I was general secretary of the movement I had done my utmost to impress upon the Working Committee the importance of establishing a newspaper as an organ of the movement. They would not hear of it, their excuse being that we would probably get ourselves embroiled in sedition cases. Personally I failed to see how any liberation movement could possibly succeed without an effective means of broadcasting its policy to the rank and file of the people. In the same way that I took the initiative over the Ghana Colleges, so I made plans to launch a newspaper.

I arranged to purchase by instalments a "Cropper" printing machine which an Accra printer allowed me to install in his Ausco Press printing office. With the help of an assistant editor and four boys to operate the machine, the first edition of my paper, the *Accra Evening News,* appeared on September 3, 1948, on the very same day that the Working Committee had relieved me of my post as general secretary.

From the beginning, the *Accra Evening News* became the vanguard of the movement and its chief propagandist, agitator, mobilizer and political educationist. Day by day in its pages the people were reminded of their struggle for freedom, of the decaying colonial system, and of the grim horrors of imperialism. At first, owing to lack of funds, we could only print a single sheet containing feature articles, an editorial, an "Agitator's Column" and the most dreaded and talked about column headed "Rambler." There were no limits to "Rambler's" jottings; his eyes and ears were everywhere and he had no hesitation in exposing whom he pleased. A certain doctor was heard to remark that it was quite impossible to hold even a private conversation with one's wife in one's own room without "Rambler" reporting it. I remember, too, an American newspaperman who visited the Gold Coast at that time and offered a thousand pounds for the chance to meet "Rambler."

The demand for the paper was so great that the limited numbers we were able to produce on our small machine were avidly awaited by the crowds and were passed from hand to hand as if they might have been currency notes, the exchange invariably increasing the value of the paper until it was often sold for sixpence a copy. Even those unable to read would gather themselves into groups while a literate person read the sheet to them from beginning to end. The mottoes appearing as part of the heading soon became household words—"We prefer self-government with danger to servitude in tranquillity." "We have the right to live as men." "We have the right to govern ourselves."

In spite of its popularity we made no profit, for all the money received from the sales was utilized in paying the employees and in buying newsprint and other equipment with which to carry on. We refused to accept any advertisements for fear that the advertisers might try to influence the policy of the paper. In any case, most of the people who could afford to advertise were the imperialist and capitalist merchants who would not have been willing to associate themselves with our paper.

When the Working Committee saw how valuable the *Accra Evening News* had become in furthering political agitation, they founded a weekly paper of their own called the *Ghana Statesman*. This disappeared a few months after its first publication and was followed by the *National Times* and another paper called *Talking Drums*. But these, like the *Ghana Statesman* soon became defunct. The *Evening News*, however, proved such a success that in January, 1949, I established the *Morning Telegraph* in Sekondi with Kwame Afriyie as editor, and followed this up with the Cape Coast *Daily*

Mail in December of that year, which was edited by Kofi Baako, now my ministerial secretary and the government chief whip.

On September 6, 1948, after I had set the wheels of the *Accra Evening News* in motion and because of the tension in the country on account of my removal from the general secretaryship of the U.G.C.C., I decided to go away for a holiday to the French Ivory Coast and French Guinea. In a way it was a busman's holiday, for one of my main reasons in going to these countries was to cover the ground that I had been forced to by-pass on my outward voyage. West African unity was still uppermost in my thoughts. I renewed my acquaintance with many of my friends of London days, who were then Deputies of the French National Assembly, and had a very successful trip.

On my return, however, I found that the *Accra Evening News* was in financial difficulties. Because it had not been possible to pay the printer for the use of his office (even though the agreement had been that we would pay him off as soon as we had made sufficient funds from the sale of the newspapers) he had decided to take over the entire finances and there was no money at all with which to pay the operators of the "Cropper" machine. There was nothing for it but to look for fresh premises, which were eventually found in Horse Road, the premises that have remained the headquarters of this newspaper to this day.

It became a common saying in the country that if you wanted to know the truth, you should read the *Accra Evening News*. Unfortunately, we were too outspoken and in next to no time I found myself involved in libel cases, the claims made against me amounting to around ten thousand pounds. All the claimants were civil servants and included the Commissioner of Police. I was not worried. I had no property to be impounded; I had nothing for them to seize except for two suits, a couple of shirts and a pair of shoes. There was no bankruptcy law in the country.

The mass of the people, who supported me wholeheartedly in the matter, came to my aid and managed to collect enough money to meet the claim of the Commissioner of Police and a few others who insisted on immediate payment. The rest were paid off over a period of time. It was not until I became Prime Minister, however, that I learnt from some of the rather less prominent people who had filed libel suits against me that they had been prompted and even urged to do so by certain Government officials who apparently hoped that by entangling me in such a mass of debt and legal action I would be overcome and, together with my *Evening News,* I would pass out into oblivion. At a later date Danquah brought an action against the *Accra Evening News* for libel in connection with an article that was written about the Kibi ritual "murder" case. He was awarded damages but, not content with this, he bought the rights of the paper. Luckily, we moved one step ahead. The Head Press, as it then was, was immediately taken over by the Heal Press which continued to publish the same newspaper under a new name—the *Ghana Evening News.*

The thing that rankled the Working Committee most strongly, however, was the fact that I was responsible for establishing the Youth Study Group which was later embodied in a nationalist youth movement with the Ashanti Youth Association and the Ghana Youth Association of Sekondi and known as the Committee on Youth Organization.

Ever since the first indication of the divergence of views between myself and the members of the U.G.C.C. during our detention together, I knew that sooner or later a final split would have to come. I was determined, therefore, to organize things in such a way that when this break came I would have the full support of the masses behind me. By gathering together the youth of Osu, a district of Accra, I formed the Youth Study Group. Owing to the fact that I was too busy with my duties as the then general secretary of the U.G. C.C., I did not want to tie myself down as chairman of this group, even though I was at the helm. It was therefore agreed that Komla Gbedemah (now Minister of Finance) with whom I was living in Accra should be the chairman. Our meetings were held regularly at Gbedemah's house.

The aim of the Committee on Youth Organization was not to work against the Working Committee of the U.G.C.C. but rather to form itself into a youth section of the national movement. It was intended as a spur to further the cause of this movement. The members of the Working Committee, however, objected strongly to its formation. They felt that with its program of "Self-Government Now," the youth were becoming too critical of the program of the U.G.C.C., "Self-Government within the shortest possible time." But basically they opposed it because it was composed of the less privileged, or radical, section of the people and voiced the economic, social and political aspirations of the rank and file. It went completely against their more conservative outlook.

They thought, and rightly so, that I had been responsible for this organization of the youth and this fact strengthened their desire to remove me from office. Unfortunately for them, they disclosed their intention of doing this and thereby brought about open conflict between the supporters of the C.Y.O. within the U.G.C.C. and the Working Committee. It became obvious to all that these men who had, until that moment, complete control of the national movement, were anxious to be rid of me because I represented the radical and progressive section of the movement.

With all this unpleasantness brewing up again, I decided to make a short trip to Nzima where, in the peace of my home surroundings, I hoped to be able to restore in some measure my equilibrium. I knew that the time was fast approaching when decisive action was going to be necessary, when in all probability control would be in my hands, and I realized how important it was to plan my next steps.

During my absence Komla Gbedemah arranged for a mass meeting of the Committee on Youth Organization in the King George V Memorial Hall. It had been advertised that I was to address the gathering. I knew nothing about this and, as the day for the meeting drew near, the organizers became more and more anxious, fearing that I would not arrive back in Accra in time and that the crowd would be disappointed. In desperation, therefore, Gbedemah set off from Accra on the evening before the day the meeting was to be held and drove his old car as fast as it would go towards Nizima. When he arrived at the Ankobra river and was waiting for the canoe to ferry him across, it so happened that at the very same time I was standing on the opposite bank about to get into the canoe. The ferry man complained that there was some impatient chap on the other bank who appeared to be trying to find somebody. At first I didn't take any notice, but suddenly, across the water, I recognized Gbedemah's voice calling out my name. I immediately shouted back in reply, much to the consternation of the ferry man who, I suppose, thought that there must be two mad men at large. It was four o'clock in the morning.

Without wasting any more time, Gbedemah hurriedly pushed me into his car, and, while he steered it round hairpin bends at a speed far too great for its age, he proceeded to tell me about the meeting and how important it was that I should be there. We arrived in Accra at about three-fifteen, just before the meeting was due to begin. The hall was packed to capacity with both Europeans and Africans from all walks of life. I spoke to them for almost two hours on the subject of "Liberty of the Colonial Subject." It was a most successful meeting from many points of view for, by charging admittance to the meeting, we collected two hundred pounds for the funds of the C.Y.O.

Soon after this we made arrangements to hold a Ghana Youth Conference in Kumasi from the 23rd to the 26th of December, 1948. To this conference all sections of the country's youth were invited.

On the very day that the conference was due to be held, however, it was announced on the radio that because it was felt that it might lead to a breach of the peace, the meeting had been banned by the police. Owing to the lateness of the announcement many people had already set out for Kumasi and we therefore got together all those who had arrived and held an informal and secret session which lasted the whole night. At that meeting we drew up the Ghana Youth Manifesto which was published under the title *Towards Self-Government*. This manifesto set out the form of a constitution which the C.Y.O. thought could be used as a basis for discussion by the Coussey Committee which was due to sit that month, and a copy of it was sent to them for this purpose.

It was then decided that we should send cablegrams to the Colonial Office protesting against the banning of the conference. We realized that it was impossible to send these off from Kumasi—or, indeed, from anywhere inside the Gold Coast, so we set out at once for Lome in French Togoland more than three hundred miles away. When we arrived, we discovered that word about us had arrived there as well and it was equally impossible to dispatch the cables from Lome. So we had to post our protests by air mail. On the way back the taxi that we had hired broke down about ninety miles out of Accra. After waiting on the roadside for an interminable time while all those who claimed even the faintest mechanical knowledge endeavored to demonstrate their skill, a hopeful noise came from the engine. With a little persuasion the car condescended to move a few yards and then, with a splutter of protest, gave up again. After several such performances the driver decided that the only thing to do was to treat the thing with care. This meant a crawl at snail-pace in low gear. It was just about the most tiring journey that I have ever made and after eight hours of it we arrived in Accra utterly exhausted.

We had arranged for another conference of the C.Y.O. to be held three weeks before Easter in order to prepare the youth for the Easter conference of the U.G.C.C. We might have saved ourselves the trouble, however, for when the U.G.C.C. held their Easter conference at Saltpond, instead of following their scheduled program, the members of the Working Committee concentrated all their attention and energy first in demanding the immediate dismissal of my private secretary, on the grounds that he had been appointed by me without their prior approval and was being paid out of the Convention funds and, second, in refusing to reinstate me as general secretary of the party. The conference dispersed and the seed of bitterness which had already been sown between the Working Committee and the C.Y.O. took deeper root.

Early in June, 1949, the C.Y.O. held a special conference in Tarkwa which was attended by all the youth organizations in the country. The discussions that took place lasted for about three nights and proceeded into the early hours of the morning. There were two matters under discussion, whether they should acquiesce to my removal from the general secretaryship of the U.G.C.C. and whether the time had arrived to turn the C.Y.O. into a real political party. As far as the first point was concerned, it was eventually decided to resist my removal from office. The second matter was more difficult. The younger elements among the youth, led by Kofi Baako and Saki Scheck, were opposed to the formation of a political party as they insisted that by remaining within the U.G.C.C. the C.Y.O.

would eventually capture the initiative. The other section, headed by Kojo Botsio, Komla Gbedemah and Denkle Dzuwu, a staunch supporter who later defected, maintained that under the circumstances the C.Y.O. should immediately capture the political initiative of the rank and file from the U.G.C.C. by completely breaking away from that movement and forming itself into a separate political party.

The matter was then referred to me. I had no hesitation whatever in making my final ruling. I pointed out that, having had ample experience of the policy and mentality of the members of the Working Committee, anything short of the formation of a political party to lead the rank and file of the people at the earliest possible moment would be disastrous. The day we appointed for the launching of this political party was June 12, 1949.

Much discussion took place on the name to be given to this party. The most popular suggestion that was made was "The Ghana People's Party." This would have been adopted but for one vital reason. Owing to the fact that the rank and file of the people had learnt to associate my name with that of the United Gold Coast Convention, I felt that by omitting the word "Convention" from the name of this new party, it would arouse doubt and suspicion in the minds of the people who would regard it as a completely new party with new ideas and new promoters. And so, in order to carry the masses with us, we all agreed that at all costs "Convention" must appear as a part of the name. The name that we eventually agreed upon was the "Convention People's Party."

We then drew up a six-point program for the C.P.P. which was as follows:

(1) To fight relentlessly by all constitutional means for the achievement of full "self-government NOW" for the chiefs and people of the Gold Coast.
(2) To serve as the vigorous conscious political vanguard for removing all forms of oppression and for the establishment of a democratic government.
(3) To secure and maintain the complete unity of the chiefs

and people of the Colony, Ashanti, Northern Territories and Trans-Volta.

(4) To work in the interest of the trade union movement in the country for better conditions of employment.

(5) To work for a proper reconstruction of a better Gold Coast in which the people shall have the right to live and govern themselves as free people.

(6) To assist and facilitate in any way possible the realization of a united and self-governing West Africa.

It was with this program that we launched the Convention People's Party and started organizing for the struggle that lay ahead.

The Birth of My Party

IMMEDIATELY AFTER THE CONFERENCE AT TARKWA THE C.Y.O. members rushed to Accra in order to organize a mass rally at the Arena for Sunday, June 12, 1949. We were hurrying to keep one step ahead of the Working Committee which had its own plans, we knew. At the same time that we were meeting at Tarkwa, the Working Committee were in conference at Saltpond, and at that meeting they decided that I should be expelled from the U.G.C.C. They took this decision without any reference to the ordinary members of the movement and their intention was to publish the fact before I had a chance of announcing the formation of my party. I learned that they had already issued a press release which was due to appear in the newspapers on Monday. By our prompt action we took the wind out of their sails, so much so, in fact, that they were completely silenced and the announcement of my expulsion from the movement was never made.

On Sunday, June 12, 1949, therefore, before an audience of about sixty thousand people, I announced the formation of the Convention People's Party. It was without doubt the largest rally ever held in Accra and the sun shone brightly in spite of it being in the middle of the rainy season. It was a great day and my heart felt very full as I stood up to acknowledge the deafening cheers of welcome from an excited crowd.

In my speech, I went over the whole of the political struggle since my return to the Gold Coast; the formation of the Ghana schools and colleges; the *Evening News* with its fight for survival against so many obstacles and the organization of the youth of the country into the C.Y.O. I pointed out that no conflict existed between the C.Y.O. and the rank and file of the U.G.C.C. They were, in fact, one and the same people since before joining the Youth Movement it was necessary for the applicant to become a member of the U.G.C.C. The actual conflict, if one existed at all, was between the C.Y.O. and the Working Committee of the U.G.C.C. owing to the demand of the former for "full self-government now" as opposed to the latter's "full self-government within the shortest possible time."

I quoted to them an extract from *The Times* of May 24, 1949, which reported that the treasurer of the nationalist party, in the Gold Coast, "a single minded and hard-working fanatic," had started a youth movement and was agitating for self-government within the year.

I went on to explain our reasons for demanding "full self-government now," pointing out that as the Labor Government was then in power in the United Kingdom it would be more favorably disposed towards our demand. If the Conservatives were returned to power the following year our struggle for independence might be suppressed. I supported this by quoting Churchill when he said: "I did not become the Prime Minister of His Majesty's Government in order to preside over the liquidation of the British Empire."

I reminded the people that our land was our own and that we did not want to continue to live in slavery and under exploitation and oppression; that it was only under full self-government that we would be in a position to develop the country so that our people could enjoy the comforts and amenities of modern civilization. I explained to them the necessity for backing our demand for "self-government now" with a program of positive action employing legitimate agitation, newspaper and political educational campaigns and the application of strikes, boycotts and non-cooperation based on the principle of non-violence. I advised against diplomacy and deception as I pointed out to them that the British, as past masters themselves of diplomatic tactics, would far prefer to have from us frankness and firmness. A policy of collaboration and appeasement would get us nowhere in our struggle for immediate self-government.

"The time has arrived," I declared, "when a definite line of action must be taken if we are going to save our country from continued imperialist exploitation and oppression. In order to prevent further wrangling between the C.Y.O., who are ready for action, and the Working Committee of the U.G.C.C., who are out to suppress this progressive youth organization, the C.Y.O. has decided on a line of action that will be consistent with the political aspirations of the chiefs and the people of the country."

The crowd cheered madly. With much effort I managed to silence them. We would stand no compromise to our demand for immediate self-government, I went on, and, provided we all stood together, there should be no fear or qualms about the momentous step that we were about to take. In anticipation of what was to follow, the crowd again cheered loudly.

"In all political struggles," I said, "there come rare moments, hard to distinguish but fatal to let slip, when all must be set upon a hazard, and out of the simple man is ordained strength."

I then proceeded on a more solemn note. I went on to tell them that the present crisis in our political struggle had placed me in a difficult position; that I was faced with three major questions and that I wanted to know there and then the wishes of the people assembled there.

"May I," I asked them, "in the present stage of our political struggle, pack my things and leave this dear Ghana of ours?"

"No! No! Certainly not!" yelled the crowd indignantly.

"Or may I remain here and keep my mouth shut?"

"No! No! Speak! Stay and open your mouth!" they cried.

"Then may I break away from any leadership which is faltering and quailing before imperialism and colonialism and throw in my lot with the chiefs and people of this country for full self-government *NOW?*"

The unanimous shouts of approval from that packed Arena was all that I needed to give me my final spur. I was at that moment confident that whatever happened, I had the full support of the people.

As soon as I could make myself heard, I thanked them for their support. "And now," I declared, "I am happy to be able to tell you that the C.Y.O., owing to the present political tension, has decided to transform itself into a fully-fledged political party with the object of promoting the fight for full self-government now."

Then, on behalf of the C.Y.O., in the name of the chiefs, the people, the rank and file of the Convention, the Labor Movement, our valiant ex-servicemen, the youth movement throughout the country, the man in the street, our children and those yet unborn, the new Ghana that is to be, Sergeant Adjety and his comrades who died at the crossroads of Christiansborg during the 1948 riot, and in the name of God Almighty and humanity, I declared to the crowd the birth of the Convention People's Party which would, from that day forward, carry on the struggle for the liberation of our dear Ghana in the recognized party system, until full self-government was won for the chiefs and people of the country.

The applause which had been tumultuous eventually died away and a deep silence followed. It was a most touching moment for each one of us there. We had decided to take our future into our own hands and I am sure that in those few minutes everyone became suddenly conscious of the burden we had undertaken. But in the faces before me I could see no regret or doubt, only resolution.

The following Thursday, the 16th of June, the Working Committee of the U.G.C.C. and the remnants of their following held a meeting at the Palladium. Obetsebi Lamptey, when referring to me in his speech, used the word "stranger" and declared to the gathering that he failed to understand why the Ga people, who form the majority of the population of Accra, should permit themselves to be led by a man who did not even come from their area. This was too much for those who happened to be present and the meeting ended in uproar and confusion against him. The foundations of age-old tribalism had suffered their first irreparable crack.

When the Working Committee braved themselves to face the fact that the C.Y.O. had actually transformed itself into an independent political party with a definite policy and a program opposed to their own, a few of the right wing members among them showed concern. They invited a barrister from Sekondi, a minister from the Methodist Mission and another from the Zion Mission, to endeavor to settle the dispute which had arisen between myself and the other members of the Working Committee. These arbitrators met and, after much deliberation of the facts leading to the rift and the subsequent formation of the Convention People's Party, they recommended that I should be reinstated as general secretary of the U.G.C.C. and that the C.P.P. should still stand but as a political party acting as the vanguard within the U.G.C.C., since the latter held itself to be a national movement as opposed to a political party.

I agreed to accept this recommendation but the other members of the Working Committee objected. As a result of this, the whole committee, with the exception of the president, Mr. George Grant, resigned *en bloc*. Such undemocratic behavior on the part of the Working Committee confirmed my earlier fears. Immediately these people resigned, I advised Mr. Grant to convene a special delegates' conference. This was held at Saltpond in July. Apart from the accredited delegates and the ex-members of the Working Committee between forty and fifty thousand people assembled for this conference. The ex-members of the Working Committee, fearing that there might be trouble, had arranged for the police to be present.

The delegates' conference endorsed the recommendation of the Sekondi arbitrators and called for the election of new Working Committee members to fill the vacancies caused by the resignations. The ex-members of the Working Committee objected strongly to this, maintaining that as they had resigned of their own accord, the delegates should offer to reinstate them first. As a complete deadlock resulted, two new arbitrators were appointed to work out a solution. This time two chiefs were selected, who recommended that I should be reinstated as general secretary of the Convention, but added that the C.P.P. should be dissolved.

In spite of all that this would mean to me and the fact that it would certainly antagonize my supporters who were not prepared to accept any compromise, I agreed to accept their decision, but on one condition only: that the delegates present should elect a new Executive Committee to work with me in carrying out the policy which the conference was to adopt. My suggestion, as might be expected, was objected to by ex-members of the Working Committee to whom it was clear that they had lost the confidence of the conference. They feared that if an election were allowed their resignations would be confirmed and a new progressive Working Committee would be elected in their place. Soon no doubt was left in their minds when the delegates passed a vote of no confidence both in the president and in the ex-members of the Working Committee.

Immediately afterwards a message was delivered asking me to go outside the conference room. There I was confronted by an excited crowd.

"Resign!" they shouted, as soon as they saw me, "resign and lead us and we shall complete the struggle together!"

I realized at once that they were sincere and determined. Above all I knew that they needed me to lead them. I had stirred their deepest feelings and they had shown their confidence in me; I could never fail them now. Quickly I made my mind up.

"I will lead you!" I said. "This very day I will lead you!"

Hurriedly I returned to the conference room and announced that I had decided to resign, not only from the general secretaryship, but also from membership of the U.G.C.C. The delegates were then as jubilant as the crowds outside.

Standing on the platform surrounded by an expectant crowd, I asked for a pen and a piece of paper and, using somebody's back as a support, I wrote out my official resignation and then read it to the people. The reaction was immediate and their cheers were deafening. Then one of the women supporters jumped up on the platform and led the singing of the hymn "Lead Kindly Light," a hymn which from that time onwards has been sung at most C.P.P. rallies.

What with the strain of it all and the excitment, the singing of this hymn was as much as I felt I could take. I covered my eyes with my handkerchief, a gesture that was followed by many others present. The overwhelming support I had received from the masses had prompted me to act, and so I had struggled to the end of one battle only to be faced with the beginning of another. But this was the one that I had wanted so badly, the conflict which could only end with the fulfilment of my promise to my people, who had shown so readily their implicit trust in my leadership. The impact of all this made me feel suddenly humble and lonely and the tears that came were shed not from sorrow but from a deep sense of gladness and dedication. Standing before my supporters I pledged myself, my very life blood, if need be, to the cause of Ghana.

This marked the final parting of the ways to right and left of

Gold Coast nationalism; from the system of indirect rule promulgated by British imperialism to the new political awareness of the people. From now on the struggle was to be three-sided; made up by the reactionary intellectuals and chiefs, the British Government, and the politically awakened masses with their slogan of "Self-Government Now."

By forming the Convention People's Party and so introducing into the country the party political system, the foundation stone of parliamentary democracy was laid. An intensive campaign was carried on throughout the length and breadth of the country and soon, with the tireless enthusiasm of young people and the ready co-operation of the masses, the party colors—red, white and green—could be seen flying on rough wooden poles in the most remote of villages.

The first Central Committee of the Party was composed of eight members and myself as Chairman. These were: Kojo Botsio (secretary), K. A. Gbedemah, N. A. Welbeck, Kwesi Plange (who has since died), Kofi Baako, Krobo Edusei and two others who later defected from the Convention People's Party—Dzenkle Dzewu and Ashie Nikoi. Since the first Central Committee was formed, other prominent party members have been co-opted. It takes two years for a co-opted member to qualify for full membership of the Committee, and even then he does not automatically become a full member unless there happens to be a vacancy.

Much of the success of the Convention People's Party has been due to the efforts of women members. From the very beginning women have been the chief field organizers. They have travelled through innumerable towns and villages in the role of propaganda secretaries and have been responsible for the most part in bringing about the solidarity and cohesion of the Party.

So fervent were these women, in fact, that while I was in jail and the Party organization was at its most critical period, I learned that at a rally in Kumasi a woman party member who adopted the name of Ama Nkrumah ("Ama" being the female equivalent of "Kwame") got up on the platform and ended a fiery speech by getting hold of a blade and slashing her face. Then, smearing the blood over her body, she challenged the men present to do likewise in order to show that no sacrifice was too great in their united struggle for freedom and independence.

Before long we managed to collect together some trucks to which we attached loudspeakers. These, together with the Accra *Evening News,* the Sekondi *Morning Telegraph* and the Cape Coast *Daily Mail,* did yeoman service in broadcasting the propaganda of the Party and in keeping alive the spirit of nationalism. We were not disturbed by those who labelled us "verandah boys, hooligans, and Communists"; we had succeeded where they had failed. We had succeeded because we had talked with the people and by so doing knew their feelings and grievances. And we had excluded no one. For, if a national movement is to succeed, every man, and woman of goodwill must be allowed to play a part.

Positive Action

IT SOON BECAME APPARENT THAT THE FEELING OF UNREST WAS rife not only among the rank and file of the people, but also among the Government officials, the chiefs and the intelligentsia. Their discontent, however, was not born of suffering but of fear—fear of what they might have to suffer if something was not done to check this surging nationalism, this sudden political awakening of the youth and of the man in the street. The words "positive action" which I had used at the June rally in Accra spelt fear in the minds of my opponents and as soon as it became generally known that I intended leading the Party in a campaign of "non-violent positive action," rumors reached me that plans were being made to deport me from Accra. In fact the local Gold Coast radio announced that I had already been banished from the capital. Shortly after this, I received a letter asking me to appear before the Ga State Council, the traditional local authority, in order to discuss "the unfortunate lawless elements in the country and any possible solution."

I went along with two of my supporters and was surprised to find that among those present were the ex-members of the Working Committee of the U.G.C.C. The agenda that had been drawn up for the meeting was never referred to. All the speeches that were made were on one subject alone, and the whole idea of the meeting appeared to be to censure me for introducing the words "Positive Action" into the country and thereby threatening violence.

"What exactly do you *mean* by Positive Action?" I was asked.

I took my time and explained to them as fully as I could but, as I might have expected, it did not satisfy certain of my long-standing political opponents who were present. The Ga Manche, the paramount chief who was presiding, then suggested that I should convene a meeting of my followers and explain to them, in the same terms that I had just used to the meeting, the meaning of Positive Action and to report to the State Council when I had done so. I agreed to do this and immediately left.

It seemed to me that this was a matter that should go down on record as a considered statement. I therefore took a pencil and paper and, a few hours later, completed a pamphlet entitled *What I mean by Positive Action.* In it I explained that because the term Positive Action had been erroneously interpreted and publicized as being a threat of violence, the imperialists and their agents were perturbed. I had been called before the Ga State Council where I had explained to those present the true meaning of the term. That meeting concluded with a recommendation that I should call a meeting of the people and make the same explanation. I denied that I was going to be deported and protested against a false report in the foreign press that the Chiefs had demanded an undertaking from me to cause no trouble when the Coussey Report was published. If I refused, the report had said, I would be deported to Nzima.

I went on to discuss the aims of self-government and affirmed that the next step was a question of strategy; that although the British Government and the British people (with the die-hard imperialists) acknowledged the legitimacy of our demand for self-government, it was only by our own exertions that we would succeed.

I pointed out that there were two ways of achieving self-government, one by armed revolution and the other by constitutional and legitimate non-violent methods. As an example I gave the repulsion by British armed might of two German attempts at invasion and the victory over British imperialism in India by moral pressure. We advocated the latter method. Freedom, however, had never been handed over to any colonial conutry on a silver platter; it had been won only after bitter and vigorous struggles. Because of the educational backwardness of the colonies, the majority of the people were illiterate and there was only one thing they could understand—action.

I described Positive Action as the adoption of all legitimate and constitutional means by which we could attack the forces of imperialism in the country. The weapons were legitimate political agitation, newspaper and educational campaigns and, as a last resort, the constitutional application of strikes, boycotts, and non-cooperation based on the principle of absolute non-violence, as used by Gandhi in India.

It would appear, the pamphlet continued, that the Government was not pleased with our warning, that they would have preferred us to have sprung a surprise on them. But we preferred justice and fair play and to act aboveboard. We had nothing to hide and the members of the C.P.P., as members of a democratic organization, had every right to be prepared for any eventuality.

The final stage of Positive Action, I stated, would not be called into play until all other avenues for obtaining self-government had been closed. We would first study the Coussey Report. If we found it favorable, all well and good; if not, we would first put forward our own suggestions and proposals. If these were rejected, then we would invoke Positive Action on the lines already explained.

We all wanted self-government and we had a legitimate right to decide for ourselves the sort of government we desired. Until the publication of the report of the Coussey Committee, I urged the people to be calm and resolute.

By nine o'clock the following morning, after having worked all night with the "Cropper" printing machine at the office of the *Evening News,* I managed to print about five thousand copies of this pamphlet. The same afternoon I called a mass meeting at the Arena and read my statement out to the crowds. I then reported to the Ga State Council that I had carried out their wishes.

Immediately after this I made a tour of the Western Province in order to explain to the people in the more inaccessible areas what Positive Action entailed and how it could be used to achieve our aim. The point I stressed everywhere, however, was that this measure would be used only when all else had failed.

The Report of the Coussey Committee had been published at the end of October, 1949. It was thought to be quite unsatisfactory as a step towards constitutional reform and the general discontent was becoming so acute that I decided some action would have to be taken. On returning from my tour, therefore, I called together the Ghana People's Representative Assembly on the 20th of November. This mammoth gathering was the first of its kind and was attended by representatives from over fifty organizations. In fact, the only two organizations in the country that were not represented (apart from the statutory Territorial Councils which refused to honor my invitation), were the executive committee of the United Gold Coast Convention and the Aborigines Rights Protection Society. The latter society, although it was still in existence, had actually ceased to play any active part in the country's affairs, but it had been my original intention to invite them to convene this Assembly. However, owing to a most insulting reception which the then president of that body gave to two of my envoys in Cape Coast, I was compelled to withdraw the invitation.

My object in calling together this Assembly was to coalesce public opinion against the Coussey Report and to urge the people into effective action. The Assembly resolved "that the Coussey report and His Majesty's Government's statement thereto are unacceptable to the country as a whole" and declared "that the people of the Gold Coast be granted immediate self-government, that is, full Dominion status within the Commonwealth of Nations based on the Statute of Westminster." They also drew up a memorandum outlining the structure of central and local government which they desired to see incorporated in a new constitution.

The chiefs at Dodowah led by Sir Tsibu Darku and Nana Ofori Atta II did not accept the views of the People's Representative Assembly. I would have been prepared to discuss the matter further in an endeavor to come to some kind of an agreement, but the speeches that were made by some members of the Council, particularly by the president, Nana Ofori Atta II, seemed to me to be so abusive and couched in such undignified terms that I felt that any hope of a compromise was out of the question. I returned to Accra dismayed by the fruitlessness of the journey and the unpleasant attitude of the chiefs, but I continued to press the Government to give consideration to the people's demand for the convening of a constituent assembly.

I called a meeting of the executive committee of the Convention People's Party and, acting on their authority, informed the Governor in a letter dated the 15th of December, that if his administration continued to ignore the legitimate aspirations of the people as embodied in the amendments to the Coussey Committee's Report by the People's Representative Assembly, then the C.P.P. would embark upon a campaign of Positive Action based upon non-violence and non-cooperation, and that they would continue with this until such time as the British Government gave consideration to the right of the people of Ghana to convene their own constituent assembly of elected representatives of the people to consider the Coussey Report and, if possible, to draw up a new constitution. In short, we were prepared for a showdown.

The same day I published on the front page of the *Accra Evening News* a stirring article headed "The Era of Positive Action Draws Nigh." Later at the Arena, before a large gathering I warned the people to prepare for Positive Action. If nothing had been done by the British Government concerning our request for a constituent assembly within two weeks from that date, I told the crowd that Positive Action would take place any time thereafter. I impressed upon them, however, that there should be no looting or burning of buildings, no rioting, damage or disturbance of any sort; that the success of our cause depended on the non-violent and peaceful character of our struggle.

Accepting this challenge, the Government took the offensive by instituting a series of prosecutions against the editors of the newspapers which I had founded and which were, quite naturally, supporting the agitation. Several of the editors had been sent to jail and I myself had been brought into court to defend a case of contempt which had been filed against me as the result of an article which appeared in the Sekondi *Morning Telegraph*. The courtroom on this occasion was so packed with people that hundreds who had been unable to squeeze themselves into the building were massed noisily outside. Because of their strenuous and uninterrupted demonstrations in support of me, it was difficult to hear what was going on in court. In the end I was faced with a fine of three hundred pounds or four months' imprisonment. Fortunately the people of Accra and various party members rallied together and managed to get enough money to pay the fine, thereby enabling me to continue my agitation and the struggle against imperialism.

Soon after this I went on another tour of the country. While I was away a dispute had arisen between the Meteorological Employees' Union and the Government. Negotiations between the two parties broke down and the meteorological workers appealed to the T.U.C., who sympathized with them and indicated their readiness to support them. It was agreed that if the demands of the Meteorological Employees' Union were not accepted, the T.U.C. would declare a strike. The threat of a strike at this particular time increased the popularity of Positive Action. When I realized on my return that all chance of settling the dispute had broken down, I made an attempt to intervene to see if I could settle it, but this was not accepted by the Government. By intervening, however, I succeeded in my intention, which was to postpone a strike at that particular time, as this might have endangered the success of Positive Action if and when it came into operation.

It appeared that while I had been away the police had been searching for me to give me a letter from the Colonial Secretary, Mr. R. H. Saloway, an ex-Indian civil servant. The letter was eventually handed to me round about midnight on the day I returned to Accra. It contained an invitation to meet the Colonial Secretary in his office the following morning. I immediately called a meeting of the Executive Committee of the Party and put the matter to them. It was unanimously agreed that I should go.

The following morning I set out with three of my colleagues who waited for me while I had my talk with the Colonial Secretary. I went straight to the point and made my position quite clear.

"It's all very well, Mr. Nkrumah," Mr. Saloway said, not unkindly, "but things are getting to a point when I've just got to find some way of bringing some kind of order into the country."

"But order as far as you Government officials are concerned," I replied, "mean suppressing the rank and file—having them where you want them, to be told what is best for them and what they have to do. The whole country is politically awakened and it cannot be lulled to sleep again so easily. The people want their grievances redressed."

"But don't you see that this Positive Action that you are planning will bring chaos and ultimate disorder into the country?" The Colonial Secretary waited for these words to sink in. "And I'm afraid I must warn you that if anything disastrous happens as a result of this Positive Action—if anybody is killed or hurt—you will be held to be personally responsible. You must think seriously before you take this step. Now take India, for instance," he went on. "Now India was a very different matter. The Indian was used to suffering pains and deprivations, but the African has not that spirit of endurance. Mark my words, my good man: within three days the people here will let you down—they'll never stick it. Now, had this been India. . . ."

I cut him short.

"I must make myself quite plain, Mr. Saloway—if I have failed to do so up to now. If the British Government refuses to consider the resolution adopted by the Ghana People's Representative Assembly, then no alternative remains to me but to keep my words with the people and to declare Positive Action. All we are asking for is a constituent assembly which necessitates dividing the country into constituencies, calling a general election and letting the people decide for themselves whether they will adopt the Coussey report or not."

He said he sympathized with me but he gave me no assurance that anything would be done—that even an attempt would be made on the part of the Government—to consider my appeal. I bade him farewell and immediately called a meeting of the Executive Committee to report to them the result of the interview. They all backed me wholeheartedly. The next meeting that I had with Mr. Saloway was attended by four of us. I had picked my three companions from among those of the Party whose views were less radical than most. We went over the same old ground and reached no agreement.

The same day an announcement was made over the local radio that Positive Action had been abandoned. Obviously the Government officials, realizing the effect that the failure of my meeting with the Colonial Secretary might have, had hurriedly taken measures to keep law and order among the masses. I immediately convened a meeting at the Arena and made it abundantly clear to the crowds who assembled there that Positive Action had certainly not been abandoned. Very much to the contrary. The following Saturday night we had an all-night session of the Executive Committee at which it was decided to declare Positive Action on the following day if no satisfactory reply had been received from the Colonial Secretary.

A letter did come from Mr. Saloway. This said that the Government was considering the whole matter that day and that, in view of this, Positive Action should be suspended. The whole morning went by and part of the afternoon. Our nerves were on edge and the atmosphere was extremely tense. The T.U.C. had already declared a strike which had been in action since midnight of the 6th of January, two days earlier. At five o'clock I decided I had waited long enough, and called a meeting at the Arena. There I declared to the people that, apart from the hospital workers, those employed on water conservancy and other public utilities, and the police, a general strike should begin from midnight. The response of the people was spontaneous. The political and social revolution of Ghana had started.

Immediately after this, I rushed off to Cape Coast, Sekondi and Tarkwa, in the mining areas, and in each of these places I formally declared Positive Action. When I returned to Accra on the 10th of January I discovered to my annoyance that the enthusiasm of the people in Positive Action was waning. Mr. Saloway's words hammered in my brain in mockery—"Now, had this been India. . . ." The reason for this dwindling of enthusiasm, however, was that the colonial Government was using the radio as a propaganda machine and announcing in each area that the people should go back to work like their brothers in other areas. As the Cape Coast *Daily Mail* described it—to the detriment of its editor—it was "A Campaign of Lies."

When I saw that some of the stores in Accra had opened and that an attempt was being made to resume normal business, I knew that further agitation was necessary. Early in the morning of the 11th of January, therefore, I left the Party headquarters, where I had taken up residence, and set out on foot, dressed in a Northern Territories smock, to the office of the *Evening News* in order to launch a fresh campaign. I had barely gone 300 yards when I was joined by an excited crowd of supporters from all walks of life. As we proceeded we were joined by more and more until, by the time we reached the middle of Horse Road, in the vicinity of the *Evening News* office, the crowd was so thick that they seemed to be wedged in a solid block and brought all traffic to a standstill. In order to disperse the crowd I announced that they should all proceed to the Arena where I would meet them in a short while. In spite of this, hundreds were still tagging along with me and the position became so desperate that I rushed for a taxi and went to the house of a friend of mine in Osu, a district of Accra. I remained there for about an hour to get my breath and to sort out my plans in peace and quietness.

Then I went on to the Arena where the whole of Accra appeared to be assembled. I spoke to them for about two hours. At the end of it no Government propaganda machine could have succeeded in pacifying them or controlling them. Their blood was fired and they wanted justice. What is more, they would not stop until they had got justice. The tension was soon sensed throughout the whole town and it was hardly surprising to any of us when at seven o'clock that evening an emergency was declared for the whole country and a curfew imposed.

Positive Action had now begun in earnest.

All the stores were closed, the trains were stationary, all Government services had closed down and the workers were sitting at home. The whole economic life of the country was at a standstill. Public meetings were forbidden and all party letters were opened and censored. The *Evening News,* the Cape Coast *Daily Mail,* and the Sekondi *Morning Telegraph* fanned the flame by exhorting the workers to stand firm and to continue Postive Action. Then the office of the *Evening News* was raided and closed down by the police and the newspaper was banned. The same was the fate of my other two newspapers.

After this, arrests began to take place, beginning with the Party leaders in Kumasi and followed by those in Sekondi. Each of my editors was in trouble. The editor of the *Evening News* was arrested on a sedition charge for publishing an article entitled "Pull for the Shore," the editor of the *Daily Mail* was similarly charged for articles appearing in that paper entitled "A Campaign of Lies" and

"We speak for Freedom," and the editor of the *Morning Telegraph* was jailed for contempt of court.

When Positive Action had almost reached its climax, an invitation arrived from the Joint Provincial Council of Chiefs asking the leaders of the Convention People's Party, the ex-servicemen and the T.U.C. to meet them at Dodowah in an endeavor to come to some understanding and to arrive at a peaceful settlement with the Government. It transpired that the Government and the Joint Provincial Council were attempting to suppress Positive Action by arresting the key supporters. Before the representatives of the T.U.C. set out from Sekondi they received a message from their headquarters that they should not attend the meeting and they accordingly stayed away. The ex-servicemen were arrested before they arrived at Dodowah and so, when I and three of my companions succeeded in getting through unscathed, we discovered that we were the only invitees who were present.

Once more I put the case of the Ghana People's Representative Assembly before the Joint Provincial Council.

"We, the people, believe that our request for the election of a constituent assembly is reasonable and just. We will not accept half measures. The report of the Coussey Committee, a committee on which the rank and file of the people were not represented, is a matter that concerns us all. It is only right that we should have a chance of rejecting or accepting this report. If our request is not given consideration, then I have to tell you that Positive Action will continue." Because I stood my ground the speeches that followed were abusive in the extreme.

"It is obvious," declared Danquah, "that the law, as far as Kwame Nkrumah is concerned, must go according to him." Then he added: "It is my opinion that those who go against constitutional authority must expect to pay for it with their neck."

This wretched meeting was followed up by various attacks on me and on the Convention People's Party in the *Gold Coast Bulletin,* now re-named the *Gold Coast Review,* a Government sponsored publication.

It was here that I said in a speech at the Arena that if the chiefs would not co-operate with the people in their struggle for freedom then a day might come when they "will run away and leave their sandals behind them."

Almost daily now the police raided the Party headquarters in an attempt to arrest as many of the leaders as they could round up. I just looked at them disinterestedly as they searched the place for I knew, as well as they did, that I was safe for the time being. I was to be their final kill. First, I must see all my comrades safely behind bars before I suffered the same fate. Perhaps they felt that my nerves would break down and that I would run to the British authorities and on bended knees seek forgiveness for my wicked ways. My nerves were steadier than they had ever been and I could hold out just as long as they.

On the 17th of January, Kojo Botsio was arrested and detained at the police station where I managed to send food to him each day. As general secretary of the Party, his office was searched with tooth-comb thoroughness and all Party literature was confiscated.

In the streets of Accra, Syrians, Lebanese and British nationals were appointed as special constables and given truncheons to help them restore order. Some of these people took the law into their own hands and seemed to take pleasure in beating up anybody who happened to be walking anywhere near them. Accra became the scene of persecution. At this period a number of peoplet disappeared and were never accounted for, and certainly many people were injured.

Things came to a head when an ex-servicemen's demonstration clashed with the police and resulted in the deaths of two African policemen. The Government nets then tightened and the daily haul increased. On Friday night, the 21st of January, they arrested most of my comrades. It was, in fact, only by mere chance that I was not among them. Had I been arrested then, I am convinced that, the tension being as it was and intensified by the deaths of the two policemen, I would probably have been torn to pieces in the excitement of what was intended to be the final roundup.

It so happened that I left the Party headquarters that day at about 4:00 P.M. in order to visit a Party member who lived at Labadi. On arrival at his house I found that he had gone out to his farm a few miles away, so I decided to await his return. When he arrived, however, it was six o'clock and, as this was the hour of the curfew, it was quite impossible for me to leave the house. My friend lent me a blanket and I slept on the floor. It was during that night that I had a most vivid dream. A big black umbrella seemed to be descending upon me like a huge tent until it completely smothered me for what seemed like five minutes, during which time I was fighting for breath. Then it lifted and I woke up lying staring as it seemed to disappear into the distance. According to the African, such a dream would be interpreted as a narrow escape from death or extreme danger.

At eight o'clock in the morning I left the house and made my way to the Party headquarters. As soon as I approached it I could see what had happened. The police had completely ransacked the place and were waiting patiently for my return. They had, I discovered later, even taken my personal servant, Nyameke, and some of his companions and brutally beaten them at the police station in the hope that they would break down and tell them where I was hiding. But the poor people had no idea at all where I was.

As soon as one of the police officers caught sight of me he hurried towards me, obviously expecting that I was going to make a dash for it. I was perfectly calm and continued to walk at the same pace and in the same direction. It seemed almost with apology that he took hold of my arm as he informed me that I was under arrest.

"That's all right," I said calmly, "but let me first go and get my things."

I was then taken in a police wireless truck where I heard on the transmitter that all was quiet. "No trouble and all quiet at the scene of arrest," it coldly announced. Had they forgotten that Positive Action was a campaign of non-violence, I wondered?

On arrival at the police station I realized for the first time that I had become quite an object of curiosity. The crowds that had assembled there—both Africans and Europeans—were, I am sure, expecting to witness a most spectacular scene, the final arrest of that elusive revolutionary. It must have been something of a disappointment to them when a very ordinary looking African walked quietly out of a police van and made his way without any fight or resistance towards the police station. It was a relief to be in the police station away from all those inquisitive eyes.

I was searched and then taken before the police magistrate where the charges were read to me. I was then taken to James Fort Prison where I was detained until my trial came up.

Anticipating my ultimate arrest, I had made it clear to the people during my recent tours of the country that, if at any time I should be arrested, it was important that they should keep calm and make no demonstration of any kind. Because of this there was no commotion when I was taken into custody.

"The people," I thought, "will support me to the end. I will not fail them—ever."

Trial and Imprisonment

DURING THE PERIOD OF MY TRIAL, WHICH MUST HAVE TAKEN about a week altogether, I was remanded in custody. At least I was able to meet my companions and discuss our common problems, but the thing that I objected to most of all was the constant interruption of being dragged backwards and forwards to the courtroom. Some of the undisciplined warders made conditions worse by their obvious delight in having so many prominent people to bully and push around. They had probably never before dealt with so many political lawbreakers and were revelling in this chance to display authority.

I was quite resigned to my fate. I had foreseen what in all probability lay in store for me and I had prepared myself to accept the consequences. It was all a part of the struggle that I had embarked upon. It was a nuisance, of course, because it meant delay in achieving the final goal of freedom, but I would be able to pick up the threads where I had left off just as soon as I had served my sentence. I had long since come to learn that in the colonial struggle, when faced with a situation of this sort, it is not a question of justice. The idea of defending my case, therefore, had never entered my head, for, whatever defense was put up, I felt that the authorities would not allow me and my colleagues to escape conviction, for the judiciary and the executive under a colonial regime are one and the same thing.

Some of my followers, however, who were unacquainted with the treatment meted out to promoters of uprisings in a revolutionary movement, pressed me to secure the services of a lawyer to defend us. Although I knew that this was going to be a complete waste of money and energy, I did not want my colleagues to feel during the long months that lay ahead of us that we had put up no legal fight. I felt that even if we failed, the fact that we had tried might make them feel happier while undergoing their sentences.

An African lawyer was out of the question and so I arranged for two barristers to come out from England. These two gentlemen did everything they possibly could to help us, but I think that even they must have known how useless it was from the very beginning to battle against so determined a power. Our defense cost two thousand pounds altogether and I had to get various loans in order to settle the amount.

I was quite prepared for a prison sentence but horrified by the rumor of a very different punishment in store for me. According to this report, someone in authority had conceived the ingenious idea that, as it had been impossible to pin the crime of murder for the two African policemen during the clash with the ex-servicemen on any individual, and because I was responsible for declaring Positive Action, then I should be linked with the deaths of these two unfortunate men. It would have suited many people to have me out of the way for all time but, as my hands were perfectly clean with regard to this incident, their investigations proved quite fruitless and the charge was never brought against me.

I appeared in the courtroom to defend the various charges against me, the main one being that I had incited others to take part in an illegal strike under the terms of Positive Action, which, in the opinion of the presiding magistrate, was a different matter from organizing a strike in furtherance of a trade dispute. What I had done, I was informed, was to endeavor to coerce the Government of the Gold Coast.

Mr. Saloway was there as one of the chief witnesses for the Crown. I sat and listened to the long story of my activities, of my warnings from the Colonial Secretary and of my determination to go ahead with my plans in spite of these warnings. My defense could hardly have been called such for, apart from denying the charge that I had anything to do with the strikes of the T.U.C. and the meteorological workers and explaining my campaign from my own standpoint and from that of the Gold Coast people, I admitted that the facts they had recited were a fairly accurate record of what had taken place. I was given two sentences of one year each. But they had not finished with me. From Accra I had to go on to Cape Coast to undergo trial on a charge for sedition as publisher of the *Daily Mail* in which an article had appeared called "A Campaign of Lies" and for which my editor, Kofi Baako, was already imprisoned.

I had forgotten for the moment that I was then a member of His Majesty's Prisons and I was rather looking forward to this trip to Cape Coast in, I thought, a reasonably comfortable car. I soon discovered how wrong I was! To begin with, although I put up not the slightest resistance, my warders were apparently not going to take any chances of losing me, for I was promptly handcuffed. Then, with both hands clamped together at the wrists, I was made to climb into the back of an old truck, a feat which would have put many experienced acrobats to shame.

One look at the truck dispelled any thought I may have had about a comfortable trip. Comfort was the least of my concerns now; the question uppermost in my mind was, how could so decrepit a vehicle possibly make the journey in one piece? I soon stopped worrying about the vehicle, however, for it became increasingly apparent, with every yard that we progressed, that the odds against *me* arriving at my destination in one piece were far heavier. For three hours I was perched sideways—on a hard bench clasping awkwardly with my shackled hands a bar that was placed in the middle of the truck. The body of the vehicle, with which I was most actively concerned, rocked and rolled as if it were a light raft on a stormy sea, and by shutting my eyes I could visualize myself as a galley slave. Every time we turned a corner—and I had no idea before that there were so many on that road to Cape Coast—every muscle of my body was brought into play in an effort to keep me from being thrown to the other side of the van.

And this was not all. Every species of insect life that could fly, tickle and bite was represented in that van and it took no time at all for them to discover my inability to knock them off the exposed parts of my body. I think the warders must have felt a little sorry for me because somewhere along the route the truck stopped and one of them brought me a bar of chocolate. As I had refused to eat anything before I left Accra, I was very thankful for it and I felt considerably happier as a result of the man's kind gesture.

A solemn crowd of tearful people had assembled around the prison entrance at Cape Coast and the sight of them touched me deeply. As soon as the truck drew up I performed another acrobatic feat as I got out and was then bustled off to a cell. There, wrapped up in a blanket on the floor, completely left to myself, I had the deepest and soundest sleep that I had had for many nights.

The following morning I appeared before the court, defended by Archie Casely-Hayford, now Minister of Communications. But here again, the defense might just as well have saved its breath, for it was all in vain. I was given another sentence of a year's imprisonment, making three years in all, each sentence to be served consecutively.

As soon as the trial was over I was given another nightmare ride back to Accra where I was safely handed over to the authorities of James Fort Prison. I was taken to cell number eleven where ten of my comrades were already installed, and I can't say that the prospect of a three years' stay in these surroundings was a very happy one.

Whilst I didn't exactly expect to be made to feel at home in James Fort, it was somewhat of a shock to me to discover that, as a political prisoner, I was treated as a criminal. Sometimes I used to speculate as to what my lot would have been as a hardened jailbird. It was difficult to imagine that there could be worse treatment if the minimum of health and sanity of the inmate were to be preserved.

For eleven men we were supplied with a bucket in one corner of the already overcrowded cell to serve as a latrine. After a few weeks most of us managed to overcome the fearful indignity of using this so very public convenience. If only we had been permitted the flimsiest of straw mats to partition the thing off, it would at least have been an attempt to preserve a sense of decency, but it seemed that, like animals in a cage, we had to act our part without complaint. We used to take it in turns to clean this receptacle each day and we did what we could to make the best of a bad job. But it was most unpleasant, especially as the wretched food that we had was invariably upsetting our stomachs. It was all most embarrassing and most degrading.

The food was both scanty and poor. For breakfast we were given a cup of maize porridge without sugar. For the midday meal and for the last meal of the day at 4:00 P.M. we were given either boiled cassava, *kenke* (cornmeal) or *gari* (a cassava farine) with red pepper. On Sundays and Wednesdays we had a watery soup with the minutest piece of meat thrown in. This was purely a gesture, for it was as hard as a bullet. Sometimes we would get a piece of smoked fish with pepper. Rice was a luxury and only given to those who were unwell and for whom it was prescribed by the prison doctor.

When we first arrived, my colleagues were so disgusted with the food that some of them went on a hunger strike. I was against this for I saw that it would get us nowhere; on the contrary, it was necessary to eat all we could in an effort to keep our strength up. There was much work to do when we were eventually released and it was going to be no good to anybody if we had to be invalided out. After much persuasion on my part, the strikers gave in.

I used to fast for one or two days a week because this had been a former habit of mine. But apart from the spiritual value derived from this, during those prison days it also helped my stomach to right itself again. I had never cared much for food in any case, so I was perhaps more fortunate than my fellow prisoners.

We were let out of our cell from seven in the morning until eleven o'clock for exercise and to work, either at weaving fishnets or at cleaning cane ready for basket making. Then we were locked up again until one o'clock and we were finally locked up for the night at 4:00 P.M. after our evening meal. All our meals were eaten in our cell, which probably added to the unpleasantness of the food.

It was of course forbidden for me to have pencil and paper or to read any newspapers and my greatest anxiety at that time was how the Party was faring during my absence. It was permitted to write one letter per month to one's parents or near relatives, but as a warder was always standing over your shoulder and the letter had to be censored by the prison authorities, there was little apart from a flourishing account of one's health that would have got through.

Fortunately, just before I was locked up I was able to have a few valuable minutes with Gbedemah who, having served his prison sentence for "publishing false news," was preparing to leave. In those few minutes I committed to his charge the full responsibility of running the *Evening News* and the Party.

"I'll do my utmost to keep in touch with you somehow," I whispered to him, "though goodness knows how!"

There was, I realized, only one way that I could keep in touch with the Party outside those whitewashed walls—by writing. My whole life then centered around the problem of how to get hold of a pencil and a supply of paper. Before long I managed to pick up a mere stump of a pencil which I kept safely hidden inside the band of my trouser top. The paper looked like being a major problem until I suddenly saw the answer staring me in the face. Each day we were given a few sheets of toilet paper. I got the bright idea of appropriating these—as many as I could get. I don't know what the other prisoners must have thought was wrong with me when I made known to them my urgent need of additional toilet paper, but they were quite willing to exchange what they could spare for bits of food and anything else I could offer them. This precious store of paper was kept carefully under my straw sleeping mat.

As soon as it was dark and we were thought to be asleep, like the many cockroaches that roamed freely about the cell I, too, started to work. Writing in that cell was no easy matter for the only light was from an electric street lamp that penetrated through the bars at the top of the wall and cast its reflection on a part of the floor and a section of the opposite wall. I used to lie in this patch of light and write for as long as I could before cramp made it unendurable, then I would change to a standing position and use the spot of light on the wall. On one occasion I remember covering fifty sheets of this toilet paper with my scribble. The written sheets were then folded minutely and wrapped in another piece of toilet paper, and this eventually found its way to Gbedemah outside. How they got there is quite another matter, but by the same means that my toilet paper scribbles found their way out of jail, so Gbedemah was able to send me from time to time a full report of what was going on outside.

It was no easy task for Gbedemah to keep the Party united and it was especially difficult when so many of the members were vying with one another for leadership. By reading out my messages from prison, however, Gbedemah managed to keep my name alive in the minds of the people and encouraged them to carry on their struggle under his guidance until the day that I would be once more able to lead them. Once or twice a week I could hear evidence of the success of this, for crowds used to assemble outside the prison and sing Party songs and hymns. One that I particularly remember was "Kwame Nkrumah's body lies a-mouldering in the cell" to the tune of "John Brown's Body." It boosted up my morale a great deal to hear these voices and to know that I had not been deserted and forgotten.

I decided to grow a beard after discovering that we were expected to share one razor blade and one shaving stick between us. Although I was rapidly learning that the sooner I lost my self-respect the sooner I would settle down in my uncomfortable and unsavory surroundings, I could never get used to the idea of a communal razor blade and shaving soap. I preferred to let my whiskers grow rather than run the risk of skin infection.

I used to look forward to Sundays more than anything as we were excused our usual labors on that day and, after washing my prison clothes, I used to search for a quiet corner in the prison yard where I could sit and reflect. One Sunday morning I gathered my fellow Party prisoners together and we organized a committee, of which I was the chairman, in order to work out the plans which the Party outside were to follow. At the same time we elected two sub-committees, one composed of the ex-servicemen and the other with Kojo Botsio as its chairman. We met regularly thereafter and discussed our common problems. This was unknown to the warders.

On Sundays also we were allowed to attend whatever service was being conducted in the prison, the most popular of which was that of the Apostolic Faith. During this particular service there was much clapping of hands and movement. Every prisoner, old and young, Christian and atheist, was glad to join in this service—in fact we looked forward to it—for we managed to get not only fresh air but also exercise and relaxation from boredom. Some of the prisoners got so carried away during the service that they shed tears like children as they reflected and confessed their past misdeeds, begging for remission of their sins. In fact some of them who confessed their sins were so repentant that when they were released they vowed they would never commit a crime again. But, in spite of these good intentions, I used to notice that in a matter of weeks the same men were back again for the same crimes.

After about a month or two the hardship and monotony of prison life began to get the better of some of us and we started quarrelling and blaming one another for what had happened. Some of them couldn't understand why we should be forced to suffer and quite a fracas ensued. Many times I had to act as mediator and often had to beg and plead with my companions to keep peace and order within the confines of our small prison cell. This feeling of general unrest and discomfort brought out feelings of bitterness, selfishness and revenge. I remember how on one occasion I had managed to get hold of a copy of the *Evening News*. As soon as we had been locked in our cell, one of our number became so embittered when he saw me reading this precious paper that he reported the whole thing to one of the warders. A search was made of our entire cell and the newspaper was run to ground and confiscated. I was so relieved that my stump of pencil had not been found and that the sheets of toilet paper were not suspected of playing a duplicate role, that I gladly accepted my punishment of short rations. The normal rations were barely adequate to keep body and soul together and any reduction in this amount was certainly no joke, but I stuck it out.

Apart from the Sunday service there were two things that supplied a little relief to the boredom. One was an occasional concert that the prisoners used to get up which, in spite of the crudeness of the performance, was, compared with the dark walls of the cell, grand entertainment. The other pastime that we enjoyed was gambling. There were three items of value in the prison: toilet paper, nut kernels, and soap. These things were so precious and so much in demand that they always represented the stakes in our gambling games, for money was quite useless to us. I became a keen gambler as far as the toilet paper was concerned, because I could never get enough of this to write all I had to say. The nut kernel was generally used by the prisoners to oil their bodies because, on account of the rotten diet and the poor quality of the soap, the skin became scaled and cracked. By chewing the nut kernel and then smearing your body with it, it was possible to get enough oil to lubricate at least the most affected parts of your skin.

The most demoralizing moments that I experienced in prison were when a prisoner was committed to be hanged. These unfortunate men were brought in in chains and were kept in solitary confinement away from the ordinary prisoners. We all knew when the day of execution arrived for we were made to get up earlier than usual and taken from our cell to an upstairs room where we were locked in before six o'clock. Some people used to try and peep through the window to see if they could catch a glimpse of what was going on, but it was quite impossible. By about ten o'clock we were let out and the only sign of the grim event was that there was sometimes an occasional blood stain on the ground near where we went to have our ablutions, for the gallows was situated in the vicinity of the washroom. To see a man brought in one day and disappear completely a few days later was something that really affected the other prisoners. There must have been an average of one execution a month during the time I was imprisoned, and most of the offences for which these men were hanged were for killing their wives or killing men whom they had believed were having illicit relations with their wives.

I used to reflect after these awful moments and I wondered whether prison punishments really did achieve their purpose in reforming the criminal, whether capital punishment was a solution to murder cases. Criminals, after all, are human beings. No man is born a criminal; society makes him so, and the only way to change things is to change the social conditions. It is only from the social standpoint that crime and punishment can be effectively approached. I have always been against the death penalty, even before I came so close to understanding what this meant during my prison life. I believe that it is a relic of barbarism and savagery and that it is inconsistent with decent morals and the teaching of Christian ethics. The aim of punishment should be that of understanding and correction.

I looked back on my own boyhood. I was brought up in a particularly primitive society, but during the whole of my eighteen years or so of boyhood life in Nzima, I can only remember there being one murder case, and that was a case in which a sexual maniac was involved. The taboos of primitive society generally curb crime. The impact of Western culture on the African mind brought in its train as much bad as good. Offences like forgery, bribery and corruption, for instance, were practically unknown in our early society.

My experience of fourteen months in prison convinced me, moreover, that in a very short time prisoners lose all their individualism and personality; they become a set type in an unhappy world of their own. They lose confidence in themselves and are so unequipped to meet the outside world that it is little wonder that they hanker for the misery and boredom of their prison cell, a protective shelter for their lost and shattered souls.

Although I suffered extreme boredom, I was luckily far too actively engaged in planning for the Party outside to allow myself to become stagnant. Very soon the time approached for the general election which was due to take place on February 8, 1951. There was much work to be done for this, for it was vital that our Party win a majority in the new Legislative Assembly. I had already made it clear to the Party organizers outside that by all means they should contest every seat in the election, and I had received word from Gbedemah that they had prepared themselves to do this.

It had not been my original intention to stand for election myself until I realized that unless I did it might be very difficult to obtain my release before my sentence ended—for I knew that if I succeeded in winning the election it would be very difficult for the authorities to insist on keeping me in prison.

The first thing I did was to insist on my name being registered on the electoral roll. I experienced much opposition over this but I was adamant and, as I was within the law in this respect, nobody could forbid it, even though I did not expect to be able to use my vote. Few people realized that by our law anyone who is convicted to a term of imprisonment not exceeding one year is entitled to be registered on the electoral roll. Although my total sentence was for a period of three years, this was made up of three separate terms of imprisonment of one year each.

After battling to get my name on the electoral roll, I went to the prison authorities and told them that I had decided to stand for election. It was no good for them to try to tell me that I was not qualified to do so, for the fact that I had been qualified to register as an elector ruled this out.

Strange to say, some of the Party members outside protested about my decision to stand election, for they held that if I was later disqualified we would lose the seat altogether. But I waved all this aside. I told them that I would stand for Accra Central in place of Gbedemah, who agreed to stand election in Keta. This sudden change made the organization somewhat difficult, but we were able to overcome it.

Acting officially through the prison superintendent, I arranged with those outside to pay my deposit, to sign my papers, and to form themselves into a campaign committee. My forms were completed and submitted to the authorities a few minutes before the registration period closed and the campaign committee got to work on my behalf.

I busied myself in rewriting the Party manifesto as the one that had been smuggled in to me was not a manifesto in the true sense of the word. In due course I completed it. As soon as it became known that I was going to stand for election, there was terrific jubilation throughout the country, for there was a general feeling that if I was elected the Government would, on the strength of it, release me and my colleagues.

On the night of the general election extra precautions were taken by the prison authorities owing to a rumor that had been circulated that the whole of Accra was going to advance on the prison and get me out. However, although it was all quiet, I was quite unable to sleep the whole night. I was both excited and anxious. I began to wonder whether everything would now prove to have been in vain, whether the people would still stand by the Party and give me the chance to finish the job. Deep down in my heart, however, I knew that my hour of victory was at hand; I had complete trust and confidence in the people and I knew that they would not let me down.

The prison superintendent had arranged for hourly reports to be given to me on the progress of the election results. At about four in the morning the news was brought to me that I had been elected for Accra Central. Not only that, but I had received the largest individual poll so far recorded in the history of the Gold Coast—22,780 votes out of a possible 23,122. I had no time for reflection for the news flashed round the prison and in a matter of seconds the place was alive with jubilation. I believe even the warders were happy. Throughout Accra the excitement of the crowds was so great that Gbedemah had the greatest difficulty in stopping a crowd, hundreds strong, from advancing on James Fort where they intended breaking down the doors and rescuing me from my prison cell. Such an act—although done in good faith—would naturally have ruined all our chances for success.

As the day wore on and the true significance of all that had happened became clearer in my mind, my feelings became a mixture of humility, of gratefulness to the people, and of peace—peace of mind, in fact, that I had long forgotten existed. I was brought back to earth by a message that was brought to me, saying that there were a number of foreign newspaper reporters clamoring for a statement from me. I promptly refused to have anything to do with them for I had long since discovered that such people rarely report you verbatim; they give their own interpretations, and the more lurid and sensational they can make these, the better they like it.

The day after the election results were announced, the Executive Committee of the C.P.P. asked the Governor if he would receive a delegation of the Committee in order to discuss the question of my release, for they held that as leader of the Party, if that Party was asked to form a government, it would be impossible for me to do so while in prison. The Governor agreed to meet this delegation and, after the meeting, arrangements were put in hand for my release. All this was done in complete secrecy as the Government did not want the news of my release to be spread abroad.

Between eleven and twelve o'clock on the morning of February 12, 1951, the prison superintendent sent for me and told me to be ready to leave the jail within the next hour. I looked around me, but the only possessions I had were my bit of pencil and a few sheets of toilet paper, and these no longer seemed valuable. I told him that I was ready to leave at a moment's notice. At about the same time, apparently, the news of my release leaked out into the town. At one o'clock when the prison gates were closed behind me I realized why the Government had tried to keep the news top secret. I don't think I have ever seen such a thickly packed crowd in the whole of my life.

I was too bewildered to do anything but stand and stare. Any emotion that I had anticipated was completely arrested and I felt like a stuffed exhibit in a museum.

Then I remember a familiar voice speaking my name and I woke from my trance to find Gbedemah standing by my side. We greeted each other and my senses came to life as I was hoisted shoulder high and carried to an open car that was standing nearby. It is difficult even now to describe all I experienced as this car moved at a snail's pace like a ship being dragged by an overpowering current in a sea of upturned faces. To look at this locked mass of struggling figures and to listen to the deafening clamor of their jubilant voices made me feel quite giddy. The only way I could steady myself was to keep my eyes averted and to gaze at the mighty expanse of sea and sky, until I was able to adjust myself and acknowledge the greetings of the people.

Slowly, as I filled my lungs with the pure air of freedom, new life was born into me. This was the greatest day of my life, my day of victory and these were my warriors. No general could have felt more proud of his army and no soldiers could have shown greater affection for their leader.

From James Fort the procession made its way to the West End Arena, taking two hours to do a normally fifteen minutes journey. At the Arena, the birthplace of my Party, the customary expiation was performed by sacrificing a sheep and by stepping with my bare feet in its blood seven times, which was supposed to clean me from the contamination of the prison. The crowd stayed with me the whole time, accompanying me in procession to the Party headquarters where, completely worn out, both physically and mentally, I crumpled into the nearest chair.

Leader of Government Business

THE DAY AFTER MY RELEASE FROM PRISON I WAS INVITED BY THE Governor to meet him at nine o'clock that morning. When I walked into the courtyard of Christianborg Castle, the official residence of the Governor, I suddenly realized that this was the very first time I had set eyes on the place. The glaring white stone of the battlements, the impressive forecourt and the beauty of this imposing building with the roaring surf battering against its foundations, seemed to me like a new world. Although Sir Charles Arden-Clarke and I had been opposing each other for so many months past, I had no idea what he looked like, for we had never met. I wondered how I should be received. Had I known this man before, I should not have doubted the courtesy that would be shown to me.

A tall, broad-shouldered man, sun-tanned, with an expression of firmness and discipline but with a twinkle of kindness in his eyes came towards me with his hand outstretched; a hand that I noticed was large and capable looking. He welcomed me and asked me how I was. As we both sat down I sensed that he must be feeling as alert and suspicious of me as I was of him. We lost little time, however, in coming down to the business on hand. I did my best to make it clear to him that I would be prepared at all times to place my cards face upwards on the table because it was only through frankness that mutual trust and confidence could be established. He agreed with me wholeheartedly in this and I sensed immediately that he spoke with sincerity. He was, I thought, a man with a strong sense of justice and fair play, with whom I could easily be friends even though I looked upon him as a symbol of British imperialism in the country.

In spite of the fact that I was fresh from the prison cell and had probably every reason to harbor hatred in my heart, I had forced myself to forget the sufferings and degradation that I had endured at the hands of the colonial administration, for I knew that revenge was bitter and that it was foreign to my make-up. It was with truth and sincerity that I made the statement soon after my release from jail that "I came out of jail and into the Assembly without the slightest feeling of bitterness to Britain. I stand for no discrimination against any race or individual, but I am unalterably opposed to imperialism in any form."

I left the Castle with instructions from the Governor to form a government. As I walked down the steps it was as if the whole thing had been a dream, that I was stepping down from the clouds and that I would soon wake up and find myself squatting on the prison floor eating a bowl of maize porridge.

I must say a word or two here about the constitution existing at this time. Contrary to the provisions of the Burns Constitution, that of the Coussey Commission recommended that the new Legislative Assembly was to consist of a Speaker, to be elected by the Assembly from among its members or outside it, and eighty-four elected members. Five seats were allocated to the municipalities—two for Accra, one each for Cape Coast, Sekondi/Takoradi and Kumasi; thirty-three rural members were to be elected in two stages, first by direct primary voting and secondly through electoral colleges; ninteen inhabitants of the Northern Territories were to be elected by the Territorial Councils of the Colony, Ashanti and Trans-Volta Togoland; six special members were to be elected in equal proportion by the Chamber of Commerce and the Chamber of Mines and three ex officio members were to be nominated by the Governor—the Minister of Defense and External Affairs, the Minister of Finance and the Minister of Justice. The result of the election showed that the Convention People's Party had won thirty-four out of a possible thirty-eight elected seats in the municipal and rural areas and that they also had a majority in the Assembly over the nominated candidates.

Immediately after I left the Castle I convened a meeting of the central committee of the Party in order to discuss with them the names of those whom I had selected to serve as ministers in the new government. The problem which faced me was that, during my discussions with the Governor, I had agreed that since the C.P.P. had won a majority only in the elected seats of the Assembly, to select my ministers solely from the ranks of the Party might bring me into conflict with the territorial members and with other independent members of the Assembly. I proposed to the central committee, therefore, that of the seven ministers, five should be party members, one should come from the Northern Territories and the other one from Ashanti. At first the central committee objected to this proposal as they felt—and understandably so—that all the ministers should be chosen from the ranks of the Party supporters. After a long discussion, however, they accepted my suggestion and I then submitted the names to the Governor. The five ministers belonging to my Party were:

Kojo Botsio—Minister of Education and Social Welfare
K. A. Gbedemah—Minister of Health and Labor
A. Casely-Hayford—Minister of Agriculture and Natural Resources
T. Hutton-Mills—Minister of Commerce, Industry and Mines
Dr. Ansah Koi—Minister of Communications and Works.

I nominated as Minister of Local Government, E. O. Asafu-Adjaye, a representative of Ashanti, and finally, to represent the Northern Territories, I selected Kabachewura J. A. Braimah, as Minister without Portfolio. Under the constitution, as leader of the majority party in the Assembly, I became the Leader of Government Business.

For the C.P.P. to win such a sweeping victory had been unexpected and must have been an unpleasant surprise for quite a number of people. The post of Leader of Government Business, for instance, had been earmarked for the Attorney General, a post held by an overseas officer. Many other members of the Assembly, who were opposed to the Convention People's Party, were expecting ministerial appointments and had made extravagant preparations in anticipation of this, believing that if the Governor, under the Coussey Constitution, was going to nominate members to the Executive Council, they stood a fair chance of being selected. Because of this new suits had been ordered to fit such offices, and wives had been dispatched to Europe to get themselves trained in the art of entertaining at a high level. But, as things turned out, the victory of the C.P.P. over the combined forces of its political opponents showered cold water on these plans.

In order to acquaint the C.P.P. Assemblymen with the policy of the Party and of the dangers and difficulties that lay ahead of them when they took their seats in the Assembly, I arranged to address them at the Arena. Because of the importance of this message, I had copies of it printed so that it would be a permanent record for them.

In this address I pointed out that the Convention People's Party, although alert to the dangers of trying to work under the existing constitution, was committed to pursue the struggle for "full self-government now." Going to the Assembly, I said is not an end but a means whereby "self-government now" can be fought for and won, both from within and from without the Assembly. Our party was the only one in the country that had this aim and therefore it would be impracticable for it to work with those who held different views.

I explained that in a democratic society, if a political party was in the minority it formed the Opposition; if it was in the majority, then it formed the Government. As far as we were concerned there should be no compromise on this point. Coalition with the other political groups in the country, as we knew them, would be dangerous.

The C.P.P., if it was to take part in forming the new government, would ask that all the eight ministerial positions should be from the Party members, but a concession might be made for the inclusion of one or two territorial members in the Executive Council. I pointed out that colonial governments did not give self-government to their colonies until circumstances and mass pressure forced them to do so and that it was only by determination, by singleness of purpose, and by effective and relentless agitation and organization that we could achieve our goal, and this regardless of victimizations, persecutions and imprisonments.

Members of the Assembly should not overlook the fact that the essential part of any proposal for a democratic government consisted in the desire to create all the conditions—political, economic, social, and cultural—necessary for a decent and full life for the people.

I warned them also that there was one great risk attached to accepting office under the present constitution: the temptation to identify oneself with such a constitution and to be swayed by considerations of temporary personal advantage instead of seeking the interests of the people. Bribery and corruption, which had been part and parcel of the colonial setup, must be stamped out. Our election to the Assembly showed that the public had confidence in the integrity of the Party. The trust which the people had placed in the C.P.P. was the most precious thing we possessed, and as long as we were able to maintain it, victory would be ours.

The people of the country needed political power to manage their own affairs, but we should not be deceived by such things as the creation of African ministers under the new constitution, for these ministers could very easily become tools and puppets in the hands of British colonial bureaucrats. It was important, therefore, that the party system should be established forthwith in the new Legislative Assembly, so that ministers could be collectively responsible to the people, whom they represented, and not to civil servants.

I also told them that it was important to remember at all times that, as members of the Legislative Assembly, we did not stand alone; as such we were leaders of the mass of the people outside the Assembly and at all times we must be conscious of this link and avoid isolating ourselves from the people. We must keep contact with those who gave birth to and nurtured the Party. This could be done by meetings and consultations with the people and by putting forward the needs of the people in the Assembly. As long as the Party preserved this link with the people, it had every chance of becoming invincible. Assemblymen should have foresight and be able to deal with matters effectively, but at the same time the policy of the Party should be explained to the people whenever a new situation arose.

An important thing that must be carried out, I went on, was to sweep away all colonial laws which restricted freedom of speech of the press and in public assembly. In particular, I quoted the need for amendments to the laws concerning trade unions, the law of sedition, and others which were aimed at hindering the progress of the people. Moreover, a citizen should be tried by a jury in all criminal cases instead of the questionable trial by assessors.

It was felt that had we not accepted office by virtue of our majority in the Assembly, but had embarked on non-cooperation and remained in the opposition, we would merely have been pursuing negative action. It was moreover the opinion of the Party Executive that by taking part in the new government, we were at least preventing the "stooges and reactionaries" from taking advantage of the position. Governmental positions could also help us to obtain the initiative in the continuing struggle for full self-government. If we were obstructed in our purpose by British bureaucratic officialdom, we did not rule out the possibility of further Positive Action.

There should be no fraternization, I said, between Assemblymen and European officials except for strictly official relations; for what imperialists failed to achieve by strong-arm methods, they might hope to bring off with cocktail parties. I emphasized, however, that we were not fighting against race or color, but against a system. To prove that we had not led this struggle for any personal aggrandizement, we had agreed that none of our Party members in the Executive Council should go to live in the palatial ministerial bungalows that had been built for the purpose.

Moreover, I continued, until such time as full self-government had been attained, I was strongly of the opinion that all Party members of the Assembly, as well as Ministers, should surrender their salaries to the Party and draw instead agreed remuneration from Party funds. This would prevent careerism and induce those in high office to live simply and modestly and so maintain contact with the common people.

By launching Positive Action the previous year, we had demonstrated to the people that we stood by our word whatever the cost might be. "The spirit of Positive Action," I declared, "has made the Party what it is today and Positive Action must maintain it."

"The die is cast," I concluded. "The exploited and oppressed people of colonial Africa and elsewhere are looking up to us for hope and inspiration. Progressive people in Britain and elsewhere are also solidly behind us. The torch of the Liberation Movement has been lifted up in Ghana for the whole of West Africa and it will blaze a trail of freedom for other oppressed territories.

"Long live the Convention People's Party! Long live the Liberation Movement throughout the world!"

The Legislative Assembly first met on February 20, 1951, for the purpose of members taking the oath of allegiance and the election of a Speaker. Much to the amazement of the people, the Speaker I proposed was in no way connected with our Party and had never shown any interest in the policy of the C.P.P. This was Mr. E. C. (now Sir Emmanuel) Quist, a distinguished barrister and former president of the Legislative Council. This nomination and that of Dr. Fiawo, as Deputy Speaker, were unanimously accepted. The Assembly then adjourned until the 26th of February when the election of ministers took place. Apart from my own nominations, the Governor nominated as ex officio ministers Mr. R. H. Saloway as Minister of Defense and External Affairs, Mr. R. Armitage as Minister of Finance, and Mr. P. Branigan as Minister of Justice and Attorney General. All the representative ministers were unanimously accepted by secret ballot of the Assembly.

The Legislature began its work in earnest. The C.P.P. representative minister with the three ex officio ministers formed the Executive Council which was presided over by the Governor. Between the two were certain Independents from the Territorial Councils who did not come under the control of either Whip and voted according to their own conscience, sometimes for the Government and sometimes for the Opposition. But although my Party held only thirty-four of the total of seventy-four seats in the Assembly, we were usually able to maneuver things in such a way that we had enough support from the Independents to give us a firm and reasonable majority to carry out our policy in legislation.

During those early days of 1951, there was so much to be attended to that, looking back, I wonder how I ever got through it all. First there was the organizing and arranging of the work of the Assembly, such as the procedure for bills, questions, preparation of standing orders, and the introduction of some method of accurately reporting the Assembly proceedings. Then I planned the Speaker's office. Coupled with this, owing to the unexpectedness of my appointment as Leader of Government Business, no provision had been made for an office for me, as, if things had gone according to plan, the position would have been in the hands of the Attorney General. I was given a room in the main Ministry Building near that of the Colonial Secretary and the services of a British Senior Assistant Secretary from the Ministry of Agriculture. Together we laid the foundations of my office.

And then there was the Party to consider. The Party headquarters was filled to capacity each day with members coming to see me with urgent problems, personal matters, or just to shake my hand, and it was all-important that I should be there to meet them. My daily program was an exhausting one. I used to get up at four in the morning to go into my study and spend a couple of hours preparing my files, speeches, or other matters that had to be dealt with during the day. Then people would start coming to the house, often long before I had finished my work, and I would spend another couple of hours talking with them and trying to sort out the hundred-and-one problems that they brought to place before me. If I had time, I would drink a cup of tea but this was often left to get cold.

I would arrive at the office around eight o'clock and go through whatever there was on my desk. If the Assembly was in session, I would go there and proceed later to the Party headquarters, otherwise I would go straight to the headquarters and spend hours there. I rarely had anything to eat in the middle of the day and it was usually late afternoon when I got back to my house to eat disinterestedly whatever had been put on the table for me—*fou-fou, kenke,* stewed fish, or a rice dish. Sometimes I would hardly have sat down to begin my meal before people arrived with more problems that they felt could not possibly wait five minutes. While I went about my business of eating, they sat and talked to me.

The evenings were as busy as the days—Party meetings, interviews, people, people and more people. It was rare that I got to bed before midnight and my hours of sleep averaged four per night.

As time went on, the disgruntled members of the Opposition, having got over the shock of having to forego their positions of high office in the new government, had started their old game of attacking me and my followers. They tried to cause discontent among the people and misunderstanding in the world press by announcing that because "these flotsams and jetsams and the popinjays of the country" had landed themselves good jobs, they had forsaken their policy of "self-government now."

In order to defend myself and the Party, I issued to these critics a challenge which I delivered in public before a large crowd in Kumasi at the beginning of October. After going through the history of the Party and reiterating to the people that our policy was as strongly for "self-government now" as it had ever been, I warned the crowd against falling into the trap of the enemies of our Party, who were now accusing me and the C.P.P. of compromising with imperialists, of deserting our sacred cause and of signing secret pacts.

"We either go forward to victory, or we pay the consequences of defeat," I said.

"What is wrong with these political charlatans and humbugs?" I asked. "It is time for them to make up their minds and I am going to help them to do so."

"What do they want of me? Let them come out openly and say it. If, after having won the election so decisively, the Convention People's Party had not accepted ministerial positions, these same people would have said that we were afraid of responsibility and it would not have been beneath them to do anything that would bring them into power."

I reminded the people that the U.G.C.C. and some of the Chiefs had accused us of rejecting the Coussey constitution but that they had agreed at the Joint Territorial Congress in Kumasi that this constitution should be given a trial.

"Can it be," I asked, "that they now want self-government immediately—today? Are they prepared for Positive Action now?"

I wondered, I said, whether, if a motion for immediate self-government, unanimously adopted by the Assembly, was rejected by the British Government, would these elements join with us in staging another Positive Action?

"In this connection," I declared, "I will now throw a challenge to the U.G.C.C. and all other political opponents. We of the Convention People's Party have made it plain that we are working according to plan, but we are nevertheless prepared to readjust—or even change—our tactics and stategy if our detractors and opponents accept the challenge to join us in declaring Positive Action for self-government now. My colleagues and I are prepared to resign from the Government immediately if the so-called opposition parties, factors, groups and caucuses come out of the conspiratorial dens and join me and my Party in staging Positive Action for full self-government now."

"To implement this challenge," I continued, "we invite Dr. Danquah, Mr. Obetsebi Lamptey, and the Executive of the United Gold Coast Convention; Mr. Ollenu, Mr. Bossman and the Executive of the National Democratic Party; the Chiefs of the Asanteman Council; Nana Ofori Atta, President of the Joint Provincial Council, and Chiefs of that Council; Mr. Kobina Sekyi and the Executive of the Aborigines Rights Protection Society—all of them to communicate with the General Secretary of the Party within fourteen days from today, the date line being midnight of October 14, 1951, whether or not they are prepared to meet the representatives of the C.P.P. in conference to plan a nation-wide campaign of Positive Action if the British Government rejects a motion for self-government now."

I amplified the conditions upon which this "united party" would treat with the British government and ended by declaring that the people of the country would now be able to judge the mettle of our political opponents. Of course, not one of them answered my challenge. But the air was cleared once more.

Tactical Action

IT HAS ALWAYS BEEN MY CONVICTION THAT AFTER ANY POLITICAL revolution, non-violent or violent, the new government should, immediately on coming into power, clear out from the civil service all its old leaders. My own experience taught me that by failing to do so, a revolutionary government risks its own destruction. In my case, however, such a course was impossible because the civil service at that time, of which about eighty per cent were British, came under the Secretary of State for the Colonies. It became obvious to me, in fact, that there existed in the civil service at that time an attitude of dual allegiance—one to our Government and the other to the Colonial Office represented by the Secretary of State.

The civil service, the police, the judiciary, defense and external affairs were all in the hands of the Governor and, as internal security was not in the hands of representative ministers, all decisions thereon had to come from Whitehall. Because of this the representative ministers quite often came into open conflict with the Governor and the ex officio ministers. I did everything in my power to ensure that such conflicts never came out in the open, for I feared that this might result in the breakdown of the Government and possibly the suspension of the Coussey Constitution. As a matter of fact, had it not been for the unique relationship and understanding that quickly developed between the Governor and myself, this would have been the only way of bringing to an end this system of diarchy.

To achieve full internal self-government and to carry out the intensive five-year development program that had been formulated for the country, I had to rely on the varied government machinery and the same civil service, police and judiciary that had participated in one way or another in my arrest and imprisonment. Both from my side and from theirs it was difficult to know where and to what extent to put one's trust and allegiance. The Commissioner of Police, for instance, who had won a libel case against me as publisher of the *Evening News*; the member of the Crown Counsel who so happily led the prosecution at my trial; the magistrate who presided at my trial; the Colonial Secretary as Crown witness and hundreds of his colleagues in the Government who had taken part in the chase, if not bodily, then certainly in spirit—all these could have been against me.

I had long ago made up my mind that it was essential from all points of view to bury the hatchet. I was not so sure, however, that those with whom I should have to work would find it possible to do the same. I found that some managed it very successfully but that a minority were unable to forget and put the past behind them.

In 1951, the twenty per cent of African government employees held only very minor posts. At the rate things were going, unless Africanization was speeded up, it looked to me as if it would be many years before our own people would be sufficiently qualified and experienced to take over responsible posts in the civil service. On the other hand, I was faced with a far more serious problem if the overseas officers, realizing that Africans were being trained to take over from them and that their days were therefore numbered, resigned *en bloc* from their posts. Some of the Europeans at that time were very much of the old colonial type. The sight of an African in any job above a messenger or a clerk would have been more than they could stand, and they would have either insisted on his removal or tendered their own resignations on the spot. Unfortunately we could not afford to wave them goodbye and I realized that the problem was going to call for much thought and tact.

From the point of view of the overseas officer I could quite understand that he had his career to consider. He had joined the Colonial Service under certain conditions, and when the amendments that I visualized were made to the existing constitution, I could see that, in a country on the verge of independence, he would not be able to retain the status which was given to him under the old colonial regime. He would be faced with a choice: to leave the country or to surrender his existing terms of apointment under the Colonial Service regulations by joining the Gold Coast service and accepting full local control.

And so I set about planning a Gold Coast local civil service in which these overseas officers could elect to serve if they wanted to. At the same time I knew that this in itself was not enough. Some inducement would have to be offered to make it worth their while to stay, otherwise there would be a general exodus which would not be in the interests of the country. I therefore formed a proposal for compensation for loss of career in order to secure the interest of the officers concerned and to retain their services as long as possible until we were in a position to put through our Africanization program.

The Secretary of State was consulted on the matter and made it clear that he was concerned particularly with two aspects of the problem. First, how to help the successful development of the country by continuing to provide an overseas staff as requested by the Gold Coast Government and to encourage overseas officers to remain in the service as long as they were needed; and, second, he was anxious to fulfill his obligations towards officers holding Secretary of State's appointments. I was equally anxious that the responsibility towards officers holding Secretary of State's appointments should be fully discharged and I realized that we had to have an efficient administrative machine to give effect to government policy. Our position was unlike that of India, Pakistan and Ceylon, for at the time they achieved independence, all three of these countries had a public service which was largely indigenous.

On July 8, 1953, I made a statement in the Assembly concerning the position of overseas officers. I pointed out that although great strides had been made in Africanization and that the foundations of the African Civil Service of the future had been laid, we had to face the fact that for some years to come we would have to continue to rely on the services of overseas officers. "It is therefore imperative that we should make our attitude clear towards them," I said. "I am aware that on the eve of fundamental constitutional changes, which must inevitably involve a change of conditions of their service, there is a feeling of uncertainty regarding their future among service officers. I want to allay this uncertainty by assuring overseas officers that a fully self-governing Gold Coast will need and want their services and that their interests will be fully safeguarded."

I then outlined the general principles which my Government proposed to adopt. "At the outset, I would remark that one of the main considerations is to provide a breathing space during which the transition to a Gold Coast Civil Service can be completed as smoothly as possible. We seek to avoid any sudden exodus of overseas officers and by safeguarding their future, to induce them to remain. While appreciating the need for accelerated Africanization, the Government does not propose that this should be achieved at the expense of efficiency, or that promotion in the Service should be on the basis of color. At the same time, changed conditions of service will be recognized by the introduction of a scheme for compensation."

Nearly eight hundred officers were involved and as the majority of these men at this time formed the backbone of the service, it was important that efforts should be made to retain as many as possible. In order to be doubly sure that there should not be a mass exodus, I devised a so-called "freezing" period of four years to give us a breathing space. By this means those concerned could elect to stay in the Gold Coast Service for a period of four years, after which they could take their compensation and go.

When the constitutional change came, many chose to stay. We lost only one hundred and forty officers and another eighty-three later on. Things went very smoothly from the civil service point of view, the credit for which must go to the Government. The Africanization program was stepped up and the overseas officers who elected to stay have for the most part adjusted themselves to their new conditions and adapted their minds to working under or side by side with African officers. Friendly co-operation has been established between them and the government machine runs reasonably smoothly.

But I must not leave the impression that everything was plain sailing. Apart from those who succeeded in making the best of things and discovered before long that their heart was really in the cause, there were others who, instead of leaving the country as their conscience dictated, chose for one reason or another to stay and battle on, making life miserable for themselves and objectionable for those with whom they came in contact. For instance it did not escape my notice that where the administrative service was concerned, if a policy was laid down for the officials by the Government with which they disagreed, means were adopted, by subterfuge or otherwise, to wreck that policy. At other times I would find that matters that I wanted to be dealt with urgently, would be delayed indefinitely (because they were not approved by some of the officials) until I had to intervene and get the job done.

In certain cases, although it was never easy to obtain evidence to prove it, it was impossible to believe that the civil service was as unbiased politically as it was supposed to be. It happened too often for it to be a coincidence that whenever government policy was put into effect, the officials either dilly-dallied or saw that nothing at all was done about it. Again, I could at one time almost guarantee that if there was any movement afoot against the Government, every attempt was made on the part of the civil service to enhance the opposition against the Government. Whether this was an example of the inherent sympathy of the British for the underdog is not clear, but it is liable to breed distrust.

Certain difficulties arose also with regard to the Chief Commissioners and the District Commissioners out in the field. Before my Party came into office the Chief Commissioners and their satellites, the District Commissioners, were actually the little governors of the rural areas over which they exercised their control. I knew by travelling through the country that many of these officers were hated by the people and that, because they represented colonialism and imperialism in practice, their presence was harmful to the country. I could not dispense with their services under this trial constitution, and in any case some measure of regional control was necessary. In an endeavor to effect a partial remedy I decided to change their titles to something more palatable to the people. I proposed that in future the Chief Commissioners would be known as Regional Officers and the District Commissioners as Government Agents. By this means I endeavored to impress upon the public that the old order had changed, that the Chief and District Commissioners were no longer a law unto themselves, agents of the archimperialists of the Colonial Office and Whitehall, but that they were the real agents of the Government of the Gold Coast.

In order to impress this upon the people and the Assembly, to whom these officers owed allegiance, I established a Chief Regional Officers' Conference to be held each month. At these conferences I was able to keep in touch with all that was going on in the Regions, to have the various problems explained to me, and to advise on the action to be taken. On the whole, I think that the Chief Regional Officers have found it more difficult than most other expatriates to accept the new order of things.

Another matter that called for careful handling but for definite action was the Swollen Shoot disease that was attacking cocoa trees in the country. This disease, which is carried from one tree to another by an insect called the Mealy Bug, was threatening the future of our cocoa crop, the country's most valuable export. Investigations into the matter confirmed my former fears, that the only solution was to cut down the affected trees. I knew the farmers would kick against this for they could not understand that although the cocoa trees were said to be infected with Swollen Shoot, they still produced apparently healthy cocoa pods. It was difficult to convince them that in a few years time the whole of their crop would fail.

A committee under Mr. Justice Korsah had been set up to look into the matter of Swollen Shoot and had recommended that the previous method of compulsorily cutting down affected trees should cease and the consent and co-operation of the farmers should be sought. The Government agreed to this and also transferred the control of the cocoa industry from the former Cocoa Rehabilitation Department to the Department of Agriculture. In order to organize the farming community and to make them feel conscious of the importance of a healthy and abundant cocoa crop and of the best means of obtaining this, it was proposed to set up a Central Advisory Board, a Farmers' Association and Cocoa Farmers' Regional Council.

In an effort to arrest the disease I launched what I called "The New Deal for Cocoa." In a broadcast speech I explained to the country that this was to take the form of a seven-year plan, "which would put the Gold Coast on the cocoa map of the world once more and keep it there, where it belongs." All farmers who had diseased trees should, I said, contact their nearest field officer of the Agricultural Department who would examine the trees and advise what should best be done. If he advised that the tree should be removed, and if the farmers consented, all possible assistance would be given both in removing the diseased trees and in protecting the healthy ones. As compensation to the farmers the Government would recommend to the Cocoa Marketing Board that they should pay to each farmer concerned four shillings as a first payment for every living large tree cut out and two shillings a year for three years as a replanting payment. Replanting payments would begin when the diseased tree had been removed and burnt and a new tree properly planted in its place.

"So enter into the New Deal for Cocoa with me," I appealed. "With voluntary effort, and absence of compulsion from the Government, or from those who do not understand the needs of the moment, we can organize our way to victory over this disease. We shall preserve our economic heritage in the hands of the people themselves. In re-establishing our cocoa, we shall not only be helping ourselves but we shall be proving to the world and to our critics and to the manufacturers who buy our cocoa that we are capable of looking after our own major industry. If there was ever a test of our fitness to control our own affairs," I concluded, "this is it."

An eight-weeks campaign was organized in order to explain the New Deal in detail to cocoa farmers in the areas affected. On the whole the response was good, but a minority group, who failed to grasp the seriousness of the problem, refused to allow their diseased trees to be cut down. The future of the cocoa industry was too important for it to be affected by the obstinacy of a few people. In October of the following year I made another broadcast on the subject stressing that the matter was one of national concern.

"It is the plain duty of everyone who owns cocoa to see that his farm is kept free from the disease," I said. "It is a duty to himself and to his family, because if he fails to cut out diseased trees his whole farm will eventually die and he will lose his livelihood. It is a duty to his neighbor, because the disease does not respect farm boundaries. It is a duty to his country because without cocoa there can be neither prosperity nor progress."

I concluded by saying that the few who were refusing to co-operate had now to fall into line and I warned them that those who refused to help would be breaking the law, and that unless they changed their ways and co-operated, the law would take its course. Because of the continued obstinacy of this minority and at the risk of my political reputation, I made it compulsory for diseased trees to be cut down. Owing to the co-operation of the Ghana Farmers' Council, I managed to succeed in getting this unpopular but very necessary measure effected.

Prior to my Party coming into power, local government was managed by the District Commissioners and the various State Councils. I realized that it was important that the people should become active participants in the affairs of their particular areas and so I set about the task of establishing local councils. Under a new ordinance that was introduced into the Assembly by the Minister of Local Government, three types of local councils were to be set up, District, Urban, and Local; the first to operate over a fairly wide rural area and the others over smaller areas. The chiefs, although they could be invited to serve in a purely formal capacity, would have no voting right and no official status in the councils. And the District Commissioners, who formerly had the say in all matters concerning their respective areas, were excluded from membership in these councils. Their new role was to act as liaison officers between the Government and the local councils and to see that the policies of the central Government were properly interpreted. The councils were to be able to raise funds by charging rates and taxes and they could also apply for grants-in-aid from the Government.

As a result of the first local government council elections that took place early in 1952, the C.P.P. secured over ninety per cent of the seats in the two hundred and seventy new councils that had been established. This placed us in a strong position. Democracy, I thought, had now succeeded in penetrating well and truly into the deep-rooted cancer of feudalism.

Then there was the important matter of foreign investment and in order to make the position clear, I made a statement on the subject in the Legislative Assembly on March 1, 1954. Apart from the proposal to produce electricity by damming the Volta River and to construct an aluminium smelter, a project that was at that time receiving detailed examination, I realized forcibly that the economy of the country should be expanded in other directions, especially with regard to industrial development. There was ample scope for the establishment of new enterprises, but I was well aware that the implementation of such projects would require the assistance of all. I realized that it would be many years before the Gold Coast would be in a position to find from its own resources people who could combine capital with the experience required in the development and management of new industries and that the country would therefore have to rely to a large extent on foreign enterprise. I made this clear in my statement to the Assembly and went on to say that it was only to be expected that foreign investors would require assurance about the conditions which would apply to their investments.

I pointed out that a condition of primary importance to my Government was that, whilst we appreciated that in industry the criterion must be that of industrial efficiency, the warmth of our welcome to both publicly and privately owned enterprises would depend on the extent to which they provided for the training of African employees for eventual employment in senior technical, professional, and managerial appointments. It was my firm intention that for the future there should be a steady increase in the number of qualified Africans to hold positions of responsibility and authority.

With this vital fact in mind, the Government would, I said, encourage as much as possible the entry and investment in industry of foreign capital. The Gold Coast had reserve funds which could be made available for investment in large scale enterprises and, where it was approached, it would be willing to participate in those that could be shown to be economically sound. In such cases where Government's participation was calculated to serve the national interest, the Government must reserve the right to insist on partnership. It was not intended, however, that foreign capital should be directly invested in public utilities, but apart from this, foreign capital should be free to invest in any other form of new industrial enterprise.

Every assistance would be given by the ministries concerned for the acquiring of suitable sites for factories, offices and staff accommodation, and investigations were being made with regard to factory sites in the principal urban centers, with particular attention to the zoning of industrial areas.

An Industries Section had, I said, been set up in the Ministry of Commerce and Industry for the purpose of advising both domestic and foreign capital in new ventures, providing assistance in locating suitable sites, obtaining priorities in the supply of public services and generally assisting in the solution of any difficulties. New industries might also be granted relief from import duties on specified raw materials.

I concluded by saying that it was my Government's earnest wish that those with capital to invest would seek the opportunity which existed in the Gold Coast in the full confidence that they would be treated as partners in the development of the country's resources.

American Interlude

In the midst of all the hurly-burly which seemed to be the pattern of my new life—an unworkable constitution, a disgruntled Opposition, an embryo office and a suspicious civil service—I had a most pleasant surpise. I received a letter from the President of Lincoln University informing me that the Board of Trustees had agreed that the Doctor of Laws degree should be conferred upon me at the Commencement Exercises in June of that year (1951). It was just over six years since I had left America and I could not believe that such an honor could be bestowed upon me in so short a space of time. I felt that I had not done enough to merit it and my first inclination was to decline it. I felt also that I was far too busy to pay a visit to America at that time. But my friends were insistent that I should accept the degree and that a trip abroad would do me a lot of good and so I wrote to the President, Dr. Horace M. Bond, accepting the offer.

On the 30th of May, accompanied by Kojo Botsio, then Minister of Education, I took off at Accra airport for London. Thousands had gathered at the airport to bid us bon voyage and the police had their work cut out keeping them from following me into the plane. It was my first long flight. Apart from the taking off and landing which I dislike intensely, I quite enjoyed the trip but I found it difficult to believe that we would land in London in a matter of eighteen or nineteen hours and I spent much of the time musing on the last time I had journeyed from Accra to London. Was it the same Kwame Nkrumah, I wondered? Kojo broke into my reverie to indicate that I should fasten my seat belt, for the last time, I was thankful to note. We circled round London airport on a clear bright morning and came in to land. The firm tarmac under my feet had never felt so welcome.

In the reception hall a familiar figure walked up towards us—George Padmore. It was a happy reunion, particularly so as it had all happened so suddenly. Together we went to George's flat where, seated around the old kitchen table, we related our activities since our last meeting. Hours later, when each one of us had exhausted his store of information, we sat back and relaxed. It was good to be back in London again and the change was certainly doing me good. Already the problems and perplexities of the past few months seemed mere trifles. In a gay mood, I made a tour of the Tower of London, Kensington Palace, Buckingham Palace, and St. James' Palace—all buildings I had attacked in my more fiery speeches as monuments of imperialism!

Two days later we boarded another plane for the United States and arrived early the following morning in New York. It was Kojo's first visit to America and I was keen to show him all my old haunts. But I had forgotten that this time I was no longer a poverty-stricken student wandering wherever the mood might dictate, looking for a room and being evicted after a week because I couldn't find the money for the rent.

"What are all these people doing?" I muttered to Kojo as a number of people walked towards us. Kojo replied that they must be extending an official welcome. Sure enough, the protocol officer from the State Department at Washington, followed by a delegation from Lincoln University, headed by the Dean and the President and members of the Lincoln Alumni Association, and the liaison officer for Gold Coast students with a large group of the students, were all there to accord me a most enthusiastic welcome. I felt honored indeed.

With flash bulbs bursting on all sides of us, we were ushered into a car and driven to our hotel with a police escort. On arrival at the hotel I held a press conference. I explained to the reporters that my visit was of a dual purpose: that I was there not only to receive an honorary degree from my old university, but that I was anxious to explore avenues in the United States for obtaining technical assistance for the development of my country.

Kojo and I lunched with a Gold Coast business man on the first day of our arrival and after this we went on to the apartment of Daniel Chapman, now Secretary to the Cabinet, but at that time working in the Division of Non-self-governing Territories of the United Nations. There we met a crowd of Gold Coast students and business men. We were most enthusiastically received and everyone was eager for the latest news of the Gold Coast. I told them as briefly as I could of the educational and economic development plans that we had in mind and emphasized to them the importance of their achieving the highest qualifications while they were in America so that they would later be able to render service to their country as technicians and advisers. It was a very happy gathering, a home from home, not only for Kojo and me, but for all those living temporarily away from our country. I remember Daniel's wife, Efua, handing me a bowl of rice and groundnut stew which I ate with the utmost appreciation sitting on a box by the kitchen door. In the evening various Negro pressmen came for an informal meeting with me and they were so enthusiastic about my appeal for technical aid and recruitment for the Gold Coast that they promised to give every assistance by way of publicity and propaganda.

The following day I travelled to Philadelphia where I was met by the Mayor and presented with the keys of the city. Philadelphia was a city with many associations for me, both good and bad, and it was a proud moment for me when I was granted its freedom. I chuckled to myself, as I thought of my interrupted sleep in Philadelphia's railway station. What would the policeman say now? It was a pity that he would never associate me with that sleepy down-and-out student and would be unable to share in the joke.

After the ceremony I was taken to the Bellevue-Stratford Hotel where I made a recording for a short broadcast acknowledging the cordial welcome that had been extended to Kojo Botsio and myself and assuring the people of America that the Gold Coast was determined to become a democratic state with the assistance of British and American friends.

I then went up to my room to wash and prepare myself for a

luncheon party that was being given at the hotel by the World Affairs Council and the Trustees of Lincoln University. When I got into my room I looked around for my suitcase. It was not apparent in any of the obvious places so I searched under the bed, in the cupboards, and in all the most unlikely places. All in vain. I checked with Kojo to see whether it had found its way to his room by mistake, and then got in touch with hotel porter. But nobody had seen my suitcase. Was I sure I had one? somebody suggested. I never discovered where it got to, but weeks later it was returned to me in the Gold Coast with everything intact. Perhaps I had been suspected of being a Communist agent and my shirts and ties were grabbed for inspection by the Federal Bureau of Investigation, but whatever the reason, it was certainly inconvenient at the time.

Both Kojo and I spoke at the luncheon. I went to some length to outline the history of my Party, the struggle for self-government and my reasons for accepting office under the Coussey Constitution despite my original objections to it. I expressed the hope that in the near future further constitutional progress would be made towards full self-government. I once again stressed the need for American and British technicians to assist in our development program. Many people came to me afterwards and promised to communicate with me concerning this appeal.

After lunch I visited the Philatelic Museum at Temple University, which I thoroughly enjoyed, as I am not only interested in philately but have a strong passion for museums of any kind. Before we knew where we were, the day had gone. I had to have a few minutes in which to prepare my Commencement Address for the following day and so I quietly escaped to my room in the hotel to write this. When I had finished I gave it to Kojo to read through and give his comments. It was around ten o'clock when Kojo very sensibly suggested going to bed, for we were both tired and the following day promised to be as hectic as ever.

"Kojo," I said suddenly, "there are two people I just must call and see. This may be the only chance I shall have. One is my dear old landlady, Mrs. Borum, and the other is Portia."

Kojo laughed, "Do you mind if I come along with you?" he asked.

"You don't think I intended leaving you behind, do you?"

As I walked up to the door of my old lodgings it felt as if I had never been away. Nothing was changed, except that I no longer had the key to the front door. Then I had the awful feeling that perhaps Mrs. Borum might not be there any more. I had never written to her and she was already an old woman six years before.

I knocked on the door. We waited a few minutes before we heard the shuffling of tired footsteps in the passage. The door was slowly opened and a sleepy head appeared. She did not recognise me at first until I asked if I could come in. Then she knew me at once by my voice.

"It's Kwame!" she exclaimed in delight. "Kwame, my boy!" We embraced. She was my American mother and it was like a home-coming to both of us.

We went in, but I told her that we would not stay long as it was late and I knew she retired early. After we had chatted about our mutual friends for a little while I got up and said we would have to go. As I was about to leave I closed her fingers firmly around a hundred dollar bill.

"I can never repay you for all the kindness you showed to me in my days of need, but this is a small contribution towards it," I whispered into her ear. Tears were streaming from her eyes as she tried to speak. I gave her an affectionate hug and told her that I would be calling again someday.

"I knew you would come one day, my boy," she said as we waved her goodbye.

It was now midnight or after and Kojo looked at his watch. "Hadn't we better put it off until another time?" he enquired anxiously. "Not on your life!" I said. "This is America. It doesn't matter how late you call on people."

I found the way to Portia's house and knocked on the door which was flung open almost immediately.

"Hello!" I said, with a broad grin on my face.

Portia's eyes nearly popped out of her head and she flung her arms round me in greeting. She had heard I was in town but my visit, at that hour, had taken her by surprise. She asked us inside and we sat talking together.

Of course, there *was* another reason for my visit as well as seeing her again, for it was with Portia that I had entrusted my precious books. I kept my eyes off them for as long as I thought polite, but she was quick to sense my feelings and, with a wave of her hand, she pointed to the bookcase.

"Your books," she said casually. "You see, I have taken good care of them for you. Whenever you want them, let me know."

"My books!" I exclaimed, trying to look as if I had quite forgotten about them. I lost no time in going to the bookcase, fingering each volume affectionately and remembering the struggle it had been procuring them. Each volume, I recalled, represented a sacrifice of some kind, mostly a meal or a bed for the night. I felt ashamed of myself all of a sudden for showering so much attention on them while Portia and Kojo quitely sat and looked on.

"Tell me about yourself," I said to Portia.

I discovered that she was married and that her husband did night work.

"You must have known," she said, with a mischievous twinkle in her eye, "calling on people at this hour of the night!"

Then I suggested that we should all three go out to one of the restaurants that Portia and I used to frequent and have a meal. "But this time," I declared, "you don't have to bring your purse, Portia! No Dutch treat tonight!"

Several hours later, tired but happy, a carefree Leader of Government Business and his Minister of Education threw themselves on their respective beds and were asleep before they had time to remove their clothes.

The following morning, I started a most memorable day with a formal Faculty breakfast at Lincoln University followed by a morning's discussion with a group of about thirty West African students of the University. At noon I attended a luncheon given by the Trustees of the University and then prepared myself for the Commencement Exercises at two o'clock. Owing to the loss of my suitcase I found that, even though I had bought several shirts, I was short of a clean one that was suitable for such an important occasion in my life. I approached Dr. Bond and explained the predicament that I was in. He at once came to my rescue and lent me a shirt.

The whole thing was still like a dream to me. I had been at several

Commencement Exercises at Lincoln during my student days there, but surely the atmosphere was never like this! There was an air of excitement so intense that I could not believe it came only from me. As I walked in the academic procession in my borrowed shirt, I suddenly felt an imposter. What had I done to merit such an honor? It seemed all wrong but I had gone too far to do anything about it. Here was the Kwame Nkrumah of 1935, who had not even enough to pay for one semester at the University but who had the nerve to persuade the Dean to give him a try. And now, sixteen years later, that same youth labelled "Leader of Government Business" was about to have a great honor bestowed upon him by his alma mater. "Truly," I mused to myself, "it is not the heights to which a man climbs that matter, but the depths from whence he came." The little village schoolteacher with his precious library of three books—the Bible, Shakespeare and Alcock's Grammar!

Suddenly I was jogged out of my daydreaming to find myself in a place of honor on the platform before a large audience among whom were some of my own tutors, my colleagues and my old classmates. The Dean, Professor Hill, was addressing them on what I had done to merit the award. He concluded his speech by saying, "I remember when Mr. Nkrumah applied for admission to this University he quoted in his letter from Tennyson's *In Memoriam* '. . . so much to do, So little done . . .' I would like to conclude by saying that I feel, as far as he is concerned, this should now read 'so much achieved in so short a time.' "

The President, Dr. Bond, then conferred upon me the degree of Doctor of Laws and I was invited to speak.

I began by outlining briefly my study days in America and later in London, explaining my political activities in London, the organization of the West African National Secretariat, the editing of the *New African* and the subsequent abandonment of my studies there in response to an invitation from the Gold Coast to become general secretary to the United Gold Coast Convention. I went on to relate the difficulties I encountered in organizing the U.G.C.C., my arrest and detention in the Northern Territories, the split with the U.G.C.C. and the formation of my own party, the Convention People's Party, with its motto "We prefer self-government with danger to servitude in tranquility" and its policy "Seek ye first the political kingdom and all things shall be added unto you." This was met with enthusiastic cheering from the audience.

I then explained how the C.P.P. had organized the masses in their fight against British imperialism; how, because of general dissatisfaction with the Coussey Constitution, I had resorted to Positive Action in an effort to coerce the British Government into granting a greater measure of self-government; and how, as a result of this, I and many others had been arrested and imprisoned on charges of sedition. I spoke of the recent general election and my Party's great victory, my release from prison and my decision to accept office in spite of the "bogus and fraudulent" constitution, because I felt that with time and patience this could be amended and in due course we would obtain full Dominion status within the Commonwealth. I explained that we felt no bitterness against Britain, that we stood for no racialism but that we would not tolerate imperialism in any form.

I then spoke about my hopes for the future. "We are aiming to work under democratic principles such as exist in Britain and in the United States. What we want is the right to govern ourselves, or even to misgovern ourselves." I again spoke of the needs of the Gold Coast for technicians, machinery and capital to develop its great natural resources and explained that I was appealing to the democracies of Britain and the United States for this assistance in the first place, but that if this should not be forthcoming, I would be forced to turn elsewhere. I said that there was much for the Negro people of America to do to help their ancestral country, both then and in the future, and that upon the attainment of Independence, it was the intention of my Party to rename the country Ghana. I concluded my speech by referring to the Doctor of Laws degree that had just been conferred upon me. "This honor," I said, "is not so much a tribute to the little work that I have done, but to the people of the Gold Coast and Africa, who, by their deep sense of responsibility and self-respect, have made my work possible. I carry home with me a lively memory of this historic occasion."

The Commencement Exercises finished up with a tea party which was held in the grounds of Dr. Bond's residence. In response to my appeal, many Negro graduates approached me and expressed a desire to go to the Gold Coast and do their bit and I asked them to write to me when I returned to my country. I explained to them that we were handicapped at the present time by our position as a colonial territory, but that as soon as we had achieved independence, we would be able to extend a hand of welcome to all those who desired to come to our country to work.

I then returned to New York where, on the following day, I paid official calls on Sir Gladwyn Jebb, the British delegate to the United Nations, and on the Mayor of New York. Just before midday I held a press conference. My speech the previous day had aroused much interest and I was bombarded with questions about how much the Gold Coast needed in dollars to help with its development, what would be the conditions of service for interested technicians, and other pertinent matters arising from my address. I quite enjoyed it and managed to fire back my replies as quickly as the questions were asked. This was followed by a television talk in which both Kojo and I took part.

After lunching at the United Nations headquarters I attended a meeting of the Trusteeship Council which was then under the chairmanship of Sir Alan Burns, a former Governor of the Gold Coast. He had already left the Gold Coast before I began my agitation, but he had naturally heard all about it and we found a lot to talk about. Later I had talks with Trygve Lie, Dr. Ralph Bunche, Mr. Wilfred Benson and other United Nations officials concerning the possibilities of assistance in the planning of the Volta River Scheme, scholarships for Gold Coast students, and technical assistance generally. These talks were most encouraging.

The next day, Kojo and I travelled by train to Washington where we were welcomed by four officers from the Department of State. Our stay there was brief but the program was full. I had talks with officers of the Department of State and other government departments, learned how the organization of the United States Government works, laid a wreath on the memorial to Abraham Lincoln, visited the Jefferson Memorial and attended two receptions, one at the British Embassy and the other immediately afterwards at the State Department.

The following day I returned to New York and prepared for my departure. In the evening the Mayor of New York arranged a large dinner party in honour of Kojo and myself. All the leading Negro dignitaries and officials were present and I gave a speech on the political development of the Gold Coast and on our hope to become self-governing in the near future. I expressed the desire that all those who wished to return to help develop the country would be most welcome after Independence, when we would be free to open our arms to whomsoever we pleased. I said how very happy I had been that I was able to pay this unexpected visit to the United States and how welcome everyone had made me feel. I would carry back with me many happy memories.

As I sat down in my place my thoughts went back to the day when I delivered my last sermon in America at the Presbyterian Church in Philadelphia. My text was "I saw a new Heaven and a new Earth" and I reminded the people of how history repeated itself. Just as in the days of the Egyptians, so today God had ordained that certain among the African race should journey westwards to equip themselves with knowledge and experience for the day when they would be called upon to return to their motherland and to use the learning that they had acquired to help improve the lot of their brethren. I impressed upon the people that they should not be despondent or impatient, for their turn would come any day now. "Be prepared," I warned them, "so that you are ready when the call comes, for that time is near at hand." I had not realized at that time that I would contribute so much towards the fulfillment of this prophecy.

On the 10th of June, Kojo and I waved goodbye to a crowd of officials, students, and other well-wishers who had assembled at the airport to send us on our way. We both felt happy in our hearts and encouraged by the talks that we had managed to have. But we were completely exhausted.

"Did we sleep at all in America?" I yawned. There was no reply from my companion, for he was already asleep with his safety belt still fastened securely round his waist.

We were a few hours late arriving in London but in spite of this George Padmore and a few African students were there waiting for us. I had the good fortune during this short visit to meet Mr. Attlee and most of the leading members of the British Labor Party and I stressed to them the urgency of granting full self-government to the Gold Coast. Whilst I admitted that it was important not to act too hastily, I urged them to do all they could to speed it up. I was invited to a reception by Mr. Lennox-Boyd, a Conservative M.P. He made me feel extremely welcome and showed keen interest in all that I told him about affairs in the Gold Coast. Little did I know then that this same man would, five years later as Secretary of State for the Colonies, serve as the connecting link between my Government and that of the United Kingdom for the negotiations concerning Independence. Another house where I was invited and where I was made to feel very much at home was that of Lord and Lady Mountbatten of Burma. With their knowledge of India and the transfer of power there, we found much to discuss of mutual interest.

It was fortunate, too, that Sir Charles Arden-Clarke was on leave from the Gold Coast at that time and I was able to have valuable discussions with him together with the Secretary of State for the Colonies and other Colonial Office officials. I paid a visit to the House of Commons where I dined with two of the members and listened to part of an all-night debate that was going on at the time.

I got through a lot in a short space of time and it was really something of a relief when I boarded the BOAC plane at London Airport. As the four engines came to life and we waited at the end of the runway to take off, I counted on my fingers the stops we should make, "Tripoli, Kano, Lagos, Accra." What had been happening in Accra while I had been away, I wondered? It seemed so long since I left. I was just a little bit anxious.

The following morning when the plane touched down at Kano to refuel, I was greeted at the airport by a delegation of the Kano Branch of the C.P.P. and other political supporters in Nigeria and I was presented by them with a ceremonial sword that had been made locally. A few hours later as we circled over Accra before landing, I observed that the whole of the airport area seemed to have been changed from grey tarmac to dark brown and black. People, thousands of them, cheering themselves hoarse. That was all the proof that I needed to show that all was well. Whatever else might be in store for me, the people, those that really mattered, were solidly behind me and my Party.

As soon as I poked my head out of the plane door and walked down the steps, the crowds broke through the barriers and in one frenzied charge they swarmed round me. In a matter of seconds I was whisked off my feet and carried shoulder-high amidst yells of greeting, party songs and cries of congratulations to "Doctor" Nkrumah. What a joyous ending to so memorable a trip!

Later in the day I arranged to speak to the people at the Owusu Memorial Park in order to greet them after my return from America. I was dressed, for the first and last time, in an army tunic. When I arrived the crowds were so dense that it was almost impossible to penetrate them. It took us over an hour to push our way, inch by inch, to the platform, because the people were so tightly jammed together that, try as they might, they could not press closer together to make a passage way for me. They were panting and groaning as their bodies were crushed one against the other and everywhere I looked I could see people fainting. When I eventually reached the platform I realized that it was useless trying to address them and told them to assemble the following Sunday at the Arena. I stood in silence as I gazed down at that thickest of gatherings, a great body of human beings that neither pain nor discomfort could distract from their purpose, proof in its most concrete form of their solidarity, and I was deeply moved at the thought that it was I who had the honor of leading them.

Prime Minister and Constitutional Reform

IN THE ROLE OF LEADER OF A MAJORITY PARTY IN THE ASSEMBLY which had been elected under a "bogus and fraudulent" constitution that in no way satisfied the political aspirations of my Party, my task was not an enviable one. The Coussey Constitution had not been formulated with the idea of a party system developing in the country. The post of Leader of Government Business had not been planned with a view to Africans taking over the Government, and, in fact, by winning the 1951 election with such a majority and by forming the Government, the position of Leader of Government Business had already become redundant. Even *The Times,* as early as February 17, 1951, pointed out the need for the creation of the post of Prime Minister, when, commenting on the title of Leader of Government Business, it observed that under the Coussey Constitution "there is no provision for a Prime Minister. That dignity exists only when the highest ministerial office is combined with the leadership of the predominant party in the Legislature."

Party members insisted strongly that my title should be changed to that of Prime Minister. There was much criticism about it as the general feeling was that the title was of no importance and that merely renaming the present post of Leader of Government Business to Prime Minister would not change the real substance of the constitution. I maintained, however, that there was something in a name, that as Prime Minister it would be necessary to abide by the conventions that go to make a prime minister, and that as my position in the Assembly as the leader of the Government was consequent upon my leadership of the majority party, the post of Prime Minister was definitely called for.

Eventually we won the day. On the afternoon of March 5, 1952, the Governor addressed a crowded meeting of the Legislative Assembly as follows:

> "Mr. Speaker, Honorable Members, I have come here this afternoon on your invitation to inform you of the text of a statement about further constitutional changes in the Gold Coast which the Secretary of State for the Colonies has just made in the House of Commons. This is the Statement:
>
> 'In the light of the working of the present Constitution and on the advice of the Governor, Her Majesty's Government have decided that the Leader of Government Business in the Legislative Assembly should disappear from the Constitution and that the Office of Prime Minister should be formally recognized. The Governor will consult the Prime Minister before submitting to the Assembly the names of the persons whom he proposes for appointment as representative members of the Executive Council or Cabinet and before allocating to them portfolios. The Prime Minister will rank in precedence in the Cabinet immediately after the Governor or the Officer Administering the Government as the case may be, and before any of the three ex officio Ministers whose position in other respects will remain unchanged.
>
> "The necessary amendment to the Constitutional Instrument to give effect to this and other consequential changes will be made very shortly.' That is the end of the Statement."

This message was received with resounding cheers and applause. Congratulations poured in to my office, to the Party headquarters, and to the Assembly from all quarters of the globe. As soon as I could escape the crowds, I went home so that my mother could share the joyous news with me.

"What does it feel like to be the mother of the first African Prime Minister?" I teased her.

She looked at me and gave a grunt as if to say "What will you be up to next?" But there was no hiding the look of pride that suddenly lit up those poor strained eyes.

Following the announcement of my appointment as Prime Minister, the Executive Council resigned, and in consultation with the Governor I created a new instrument of Government, to be known as the Cabinet. This was submitted to the Legislative Assembly for approval.

On the 21st of March the Legislative Assembly approved my appointment as Prime Minister and also the appointments as Representative Members of the Cabinet of the following:

Kojo Botsio—Minister of Education and Social Welfare
K. A. Gbedemah—Minister of Commerce and Industry
A. Casely-Hayford—Minister of Agriculture and Natural Resources
E. O. Asafu-Adjaye—Minister of Local Government
J. A. Braimah—Minister of Communications and Works
T. Hutton-Mills—Minister of Health and Labor
Ansah Koi—Minister of Housing

I elected to become Minister of Development in addition to my duties as Prime Minister.

The task now facing us was the final struggle for complete independence and the formation of a policy for fighting both inside and outside the Assembly in order to achieve this aim. Meanwhile, certain amendments to the constitution had to be carried out which would fit in with the conditions existing in this transitional period through which we would have to pass before the attainment of full self-government. This was, one might say, a probationary period wherein we had to prove our worth and demonstrate our ability to manage our own affairs.

I initiated discussions with the Governor on the subject of these amendments to the constitution and when in June of that year (1952) Mr. Oliver Lyttelton, then Secretary of State for the Colonies, paid a visit to the country, I took the matter further. I pointed out that we desired full self-government and that, in order to work satisfactorily during the transitional period before our goal was reached, certain constitutional changes were necessary. Mr. Lyttelton agreed that when proposals had been formulated by the Gold Coast Government, after consultation with the chiefs and people of the country, they would be examined and discussed by Her Majesty's Government and the Government of the Gold Coast. This showed clearly that in order to gain our independence, it was incumbent upon the Gold Coast Government to take the initiative. In other words, the Government should initiate consultation with the chiefs and people of the Gold Coast as to the necessary changes in the Coussey Constitution.

The first step that I took in regard to that consultation was to make a statement in the Legislative Assembly in October. I began by mentioning the principal features of the present constitution which, in the light of experience gained during the past twenty-one months during which it had been in operation, showed that it could be reviewed and amended. It was necessary to examine the matter fully, I said, so that it could never be said at a later date, either inside or outside the Gold Coast, that the proposals which we would eventually make to the United Kingdom Government were not based, on our part, on a full realization of the issue at stake.

The object of the consultations was to enable discussions to take place between our Government and that of the United Kingdom, and the proposals that we put forward should indicate clearly what further functions and responsibilities we considered we should now assume. I urged them strongly that, whatever interest, party or group they represented, those who took part in the consultations should participate with a proper sense of the gravity of the issues involved. It was important that we conducted our discussions with statesmanship of a high order and avoided every idle or ill-considered word, spoken or written.

I dealt first with the question of the ex officio ministers. We should consider, I said, whether these three ministers should be retained in the Cabinet or replaced by representative ministers. In the case of the ex officio Minister of Finance, were he to be replaced by a representative minister, the Government would have to ensure that expert financial advice continued to be available. This could best be done by appointing a Financial and Economic Adviser to the Government who would attend Cabinet meetings when required, but would have no vote and would be neither a member of the Cabinet nor of the Assembly.

The present ex officio Minister of Justice combined his duties with those of Attorney General, the Government's legal adviser. It was possible to dispose of the position of Minister of Justice and appoint an Attorney General who would continue to be the legal adviser of the Government and who would attend Cabinet meetings when required to do so, but would have no vote and would be a member neither of the Cabinet nor the Assembly.

With regard to the ex officio Minister of Defense and External Affairs, were he to be replaced by a representative minister, one implication would be that the Gold Coast was prepared to immediately take over full responsibility for its own defense—the main burden of which, I pointed out, was borne by the armed naval, military, and air forces of the Commonwealth. We possessed only a very small military force and contributed only a proportion of its cost.

Another implication would be that the maintenance and protection of our external trade relations would cease to be the direct responsibility of the United Kingdom and would become our own concern. We would have to be responsible for our own direct representation in the foreign countries with which we traded and be in a position to protect our trade with foreign countries from discriminatory practices.

"It is for the chiefs and people," I said, "bearing these implications in mind, to consider whether all or any of the ex officio ministers should be replaced by representative ministers."

I pointed out that at present the appointment of the Prime Minister and of his representative ministers depended on resolutions of the Assembly, that the name of the Prime Minister was proposed by the Governor and those of the representative ministers by the Governor after consultation with the Prime Minister. "It would be more in accordance with British constitutional practice," I said, "if the Prime Minister were free to select his representative colleagues without a resolution of the Assembly, the Governor having no power to reject his choice." I suggested also that, in accordance with British practice, the appointment of Prime Minister should depend not on a resolution of the Assembly, but on his willingness and ability to form a majority Government at the invitation of the Governor. If such a change took place, it would follow that the Prime Minister would be the authority, when occasion arose, for deciding whether any representative minister should be removed from office.

"It is for the chiefs and people to consider whether there should now be any change in the procedure for appointing the Prime Minister and other representative ministers and, if so, what that change should be," I declared.

With regard to the assignment of portfolios, this was clearly a question which would have to be considered in the light of any constitutional change that might be introduced affecting the continuance of ex officio ministers and the appointment of representative ministers.

I then turned to the constitution of the Legislative Assembly. The Assembly, I pointed out, consisted of three ex officio members, six special members (of whom only two had a vote) and seventy-five other members. Of the fifty-six members representing the Colony, Ashanti and Southern Togoland, eighteen or one-third represented the chiefs and traditional authorities and were elected not by universal adult suffrage but by the Joint Provincial Council, the Asanteman Council and the Trans-Volta Southern Togoland Electoral College. The nineteen members representing the Northern Territories were elected by a system peculiar to the Northern Territories. Constituencies varied in size and their representation in the Assembly was disproportionate.

"It is for the chiefs and people," I said, "to consider whether the Assembly as at present constituted affords the best representation of the country which can be devised; and whether a second House should be established, and if so, its composition and powers."

It was clear that a Commission of Enquiry would have to be established to look into representational and electoral reform and it was for the chiefs and people to consider what the composition and terms of reference of this Commission should be.

Part V of the Constitution Order in Council, which dealt with legislation and procedure in the Assembly, contained a provision which gave power to the Governor, acting in his descretion, to control the introduction of any bill or motion which, in the opinion of the Speaker or the Attorney General, would provide for the final determination of local constitutional matters otherwise than by the Governor acting in his decretion.

"It is for the chiefs and people to consider," I said "whether there should be any change in the provisions of this part of the Order relating to bills or motions for determination otherwise than by the Governor of questions relating to the following local constitutional matters:

(a) The election, installation, deposition or abdication of my chief, or the right of any person to take part in any such election, installation or deposition.
(b) The recovery or delivery of Stool Property in connection with any such election, installation, deposition or abdication.
(c) Political or constitutional relations between chiefs under native customary law."

Part VI of the Order in Council, I continued, prescribed certain safeguards for the Public Service designed to protect the Service from political influence or control. The Service was controlled by the Governor, acting in his descretion, and provision was made for the establishment of an independent Public Service Commission advisory to the Governor. The Order did not preclude the Assembly from exercising its control over the establishment of the Public Service. It should be borne in mind that the Service was the instrument of Government policy, without which that policy could not be carried into effect. Although political advance had outstripped the advance of Africanization, it should be remembered that the Civil Service, designed to perpetuate the best British tradition, should be kept free from political influence. The preservation of high standards in the Public Service was an administrative question and no opinion could faithfully be given to a revision of the provisions of the Constitution under reference without giving careful study to:

(1) the prospective rate of Africanization in relation to future requirements.
(2) the extent to which overseas officers are, and must for some time continue to be, a necessity.
(3) the effect on serving officers, and on future recruitment, of any change in the present safeguards and the probability that, if any material diminution of existing safeguards were accepted by the United Kingdom Government, that acceptance would be on terms which would stipulate the payment of compensation for loss of career to serving officers.

"It is for the chiefs and people, having taken all those factors into account, to consider whether the provisions of the Constitution relating to the Public Service should be altered and, if so, in what respect."

It was possible, I went on, that the chiefs and people would find other questions on which they would wish to express their opinions, and these would be welcomed. The Government would not formulate its policy in regard to the questions I had mentioned until the fullest opportunity had been allowed for consultation and until the Government had studied the views submitted to it. In order to prevent the preliminary discussions from being influenced by a declaration of government policy, I had refrained from putting forward a statement of government policy in advance of the consultations that were to take place.

I proposed to send copies of my statement to every council, political party or representative group throughout the country, inviting them to submit their views to my office by the end of March. These written statements would be collated and published. The Government would then formulate its views and embody them in a White Paper for debate in the Assembly at the June meeting.

"Finally, Mr. Speaker," I concluded, "I would remind Honorable Members, and everyone who reads this statement, that we are now, in response to the invitation of the Secretary of State given at our request, embarking on an enterprise which imposes a very heavy responsibility on all who participate in it. The responsibility lies most heavily on the Government which must ultimately determine, in the light of the views which the country after due deliberation express, the proposals which are to be conveyed to the United Kingdom Government. The world, which is both critical and sympathetic, will watch with the closest attention how we deal with this problem. All I ask of the chiefs and people is that they should place at the disposal of the Government the best advice that they can give."

One hundred and thirty-one organizations submitted their views by the end of March. The Territorial Councils, the Ghana Congress Party, the Ghana Nationalist Party, and the Gold Coast Trades Union Congress all disagreed with the proposed method of consulting the chiefs and people on the desired amendments to the constitution. I had to follow this procedure, however, because the Legislative Assembly, under the Coussey Consitution, was not a fully elected Assembly.

These discussions and consultations formed the basis of the Government's White Paper on Constitutional Reform of 1953 which in its turn, after months of negotiations with the Secretary of State, formed the basis of this present constitution which is commonly known as the Nkrumah Constitution, but which I prefer to call the Nkrumah/Arden-Clarke Constitution. This did not come into being for a year after the publication of the White Paper and in the meantime I battled on as best I could.

Soon after the October statement I went on a tour of the country to see how the organization of the Party was progressing. I was greatly encouraged to find widespread enthusiasm for, and mass solidarity behind the Party. I stressed the importance of new Local and Urban Councils working in close harmony with the people who had elected them, for I said that independent and vigorous local government is the only staying power of a free and democratic self-government, and that it was our aim to foster the growth of such institutions. I took note of the most urgent needs of the people in the towns and villages through which I passed and returned with a long list of requirements, roads, schools, hospitals, dispensaries, water supplies, post offices, telephones and houses.

On my return to Accra in November I called an emergency

Delegates' Conference of the C.P.P. in order to discuss vital matters affecting the solidarity of the Party. I reported to the meeting the results of my recent country-wide tour and impressed upon the delegates that today, more than ever before, our predominant slogan should be "Organize," for the task that lay ahead of us was a very arduous one. Despite our present political achievement, I pointed out that to pass through the next phase successfully we would have to make sure that we were well organized, strong and formidable. "The next phase of our political advancement may entail general elections," I warned, "and we cannot afford to rest on our oars on account of present achievements."

We were in the unfortunate position of having two Trades Union Congresses in the country. No army can strike effectively if its forces are divided and fighting among themselves. Even though each T.U.C. was one hundred per cent in support of the C.P.P., I insisted that the movement must be led by only one Congress. I told them that I had recommended that a Committee for Industrial Organization should be set up to help promote trade unionism in the country.

I then referred to my recent statement in the Assembly on constitutional reform. I told them that I had made that statement as Prime Minister and head of the Government of the day, but that I was addressing them now as Life Chairman of the C.P.P. and Leader of the Party. The proposal I was about to put to them on behalf of the National Executive of the Party did not detract from the undertaking I gave on behalf of the Government that the views of the chiefs and people and of other political groups would be fully considered before the final proposals were formulated. It had been decided by the National Executive, I said, that the delegates' conference there assembled should recommend that the Government of the Gold Coast make representations to the Queen in Council through the Secretary of State for the Colonies, that the chiefs and people of the Gold Coast demand immediate self-government, and that an Act of Independence be simultaneously passed by the United Kingdom Parliament and the Gold Coast Legislative Assembly declaring the Gold Coast to be, under the new name of Ghana, a sovereign and independent state with Her Majesty Queen Elizabeth II as Head of State.

This suggestion was received enthusiastically. I felt that unless the pot was kept constantly stirred, the contents would go stale. I knew from experience how long it took to get anything done, especially when the ideas involved were somewhat revolutionary but if a constant agitation was kept up, I could not see how we would fail to to reach the goal of Independence.

State Visit to Liberia

TOWARDS THE END OF 1952, I RECEIVED AN INVITATION FROM PRESident W. V. S. Tubman to pay a state visit to Liberia. He was kind enough to offer to send his yacht, the *President Edward J. Roye* to come for me and bring me back.

As it was not possible to make any further headway with constitutional reform until April, when the views of various organizations were due, the more I thought about a change of scene and a breath of sea air, the more attractive the idea became. My ministers and party executive members were unanimous in their advice to accept the invitation, so I decided that I would discuss the matter with the Governor.

"You certainly look as if you could do with a rest, P. M.," His Excellency said as he looked thoughtfully into my face. "But I wonder if you will get much of that on a state visit?"

The same thought had occurred to me, but at least I would get a three days' sea trip to Liberia and three days back in which to relax on the yacht. Also, if I did not take the opportunity then, it would probably be years before I would be able to get away again, if things moved in the country as I hoped they would. So I decided to accept the invitation.

On a morning in mid-January, 1953, therefore, I set out for Takoradi where the President's yacht was waiting. I have no idea how many people accompanied me, but there was certainly a boat load of them and a surprising number flew at their own expense to welcome me in Liberia and join in the occasion.

On the outskirts of Takoradi the car was brought to a standstill by crowds of people dancing and singing, mothers with small babies tied to their backs swaying their hips to the rhythm of the drumming, young children with a look of deep concentration on their small faces as they imitated the action of their elders. Men and women of all ages arrayed in their most colourful clothes were clashing cymbals, beating drums, laughing and singing. When we eventually arrived at the docks there was more ceremony to be observed—speeches of goodwill and wishes for a safe journey, the pouring of libations and handshaking. The Dutch captain welcomed me as I stepped aboard and introduced me to his all-Dutch crew. I was shown into the President's suite which I shared with Kojo Botsio.

"Have you ever seen such luxury on the high seas?" I asked Kojo when, left to ourselves, we examined our surroundings. I threw myself on to one of the beds with a sigh of pleasure and delight. It was a mistake, I thought, to provide me with such a comfortable bed; the way I felt I would never want to leave it until I arrived in Monrovia.

I must have been the only one feeling in need of such relaxation, however, for as soon as the rest of my entourage had acquainted themselves with the geography of the yacht, one by one they opened my door to see what had happened to me. They were most concerned to see me lying on my bed apparently comatose and asked if I was feeling ill. They could not believe that I was just tired, for nobody seems to think that I get tired. I am an automaton that is wound up in the morning and needs neither food nor sleep; when the spring runs down I simply wind it up again!

And so I gave the "spring" a wind and went out to join everybody else. They appeared to have made themselves very much at home, drinking and shouting in order to make themselves heard above the sound of a radio-phonograph which somebody had discovered and which was never allowed to rest for the whole of the trip.

I have always been keenly interested in boats and it was not long before I had cornered the captain and was firing questions at him about the *President Edward J. Roye*. The yacht was named after the first all-black President of Liberia, who was elected in 1870. It is of four hundred and sixty-three tons and was bought in Holland a few years ago when the President in his go-ahead manner had recognized the necessity of travelling along the coast instead of relying on the dust tracks that formed most of the country's highways. These, during the rainy season, were often quite impassable.

"In fact, sir," the Captain said, with a smile and a salute, "this is the President's Navy!"

"I can't wait to get my own navy in that case," I declared. "At the moment my navy consists of a very gallant but badly equipped fleet of fishing boats." I made a mental note about yachts and Holland and amused myself for some time in thinking up a suitable name for the boat I had in mind.

In spite of the general activity pervading the yacht, I felt quite rested by the time we arrived at the port of Monrovia. This was fortunate, for in my wildest imaginings I had never visualized such a reception as had been prepared. The President and the Vice-President with their ladies, members of the House of Representatives and the Senate, high government officials, chiefs and a cheering crowd of onlookers were all waiting at the port. After shaking hands all round we set off in state procession through the streets of Monrovia.

As I looked around it became increasingly difficult to believe that this was the same city that I had visited in 1947. I said so to President Tubman who was sitting by my side and congratulated him on the development that had taken place during his term of office. Prior to his election as President, Liberia was far from being an encouragement and an incentive to countries aspiring to independence. Even today there is much to be done in the Republic to make it a model independent state in West Africa, for the roads are about the worst that I have seen in any country, and without good roads the hinterland is cut off from the coastal belt. There is also much evidence of poverty among the masses, even in Monrovia itself. But with the greatest will in the world, such improvements take time, and when I saw how much had been done in that short space of five years, I felt that with President Tubman at the helm for another five or ten years Liberia could solve many of her difficulties. One thought then struck me very forcibly. If Liberia, with her limited resources of about two million pounds at that time, could manage to govern herself, there was indeed hope for the Gold Coast with her revenue of over thirty-six million pounds.

My program was a very full one but carefully planned, so that I was able to see every aspect of life in the country. I addressed both Houses of the Legislature; visited almost all the Government departments and was shown how they operated; went round the iron mines; visited the homes of Gold Coasters resident in Liberia and attended receptions, garden parties and several night clubs. The pace of their hospitality was such that in each moment of leisure I felt as if I had just stepped off a carousel.

One day the President invited me up to his country villa at a place called Totota which is sixty miles inland from Monrovia. The villa and the surrounding country were so beautiful that it was well worth the bumpy and dusty trip we made by road there and back. Luckily it had not been raining, for otherwise I doubt whether we would have got through. A most sumptuous luncheon had been laid—to which all the chiefs had been invited. There must have been about a thousand people there altogether, I suppose. Mrs. Tubman, a quiet and unassuming lady, was tireless in her attention to her guests and seemed to have the knack of being everywhere at once without being in the least obtrusive. It was a most enjoyable reception.

Both the British Embassy staff and the Gold Coast people resident in the country held receptions in my honour. I made a number of speeches but the most memorable, and the one that I enjoyed delivering more than any other, was made without notes or preparation at a mass meeting held at the Centennial Pavilion in Monrovia. I knew from past experience that the sight of a crowd before me was all I needed to encourage the words to flow; I knew, also, that such a speech would be composed of words from the heart, words that the people wanted to hear and would remember.

As I stood up to speak, I could sense the tension of the crowd. That brief moment of suspense, when it seemed as if by a wave of the hand I could, like a hypnotist, control very action and every emotion of the people before me, was the most vivid memory of my trip to Liberia. I spoke on "The Vision that I See."

I began by thanking the people of Liberia for the wonderful reception they had accorded us and conveyed to them the greetings of the chiefs and people of the Gold Coast. I had visited the State Department, the Treasury and other government departments, I told them, and had seen how the machinery of the Liberian Republic worked. "If you will allow me to muse a little over what I saw," I said, "it is better to be free to manage, or mismanage, your own affairs, than not to be free to mismanage or manage your own affairs." This was greeted with loud applause. "It was this spirit which really motivated me when, in 1949, in the heyday of our agitation in the Gold Coast, I founded a newspaper. The name of the newspaper is the *Accra Evening News*—and listen to the motto of that paper: 'We prefer self-Government with danger to servitude in tranquility!' "

Both the past and present achievements in Liberia, I said were proof enough that the African is capable of governing himself. I judged Liberia not from the heights it had reached, but from the depths whence it had come. "Those who wanted to enslave Liberia have enslaved themselves!" I declared, amidst resounding cheers.

I pointed out that it was providence that had preserved the Negroes during their years of trial in exile in the United States of America and the West Indies; that it was the same providence which took care of Moses and the Israelites in Egypt centuries before. "A greater exodus is coming in Africa today," I declared, "and that exodus will be established when there is an united, free and independent West Africa. Look at the whole country of Africa today! With the possible exception of Liberia, Egypt and Ethiopia, the entire continent is divided and sub-divided, partitioned and re-partitioned—look at the map!" I declared indignantly.The continent looked like a patchwork quilt, each color representing the interest of a foreign power.

I was getting into my stride and receiving as much encouragement from the enthusiastic crowds as I did from my own people at the Arena in Accra.

"Africa for the Africans!" I cried. "Africa for the Africans—but not the kind of philosophy that Marcus Garvey preached. No! We are bringing into being another Africa for the Africans with a different concept, and that concept is what?" I paused for a moment. "A free and independent state in Africa. We want to be able to govern ourselves in this country of ours, without outside interference—*and we are going to see that it is done!*" My words were lost in a roar of acclamation and it was several minutes before it was quiet enough for me to proceed.

I pointed out that a people without a government of their own was "silly and absurd." It was important, therefore, to forge ahead and develop our respective countries, both politically and economically. We should aim at an even greater glory and majesty than that which existed in the days of ancient Ghana, the land of our forebears. I explained that long before the slave trade and the imperialistic rivalries in Africa began, the civilizations of the Ghana Empire were in existence. At that time, in the ancient city of Timbuktu, Africans versed in science, arts and learning were having their works translated into Greek and Hebrew and were, at the same time, exchanging teachers with the University of Cordova in Spain. "These were the brains!" I declared proudly, "And today they come and tell us that we cannot do it. We have been made to believe that we can't do it. But have you forgotten? You have emotions like anybody else; you have feelings like anybody else; you have aspirations like anybody else—and you have visions. So don't let people come and bamboozle us that the African is incapable of governing himself!"

As instances of Africans who had already proved their capabilities to the world, I instanced Anthony William Amoo,* Professor of Philosophy at the University of Berlin, and Toussaint L'Ouverture, a hero in the field of battle.

"We believe in the equality of races. We believe in the freedom of the peoples of all races. We believe in co-operation. In fact it has been one of my theses that in this struggle of ours, in this struggle to redeem Africa, we are fighting not against race and color and creed. We are fighting against a system, a system which degrades and exploits; and wherever we find the system, that system must be abolished. Yes, we believe in peace and co-operation among all countries, but we also abhor colonialism and imperialism. We abhor man's inhumanity to man."

* In America I discovered that Amoo, an Nzima man from Axim, had written a thesis *Tractatus de arte sobrie et accurate philosophandi,* etc. published at Halle in 1738. I learned also that a copy had been lodged in the British Museum and I planned to produce a pamphlet on the work of this scholar, the first from the Gold Coast. When I arrived in London I eagerly visited the British Museum. Alas, Amoo's thesis had been destroyed by a German bombing raid in May, 1941.

"We must learn to live together. The age of aristocracy is gone. God made all of us equal—if you can create a state and create a government for your people, then it is for the state to see to the interests of that people. You leaders of Liberia have done a lot for your people."

I then illustrated to the people how we of the Gold Coast felt that we had played our part in making our country's history. I recalled the Bond of 1844, which gave Britain a political footing in the country, and the forming of the Fanti Confederacy in an effort to oppose British imperialism. "What was the result?" I asked. "They were arrested and charged with treason."

Then the Aborigines Rights Protection Society was formed to fight against their land being taken away. The result was that today the land belonged to the chiefs and people of the Gold Coast. Then came the National Congress of British West Africa which, because of the machinations of some of its members, was allowed to fall into disrepute. Twenty years ago a man came to the country called Aggrey. He said, "You look back. Don't mind what is happening, or don't mind what has happened. A new day is coming when the youth of Africa is going to wake up, and that reawakening is going to be a challenge to civilization."

I related the story of my return to the Gold Coast to be Secretary of the United Gold Coast Convention and how in a few months the whole country became politically awakened and all were demanding in one voice their liberation from British rule. Then speaking of present affairs I went on.

"So now we have arrived at a new stage. We have put our case again to Britain. At the last conference of my Party, the whole of the Gold Coast people have been united on one ground—the sovereignty and independence of the Gold Coast. The Gold Coast is going to have a new name—not 'Gold Coast,' because this gives us memories of the past—but a new 'Ghana.' And here, mark you, a sovereign and independent State, but within the British Commonwealth, because we still associate ourselves with what Britain has done. We are not ungrateful beasts. We shall continue to be friends if and when we are managing or mismanaging our own affairs."

I told them that the campaign for a United West Africa had begun and that all the various territories on the West Coast of Africa should now think in terms of unity and solidarity with one another. It was only by uniting the people that we would be able to hold our own in the world, that we would demand respect from other nations because we would have force behind us.

I sumarized what I had said in a few words and added my thanks for their hospitality. "Long Live the Republic of Liberia."

The fortnight of extravagant celebrations was over. As I joined in the dancing of the people at the dock who came to bid us farewell I realized how much both I, representing the Gold Coast people, and the Liberians had learnt about one another. Although, through circumstances outside our control, they had been educated by the Americans and my people had been educated by the British and those between our frontiers had been influenced by the French, it now seemed very clear that we all belonged to one family and that we were all anxious for one big reunion of that family.

The engines of the *President Edward J. Roye* started up. Last minute farewells and messages were called as the gulf of water widened, and soon we had had our last glimpse of Liberia and its warmhearted people.

So we returned to Takoradi. Again the reception from my own people was something to remember. Never have I seen such a mass of people. They were almost delirious with excitement—waving arms, flags or garments, singing, shouting, dancing and drumming. Looking down on them I felt giddy at the sight; with the swaying of the bodies to the rhythm of the drums it was as if we were about to disembark onto a moving raft in a strong swell. And their welcome was in evidence all along the hundred and sixty-five miles to Accra where flags and signs of welcome were hoisted across the road and villagers came out in their gayest of clothes to shout "Freedom!" "Welcome!" and "*Akwaaba!*"

The Motion of Destiny

FROM APRIL TO JUNE OF 1953, I MET MANY GROUPS AND ORGANIZATIONS throughout the country, collating views on constitutional reform. The following month the Government White Paper was published and on July 10, 1953, I moved a motion on constitutional reform—my Independence Motion which has become popularly known as "The Motion of Destiny."

On this day, every seat in the Assembly was filled and crowds were standing outside anxious to take part in what was going on in the House. The atmosphere was one of rejoicing—almost as if independence had already been won. A cheer went up as I entered and took my place, and again as I stood to deliver my motion. This was followed by deep silence.

"Mr. Speaker," I began, "I beg to move that this Assembly in adopting the Government's White Paper on Constitutional Reform do authorize the Government to request that Her Majesty's Government as soon as the necessary constitutional and administrative arrangements for independence are made, should introduce an Act of Independence into the United Kingdom Parliament declaring the Gold Coast a sovereign and independent State within the Commonwealth; and further, that this Assembly do authorize the Government to ask Her Majesty's Government, without prejudice to the above request, to amend as a matter of urgency the Gold Coast (Constitution) Order in Council 1950, in such a way as to provide *inter alia* that the Legislative Assembly shall be composed of members directly elected by secret ballot, and that all members of the Cabinet shall be members of the Assembly and directly responsible to it.

"Mr. Speaker, it is with great humility that I stand before my countrymen and before the representatives of Britain, to ask this House to give assent to this Motion. In this solemn hour, I am deeply conscious of the grave implications of what we are about to consider and, as the great honour of proposing this Motion has fallen to my lot, I pray God to grant me the wisdom, strength and endurance to do my duty as it should be done.

"We are called upon to exercise statemanship of a high order, and I would repeat, if I may, my warning of October, that 'every idle or ill-considered word . . . will militate against the cause which we all have at heart.' It is, as Edmund Burke said a long time ago (and I am quoting him here): 'our business carefully to cultivate in our minds, to rear to the most perfect vigor and maturity, every sort of generous and honest feeling that belongs to our nature. To bring the dispositions that are lovely in private life into the service and conduct of the commonwealth, so to be patriots as not to forget we are gentlemen.'

"At the outset, I would like to remind Honorable Members of a passage in the White Paper, that 'only after the Legislative Assembly debate will the proposals of this Government take their final shape and be communicated to the United Kingdom Government.' Therefore, let your arguments be cogent and constructive. The range of this debate must be national, not regional; patriotic, not partisan; and I now ask that a spirit of co-operation and goodwill pervade this debate. It was Aristotle, the master who knows, who said:

> 'In practical matters the end is not mere speculative knowledge of what is to be done, but rather the doing of it. It is not enough to know about virtue, then, but we must endeavor to possess it, and to use it. . . .'

As with virtue, so with self-government: we must endeavor to possess it, and to use it. And the Motion which I have prepared is the means to possess it.

"In seeking your mandate, I am asking you to give my Government the power to bring to fruition the longing hopes, the ardent dreams, the fervent aspirations of the chiefs and people of our country. Throughout a century of alien rule our people have, with ever increasing tendency, looked forward to that bright and glorious day when they shall regain their ancient heritage, and once more take their place rightly as free men in the world.

"Mr. Speaker, we have frequent examples to show that there comes a time in the history of all colonial peoples when they must, because of their will to throw off the hampering shackles of colonialism, boldly assert their God-given right to be free. Today we are here to claim this right to our independence.

"Mr. Speaker, the Motion is in two parts. The first part not merely states our aim, but poses the question to Her Majesty's Government which is more fully set out in the White Paper. There is a general demand in the Gold Coast for self-government within the Commonwealth, and the United Kingdom Government should be informed of this demand, and be requested to make a declaration recognizing the existence of this demand, and expressing Her Majesty's Government's readiness to introduce an Act of Independence. This is the question which we are asking Her Majesty's Government in terms which clearly require an answer. That is the first thing we want: a declaration. But, even more important, we want to possess our self-government; we want an Act of Independence.

"The second half of the Motion sets out in a straightforward manner to obtain the authority of the House for the presentation to Her Majesty's Government of the detailed proposals which we have made for immediate constitutional reform. We ask that these proposals may be considered on their merits and without prejudice to the request which has been made in the first half of the Motion. We request that the composition of our Assembly may be so amended that all its members shall be directly elected by secret ballot. Similarly, we have gone forward to request that the whole Cabinet may be composed of representative Ministers. We have also made other proposals of immediate and striking importance, and I am confident that this Assembly will give the Motion before it its unanimous endorsement and support.

"Last year, I brought this House changes in the Constitution which were, at the time, regarded as of minor importance. I was accused, indeed, of personal ambition in seeking the title of Prime

Minister. We can now, Mr. Speaker, see the result for ourselves. Certainly nobody outside the Gold Coast has regarded my position as anything but what the name implies. The prestige of the Gold Coast Government overseas has, in fact, been enhanced by this change. Even the co-ordination of the functions of my own colleagues has been made more successful by the increase in status. I believe that there is more decision in our activities as a Cabinet than there was before, and that we are better equipped to get things done. The freedom we demand is for our country as a whole—this freedom we are claiming is for our children, for the generations yet unborn, that they may see the light of day and live as men and women with the right to work out the destiny of their own country.

"Mr. Speaker, our demand for self-government is a just demand. It is a demand admitting of no compromise. The right of a people to govern themselves is a fundamental principle, and to compromise on this principle is to betray it. To quote you a great social and political scientist:

> 'To negotiate with forces that are hostile on matters of principle means to sacrifice principle itself. Principle is indivisible. It is either wholly kept or wholly sacrificed. The slightest concession on matters of principle infers the abandonment of principle.'

"The right of a people to decide their own destiny, to make their way in freedom, is not to be measured by the yardstick of color or degree of social development. It is an inalienable right of peoples which they are powerless to exercise when forces, stronger than they themselves, by whatever means, for whatever reasons, take this right away from them. If there is to be a criterion of a people's preparedness for self-government, then I say it is their readiness to assume the responsibilities of ruling themselves. For who but a people themselves can say then they are prepared? How can others judge when that moment has arrived in the destiny of a subject people? What other gauge can there be?

"Mr. Speaker, never in the history of the world has an alien ruler granted self-rule to a people on a silver platter. Therefore, Mr. Speaker, I say that a people's readiness and willingness to assume the responsibilities of self-rule is the single criterion of their preparedness to undertake those responsibilities.

"I have described on a previous occasion in this House what were the considerations which led me to agree to the participation of my party in the General Election of 1951, and hence in the Government of the Gold Coast under the terms of the 1950 Constitution Order in Council. In making that decision, I took on the task of proving to the world that we were prepared to perform our duties with responsibility, to set in motion the many reforms which our people needed, and to work from within the Government and within the Assembly, that is, by constitutional means, for the immediate aim of self-government. We have only been in office, Mr. Speaker, for two and a half years, and we have kept these objectives constantly in mind. Let there be no doubt that we are equally determined not to rest until we have gained them. We are encouraged in our efforts by the thought that in so acting we are showing that we are able to govern ourselves and thereby we are putting an end to the myth that Africans are unable to manage their own affairs, even when given the opportunity. We can never rest satisfied with what we have so far achieved. The Government certainly is not of that mind. Our country has proved that it is more than ready. For despite the legacies of a century of colonial rule, in the short space of time since your Representative Ministers assumed the responsibilities of office, we have addressed ourselves boldly to the task of laying sound economic and social foundations on which this beloved country of ours can raise a solid democratic society. The spirit of responsibility and enterprise which has animated our actions in the past two years will continue to guide us in the future, for we shall always act in the spirit of our party's motto: 'Forward ever, backward never.' For we know notwithstanding that the essence of politics is the realization of what is possible.

"Mr. Speaker, we have now come to the most important stage of our constitutional development; we can look back on the stages through which we have passed during these last few years: first, our discussions with the Secretary of State leading to the changes of last year; then the questions posed in the October statement, which were to be answered by all parties, groups and councils interested in this great issue; the consultations with the Territorial Councils, with the political parties, with the Trades Union Congress. We have proceeded logically and carefully, and as I view it, the country has responded fully to my call. Every representation which we received—and there were many—has received my careful consideration. The talks which I had with the political parties and the Trades Union Congress, and the committees of the Asanteman and Joint Provincial Councils, were frank and cordial.

"I had also received a special invitation to attend a meeting in Tamale with the Territorial Council, the Traditional Rulers and the Members of the Legislative Assembly. Naturally, I accepted the invitation, because it was clear that if I had not held discussions with the Northern Territories, the unity of the Gold Coast might have been endangered and our progress towards self-government might have been delayed. The reverse has been the case. We have adapted some of our proposals to meet Northern Territories wishes, and have been able to set their minds at rest on several issues of the greatest importance, to them, and to the Gold Coast as a whole. Mr. Speaker, sir, the days of forgetting about our brothers in the North, and in the Trust Territory, are over.

"Criticisms have been levelled against the Government for the secrecy with which these talks were surrounded, and I should like to tell the country why this was necessary. When we went to the talks, of course, the Government members had some idea of the way their collective view on the representations were being formulated. We carefully explained, however, that our views were not finally decided and they would not be until we had had an opportunity of hearing any further views which these bodies might care to express in addition to their memoranda submitted. Having heard these views, we also sought an expression of opinion on specific problems which had occurred to us. But in order that our discussions could be of true value, frank and unreserved, I stated at an early stage that I should be grateful if the conversations could be regarded as strictly confidential. I am glad to place on record the value of the discussions which we held and the extent to which the undertaking which I was given was honored. I hope that the bodies which were consulted also feel that the discussions were worthwhile.

"Mr. Speaker, knowing full well, therefore, the will of the chiefs and people whom we represent, I am confident that with the support of this House, Her Majesty's Government will freely accede to our legitimate and righteous demand to become a self-governing unit within the Commonwealth.

"I put my confidence in the willing acceptance of this demand by Her Majesty's Government, because it is consistent with the declared policy of successive United Kingdom Governments. Indeed, the final transition from the stage of responsible government as a colony to the independence of a sovereign state guiding its own policies, is the apotheosis of this same British policy in relation to its dependencies.

"Mr. Speaker, pray allow me to quote from Britain's own Ministers. Mr. Creech Jones, as Colonial Secretary in the first post-war Labor Government, stated that 'the central purpose of British Colonial policy is simple. It is to guide the Colonial Territories to responsible self-government within the Commonwealth in conditions that ensure to the people concerned both a fair standard of living and freedom from oppression from any quarter.'

"Again, on July 12, 1950, in the House of Commons, Mr. James Griffiths, Mr. Creech Jones' successor, reiterated this principle: 'The aim and purpose,' he said, 'is to guide the Colonial Territories to responsible self-government within the Commonwealth and, to that end, to assist them to the utmost of our capacity and resources to establish those economic and social conditions upon which alone self-government can be soundly based.'

"Last, I give you the words of Mr. Oliver Lyttelton, Colonial Secretary in Her Majesty's Conservative Government of today: 'We all aim at helping the Colonial Territories to attain self-government within the Commonwealth.'

"Nor is this policy anything new in British colonial history. The right to self-government of Colonial Dependencies has its origin in the British North American Act of 1867, which conceded to the provinces of Canada complete self-rule. The independence of the other white Dominions of Australia and New Zealand were followed by freedom for South Africa. And since the end of the Second World War, our colored brothers in Asia have achieved independence, and we are now proud to be able to acknowledge the Sovereign States of India, Pakistan, Ceylon and Burma.

"There is no conflict that I can see between our claim and the professed policy of all parties and governments of the United Kingdom. We have here in our country a stable society. Our economy is healthy, as good as any for a country of our size. In many respects, we are very much better off than many Sovereign States. And our potentialities are large. Our people are fundamentally homogeneous, nor are we plagued with religious and tribal problems. And, above all, we have hardly any color bar. In fact, the whole democratic tradition of our society precludes the *herrenvolk* doctrine. The remnants of this doctrine are now an anachronism in our midst, and their days are numbered.

"Mr. Speaker, we have travelled long distances from the days when our fathers came under alien subjugation to the present time. We stand now at the threshold of self-government and do not waver. The paths have been tortuous, and fraught with peril, but the positive and tactical action we have adopted is leading us to the New Jerusalem, the golden city of our hearts desire! I am confident, therefore, that I express the wishes and feelings of the chiefs and people of this country in hoping that the final transfer of power to your Representative Ministers may be done in a spirit of amity and friendship, so that, having peacefully achieved our freedom, the peoples of both countries—Britain and the Gold Coast—may form a new relationship based on mutual respect, trust and friendship. Thus may the new partnership implicit in the Statute of Westminster be clothed in a new meaning. For then shall we be one of the 'autonomous communities within the British Empire, equal in status, in no way subordinate one to another in any aspect of their domestic or external affairs, though united by a common allegiance to the Crown, freely associated as members of the British Commonwealth of Nations,' in accordance with the Balfour Declaration of 1926, which was embodied in the Statute of Westminster in 1931.

"Today, more than ever before, Britain needs more 'autonomous communities freely associated.' For freely associated communities make better friends than those associated by subjugation. We see today, Mr. Speaker, how much easier and friendlier are the bonds between Great Britain and her former dependencies of India, Pakistan and Ceylon. So much of the bitterness that poisoned the relations between these former colonies and the United Kingdom has been absolved by the healing power of a better feeling so that a new friendship has been cemented in the free association of autonomous communities.

"These, and other weighty reasons, allied with the avowed aim of British colonial policy, will, I am confident, inspire Britain to make manifest once more to a sick and weary world her duty to stand by her professed aim. A free and independent Gold Coast, taking its rightful place in peace and amity by the side of the other Dominions, will provide a valid and effective sign that freedom can be achieved in a climate of good will and thereby accrue to the intrinsic strength of the Commonwealth. The old concepts of Empire, of conquest, domination and exploitation are fast dying in an awakening world. Among the colonial peoples, there is a vast, untapped reservoir of peace and goodwill towards Britain, would she but divest herself of the outmoded, moth-eaten trappings of two centuries ago, and present herself to her colonial peoples in a new and shining vestment and hand us the olive branch of peace and love, and give us a guiding hand in working out our own destinies.

"In the very early days of the Christian era, long before England had assumed any importance, long even before her people had united into a nation, our ancestors had attained a great empire, which lasted until the eleventh century, when it fell before the attacks of the Moors of the North. At its height that empire stretched from Timbuktu to Bamako, and even as far as the Atlantic. It is said that lawyers and scholars were much respected in that empire and that the inhabitants of Ghana wore garments of wool, cotton, silk and velvet. There was trade in copper, gold and textile fabrics, and jewels and weapons of gold and silver were carried.

"Thus may we take pride in the name of Ghana, not out of romanticism, but as an inspiration for the future. It is right and proper that we should know about our past. For just as the future moves from the present, so the present has emerged from the past. Nor need we be ashamed of our past. There was much in it of glory. What our ancestors achieved in the context of their contemporary society gives us confidence that we can create, out of that past, a glorious future, not in terms of war and military pomp, but in terms of social progress and of peace. For we repudiate war and violence. Our battles shall be against the old ideas that keep men trammelled in their own greed; against the crass stupidities that breed hatred, fear and inhumanity. The heroes of our future will be those who can lead our people out of the stifling fog of disintegration through serfdom, into the valley of light where purpose, endeavor and determination will create that brotherhood which Christ proclaimed two thousand years ago, and about which so much is said, but so little done.

"Mr. Speaker, in calling up our past, it is meet, on an historic occasion such as this, to pay tribute to those ancestors of ours who laid our national traditions, and those others who opened the path which made it possible to reach today the great moment at which we stand. As with our enslaved brothers dragged from these shores to the United States and to the West Indies, throughout our tortuous history, we have not been docile under the heel of the conqueror. Having known by our own traditions and experience the essentiality of unity and of government, we constantly formed ourselves into cohesive blocs as a means of resistance against the alien force within our borders. And so today we recall the birth of the Ashanti nation through Okomfo Anokye and Osei Tutu and the symbolism entrenched in the Golden Stool; the valiant wars against the British, the banishment of Nana Prempeh the First to the Seychelles; the temporary disintegration of the nation and its subsequent reunification. And so we come to the Bond of 1844. Following trade with the early merchant adventurers who came to the Gold Coast, the first formal association of Britain with our country was effected by the famous Bond of 1844, which accorded Britain trading rights in the country. But from these humble beginnings of trade and friendship, Britain assumed political control of this country. But our inalienable right still remains, as my friend, George Padmore, puts it in his recent book, *The Gold Coast Revolution,* and I quote: 'When the Gold Coast Africans demand self-government today they are, in consequence, merely asserting their birthright which they never really surrendered to the British who, disregarding their treaty obligations of 1844, gradually usurped full sovereignty over the country.'

"Then the Fanti Confederation: The earliest manifestation of Gold Coast nationalism occurred in 1868 when Fanti Chiefs attempted to form the Fanti Confederation in order to defend themselves against the might of Ashanti and the incipient political encroachments of British merchants. It was also a union of the coastal states for mutual economic and social development. This was declared a dangerous conspiracy with the consequent arrest of its leaders.

"Then the Aborigines Rights Protection Society was the next nationalist movement to be formed with its excellent aims and objects, and by putting up their titanic fight for which we cannot be sufficiently grateful, formed an unforgettable bastion for the defence of our God-given land and thus preserved our inherent right to freedom. Such men as Mensah-Sarbah, Atta Ahuma, Sey and Woode have played their role in this great fight.

"Next came the National Congress of British West Africa. The end of the first Great War brought its strains and stresses and the echoes of the allied slogan, 'We fight for freedom' did not pass unheeded in the ears of Casely-Hayford, Hutton-Mills and other national stalwarts who were some of the moving spirits of the National Congress of British West Africa. But the machinations of imperialism did not take long to smother the dreams of the people concerned, but today their aims and objects are being more than gratified with the appointment of African judges and other improvements in our national life.

"As with the case of the National Congress of British West Africa, the United Gold Coast Convention was organized at the end of the Second World War to give expression to the people's desire for better conditions. The British Government, seeing the threat to its security here, arrested six members of the Convention and detained them for several weeks until the Watson Commission came. The stand taken by the Trades Union Congress, the Farmers, Students and Women of the country provides one of the most epic stories in our national struggle.

"In June 1949, the Convention People's Party with its uncompromising principles led the awakened masses to effectively demand their long lost heritage. And today the country moves steadily forward to its proud goal.

"Going back over the years to the establishment of constitutional development, we find that the first Legislative Council to govern the country was established in 1850; thirty-eight years later the first African in the person of John Sarbah was admitted to that council. It was not until 1916 that the Clifford Constitution increased the number of Africans—which was four in 1910—to six. But these were mainly councils of officials.

"The Guggisberg Constitution of 1925 increased the unofficial representation in the council, making it almost at par with the officials. This position was reversed by the Burns Constitution of 1946 which created an unofficial majority. The abortive Colony-Ashanti Collaboration of 1944 was the prelude to this change.

"The Coussey Constitution of 1951 further democratized the basis of representation; and now, for the first time in our history, this Government is proposing the establishment of a fully elected Assembly with Ministers directly responsible to it.

"We have experienced Indirect Rule, we have had to labor under the yoke of our own disunity, caused by the puffed-up pride of those who were lucky to enjoy better opportunities in life than their less fortunate brothers; we have experienced the slow and painful progress of constitutional changes by which, from councils on which Africans were either absent or merely nominated, this august House has evolved through the exercise by the enfranchised people of their democratic right to a voice in their own affairs and in so doing they have shown their confidence in their own countrymen by placing on us the responsibility for our country's affairs.

"And so through the years, many have been laid to final rest from the stresses and dangers of the national struggle and many, like our illustrious friends of the Opposition who, not withstanding the fact that we may differ on many points, have also contributed a share to the totality of our struggle. And we hope that whatever our differences, we shall today become united in the demand for our country's freedom.

"As I said earlier, what we ask is not for ourselves on this side of the House, but for all the chiefs and people of this country—the right to live as free men in the comity of nations. Were not our ancestors ruling themselves before the white man came to these our shores? I have earlier made reference to the ancient history of our more distant forebears in Ghana. To assert that certain people are capable of ruling themselves while others are not yet 'ready,' as the saying goes, smacks to me more of imperialism than of reason. Biologists of repute maintain that there is no such thing as a 'superior' race. Men and women are as much products of their environment—geographic, climatic, ethnic, cultural, social—as of instincts and physical heredity. We are determined to change our environment, and we shall advance in like manner.

"According to the motto of the valiant *Accra Evening News*—'We prefer self-government with danger to servitude in tranquility.' Doubtless we shall make mistakes as have all other nations. We are human beings and hence fallible. But we can try also to learn from the mistakes of others so that we may avoid the deepest pitfalls into which they have fallen. Moreover, the mistakes we may make will be our own mistakes, and it will be our responsibility to put them right. As long as we are ruled by others we shall lay our mistakes at their door, and our sense of responsibility will remain dulled. Freedom brings responsibilities and our experience can be enriched only by the acceptance of these responsibilities.

"In the two years of our representative Government, we have become most deeply conscious of the tasks which will devolve upon us with self-rule. But we do not shrink from them; rather are we more than ever anxious to take on the reins of full self-government. And this, Mr. Speaker, is the mood of the chiefs and people of this country at this time; on the fundamental choice between colonial status and self-government, we are unanimous. And the vote that will be taken on the motion before this Assembly will proclaim this to the world.

"Honorable Members, you are called, here and now, as a result of the relentless tide of history, by Nemesis as it were, to a sacred charge, for you hold the destiny of our country in your hands. The eyes and ears of the world are upon you; yea, our oppressed brothers throughout this vast continent of Africa and the New World are looking to you with desperate hope, as an inspiration to continue their grim fight against cruelties which we in this corner of Africa have never known! Cruelties which are a disgrace to humanity and to civilization, which the white man has set himself to teach us. At this time, history is being made; a colonial people in Africa has put forward the first definite claim for independence. An African colonial people proclaim that they are ready to assume the stature of free men and to prove to the world that they are worthy of the trust.

"I know that you will not fail those who are listening for the mandate that you will give to your Representative Ministers. For we are ripe for freedom, and our people will not be denied. They are conscious that the right is theirs, and they know that freedom is not something that one people can bestow on another as a gift. They claim it as their own and none can keep it from them.

"And while yet we are making our claim for self-government I want to emphasize, Mr. Speaker, that self-government is not an end in itself. It is a means to an end, to the building of the good life to the benefit of all, regardless of tribe, creed, color or station in life. Our aim is to make this country a worthy place for all its citizens, a country that will be a shining light throughout the whole continent of Africa, giving inspiration far beyond its frontiers. And this we can do by dedicating ourselves to unselfish service to humanity. We must learn from the mistakes of others so that we may, in so far as we can, avoid a repetition of those tragedies which have overtaken other human societies.

"We must not follow blindly, but must endeavor to create. We must aspire to lead in the arts of peace. The foreign policy of our country must be dedicated to the service of peace and fellowship. We repudiate the evil doctrines of tribal chauvinism, racial prejudice and national hatred. We repudiate these evil ideas because in creating that brotherhood to which we aspire, we hope to make a reality, within the bounds of our small country, of all the grandiose ideologies which are supposed to form the intangible bonds holding together the British Commonwealth of Nations in which we hope to remain. We repudiate racial prejudice and national hatred, because we do not wish to be a disgrace to these high ideals.

"Her Majesty, Queen Elizabeth the Second has just been crowned —barely one month ago—the memory is still fresh in our minds; the Queen herself has not forgotten the emotions called forth as she first felt the weight of the Crown upon her head; the decorations in London streets are hardly down; the millions of words written about the Coronation and its meaning will endure for centuries; the prayers from millions of lips are still fresh; the vows of dedication to duty which the Queen made are a symbol of the duties devolving on the Commonwealth. And so, we repudiate the evil doctrines which we know are promulgated and accepted elsewhere as the truth.

"To Britain this is the supreme testing moment in her African relations. When we turn our eyes to the sorry events in South, Central and East Africa, when we hear the dismal news about Kenya and Central African Federation, we are cheered by the more cordial relationship that exists between us and Britain. We are now asking her to allow that relationship to ripen into golden bonds of freedom, equality and fraternity, by complying without delay to our request for self-government. We are sure that the British Government will demonstrate its goodwill towards the people of the Gold Coast by granting us the self-government which we now so earnestly desire. We enjoin the people of Britain and all political parties to give our request their ardent support.

"The self-government which we demand, therefore, is the means by which we shall create the climate in which our people can develop their attributes and express their potentialities to the full. As long as we remain subject to an alien power, too much of our energies is diverted from constructive enterprise. Oppressive forces breed frustration. Imperialism and colonialism are a twofold evil. This theme is expressed in the truism that 'no nation which oppresses another can itself be free.' Thus we see that this evil not only wounds the people which is subject, but the dominant nations pays the price in a warping of their finer sensibilities through arrogance and greed. Imperialism and colonialism are a barrier to true friendship. For the short time since we Africans have had a bigger say in our affairs, the improved relations between us and the British have been most remarkable. Today there exists the basis of real friendship between us and His Excellency the Governor, Sir Charles Arden-Clarke, and the ex officio Ministers of Defense and External Affairs, of Finance and of Justice. I want to pay tribute to these men for their valuable co-operation in helping us to make a success of our political advance. I feel that they have done this, firstly because as officers in the British Colonial Service, it is their duty to guide the subject territory in the attainment of self-government in accordance with the expressed aim of British colonial policy and, secondly, because we have, by our efforts in managing our own affairs, gained their respect, and they are conscious of the justice of our aspirations.

"Let me recall the words of the great Casely-Hayford which he spoke in 1925:

> 'It must be recognized that co-operation is the greatest word of the century. With co-operation we can command peace, goodwill and concord. Without: chaos, confusion and ruin. But there can really be no co-operation between inferiors and superiors. Try as they may, there must come a time when the elements of superiority will seek to dictate, and the inferior ones will resent such dictation. It logically follows, therefore, that unless an honest effort is made to raise the inferior up to the prestige of the superior, and the latter can suffer it, all our talk of co-operation is so much empty gas. . . .'

"Unless, therefore, our claim to independence is met now, the amicable relations which at present exist between us and the British may become strained. Our chiefs and people will brook no delay. But I feel confident that our claim, because of the reasons I have already given, will be accepted and our amity towards Britain will be deepened by our new association.

"The strands of history have brought our two countries together. We have provided much material benefit to the British people, and they in turn have taught us many good things. We want to continue to learn from them the best they can give us and we hope that they will find in us qualities worthy of emulation. In our daily lives, we may lack those material comforts regarded as essential by the standards of the modern world, because so much of our wealth is still locked up in our land; but we have the gifts of laughter and joy, a love of music, a lack of malice, an absence of the desire for vengeance for our wrongs—all things of intrinsic worth in a world sick of injustice, revenge, fear and want.

"We feel that there is much the world can learn from those of us who belong to what we might term the pre-technological societies. These are values which we must not sacrifice unheedingly in pursuit of material progress. That is why we say that self-government is not an end in itself.

"We have to work hard to evolve new patterns, new social customs, new attitudes to life, so that while we seek the material, cultural and economic advancement of our people, while we raise their standards of life, we shall not sacrifice their fundamental happiness. That, I should say, Mr. Speaker, has been the greatest tragedy of Western society since the industrial revolution.

"In harnessing the forces of nature, man has become the slave of the machine, and of his own greed. If we repeat these mistakes and suffer the consequences which have overtaken those that made them, we shall have no excuse. This is a field of exploration for the young men and women now in our schools and colleges, for our sociologists and economists, for our doctors and our social welfare workers, for our engineers and town planners, for our scientists and our philosophers.

"Mr. Speaker, when we politicians have long passed away and been forgotten, it is upon their shoulders that will fall the responsibility of evolving new forms of social institutions, new economic instruments to help build in our rich and fertile country a society where men and women may live in peace, where hate, strife, envy and greed, shall have no place.

"Mr. Speaker, but we can only meet the challenge of our age as a free people. Hence our demand for our freedom, for only free men can shape the destinies of their future.

"Mr. Speaker, Honorable Members, we have great tasks before us. I say, with all seriousness, that it is rarely that human beings have such an opportunity for service to their fellows.

"Mr. Speaker, for my part, I can only re-echo the words of a great man: 'Man's dearest possession is life, and since it is given him to live but once, he must so live as not to be besmeared with the shame of a cowardly existence and trivial past, so live that dying he might say: all my life and all my strength were given to the finest cause in the world—the liberation of mankind.'

"Mr. Speaker, 'Now God be thank'd Who has match'd us with His hour!' I beg to move."

The acclamation that burst forth was such that one expected the roof and walls to collapse. As soon as the cheering was heard by those waiting outside, they took it up as well. Members from both sides of the House came to congratulate me and, in the words of the official Legislative Assembly debates, "The House was suspended for fifteen minutes."

J. A. Braimah, Minister of Communications and Works, then seconded the motion and, after it had been debated upon for a few days, it was carried unanimously.

With this amended constitution, the anomalies in the Coussey Constitution were more or less eradicated, but in order to give effect to this, it was necessary to call a general election.

I realized more than ever before how vital at this particular time was the organization and discipline of my party, and at the Annual Delegates' Conference, which was held in Tamale in the Northern Territories in August, I stressed this point and impressed upon them the importance in the selection of candidates. I warned them against recurrences of party members contesting official candidates, as had happened recently in by-elections in at least four constituencies. Unless we enforced discipline and organized ourselves in a recognized democratic manner, we faced the danger of a split and of failing to reach our goal at the eleventh hour. The success of the next phase of our struggle, I told them, depended very much upon the loyalty, honesty and sincerity of the men and women we sent to the next Assembly. Each constituency, I said, should nominate, through its Executive, one candidate for the scrutiny and approval of the Central Committee acting on behalf of the National Executive of the Party, who would have the final say in the choice of the candidates. This means would ensure that only members who had respect for the party policy and leadership and who had proved themselves loyal would be eligible for election.

And I warned them not to underrate the enemy. "Nothing must be left to chance and there is no room for complacency."

The 1954 General Election

AS A RESULT OF THE CONSTITUTIONAL FORM OF THE COUSSEY CONstitution which was to give the country a larger measure of internal self-government, it was necessary to increase the membership of the Legislative Assembly and to change its composition. To implement these reforms, a commission was set up under the chairmanship of Mr. Justice W. B. van Lare, to enquire into representational and electoral reform. As a result, the country was divided up into one hundred and four constituencies. During the general election of 1954 the Convention People's Party contested every one of these seats.

I don't think I have ever made so many speeches in one month in my life! I toured the entire country and visited every constituency. At each one I made a fiery speech. "This is your chance! This is what we have been planning for, suffering for, slaving for! The fulfillment of our promise of 'Freedom Now' is at hand!" Sometimes, towards the end of the day, the strain began to tell on my voice, but it never once let me down. Apart from my public speeches every spare minute was taken up by one or another of the Party followers seeking advice or a special word of encouragement from me.

Then an unfortunate incident occurred. I had previously warned candidates that they should not put themselves up to oppose the official Party candidates, as had happened in some previous by-elections. It was with disappointment and anger, therefore, that I discovered that eighty-one Party members had put themselves up to stand against official Party candidates. I called these people "rebels." Firm action had to be taken. It was vital that the Party should not be allowed to become disorganized or to be weakened by the split that this would ultimately bring about. I therefore called a meeting in Kumasi and, feeling rather as an executioner must do when he has to carry out his distasteful job because of duty and justice, I expelled each of the eighty-one "rebels" from the Party. I turned a deaf ear to pleas and excuses. They had known the rules of the game but they had chosen to put their own interests before those of the Party; they lacked team spirit and they should be made an example of.

I was aware of the probable outcome of this, namely that with so little feeling of loyalty towards the C.P.P. most of the "rebels" would support any party that offered them the chance to stand. By the time I arrived back in Accra I learnt that a new party had been formed in the Northern Territories called the Northern People's Party. I at once dashed to the North, but this time it was too late to do very much. Candidates—one of whom was my late Minister of Communications and Works—had been found to oppose each of the twenty-one constituencies in the North.

In the meantime much speculation was going on as to the outcome of the election and among the Europeans there was a certain amount of anxiety as to the possibility of violence, riots and general unrest. The emergence of the N.P.P. was welcomed by many of them as being a challenge to the C.P.P. As Election Day drew near, the army and the police prepared themselves for possible action. But nothing happened.

On the day, June 15, 1954, Accra could hardly have been quieter and more orderly. People queued up patiently at the polling stations; business men, workers and petty traders carrying their wares on their heads and babies strapped to their backs. Shop assistants, clerks—men and women in all walks of life. One by one they went in to vote, placing their voting slip into the box bearing the symbol of their choice. The symbol chosen to represent the Convention People's Party was a red cockerel. There was no excitement at all, in fact the people were on the whole so casual about the whole thing that the morning queues at the bus terminals were a riot by comparison.

A large board had been erected on a platform on the old Polo Ground in the center of the town in order to display the results as soon as each one was known. By late afternoon almost every African in Accra began to wander there, preparing to wait all night to cheer or boo, as the case might be, the successful candidates as they were announced.

I was becoming increasingly restless as the evening wore on. I had plenty of callers, as usual, and the telephone never stopped ringing. I paced from room to room followed by an anxious tabby cat who was beginning to despair of my ever going to the dining room to have a meal, the time of day when she always displayed a strong affection for me.

"It's no good following me like that," I said as I nearly tripped over her, "I don't feel like eating yet."

I suddenly felt that I needed company. The hours were passing so slowly and for once in my life I doubted whether sleep would come as spontaneously as it usually did when my head touched a pillow. I rang up a friend of mine.

"I'm just about to have supper and have got the radio on listening for the results. Why don't you come and join me?" the voice said at the other end of the wire.

So I went along. It was certainly better to have somebody to share the suspense, the hours of waiting and the rejoicing as successful party candidates were announced. Between the announcements we could hear the singing of the waiting crowds and the buzz of shouting and laughter.

"There must be thousands down there!" I remarked, "How I wish I was a normal person!"

"Whatever do you mean, P. M.?" my companion asked.

"It's my head!" I moaned. "I can never hide myself. Even on the blackest night my high forehead gives me away. If the people see me—"

I was interrupted by a burst of enthusiasm from my friend.

"I'll take you and I guarantee that nobody will recognize you. You can cover your head with a red cap that I've got and my car is so small and dark inside that nobody can see who is in it even in daylight!"

I tried on the cap and examined myself in a mirror. The sight gave me a start! But it was true. In this comic cap I should not be easily recognized as Kwame Nkrumah.

Lunch aboard the yacht—*President Edward J. Roye*

Arriving at the Free Port of Monrovia and standing while the British and Liberian National Anthems are being played—January 21, 1953

At a reception given in my honor in Monrovia by the C.P.P. supporters there

Arriving at a Party rally

One of the patient and orderly queues outside a polling station at the 1954 General Election

My appearance at the Old Polo Ground, Accra, in the early hours of the morning when I had been re-elected in 1954

With the Governor after he had asked me to form a new Government—June 17, 1954

The Ceremonial Opening of the 1954 Legislative Assembly by His Excellency the Governor

The Cabinet, 1954–56.

At work in my study at home

With some of the Northern Territories' Chiefs in my office

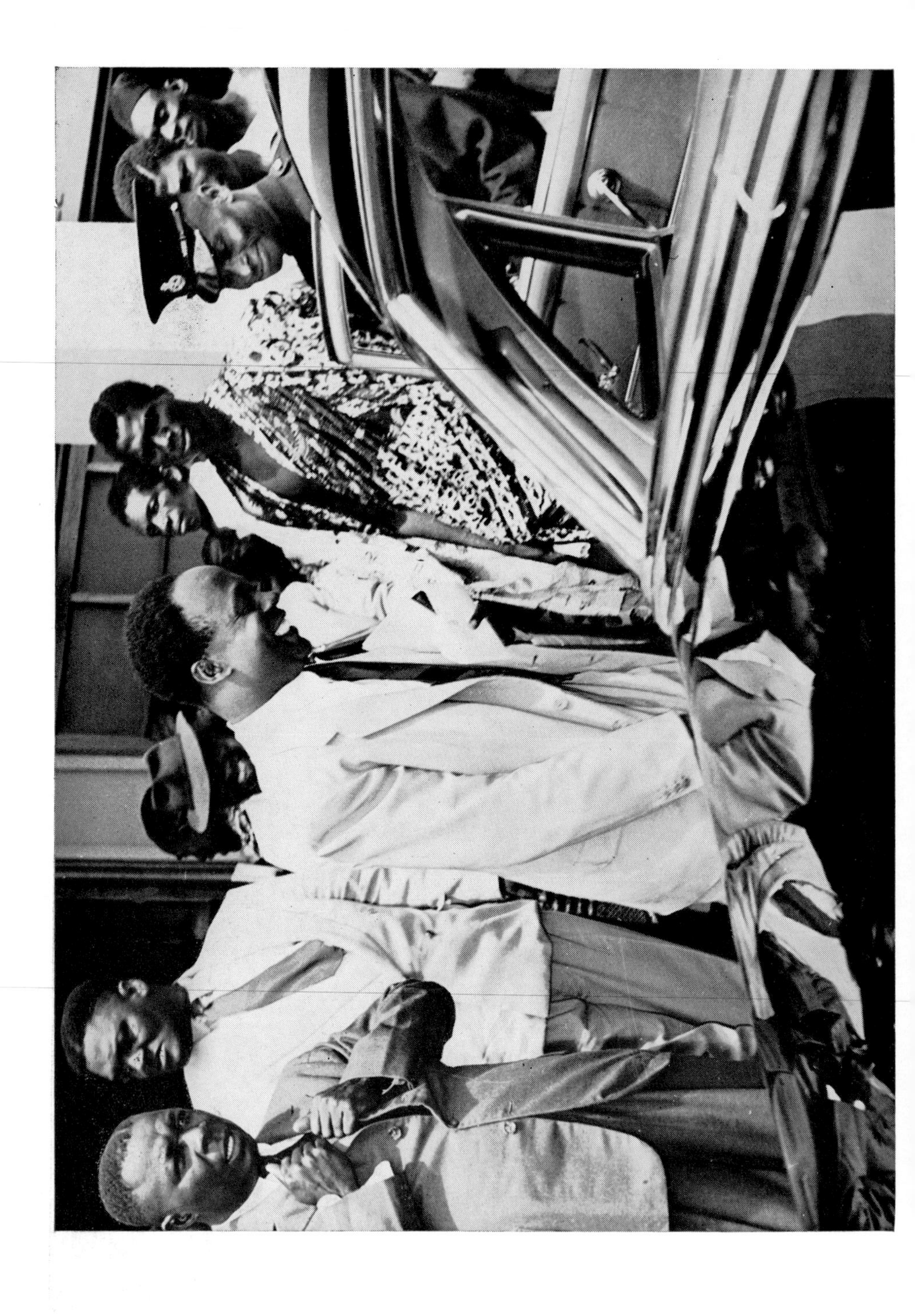

Aboard the *Nigerstroom* with the Captain, the Chief Steward, the Dutch Consul, Mr. and Mrs. D. Chapman, and Miss Erica Powell

At the helm of the *Nigerstroom*—September, 1955

Inspecting a cocoa bean for marks of disease
during a tour of cocoa growing areas

A dinner in the Cabinet Room given in honor of Mr. Adlai Stevenson
who visited the Gold Coast in 1955

On a tour of inspection at Tema Harbor (1956)
with K. A. Gbedemah and K. Botsio

Model of the Volta Dam at Ajena

Prime Minister, Ministers and Ministerial Secretaries with the Governor after the General Election of 1956

TOP:
Entering the House of Assembly to announce the grant of Independence, September, 1956

BOTTOM:
Being carried out of the Assembly after announcing the date of Independence, September 18, 1956

Kwame Nkrumah

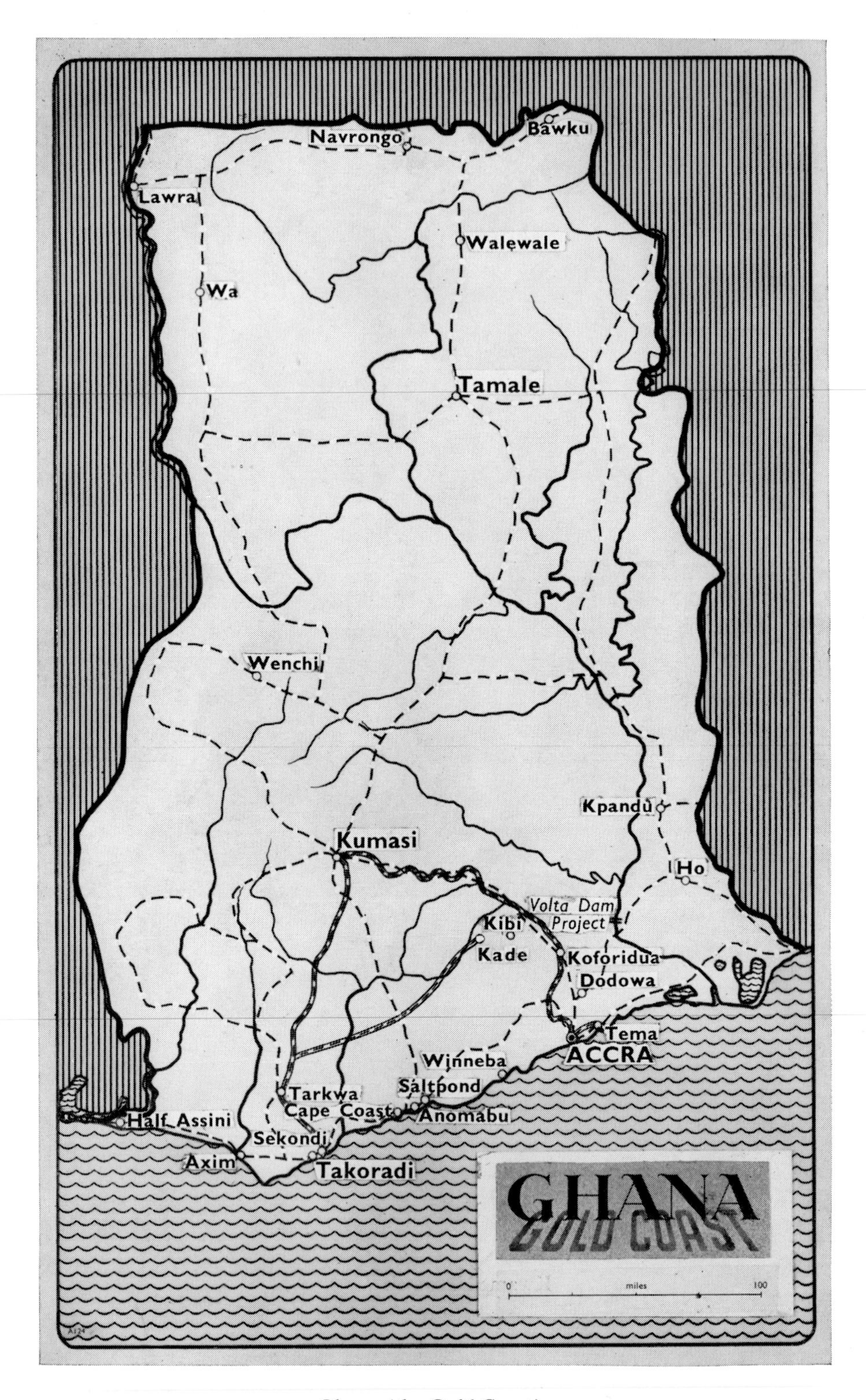

Ghana (the Gold Coast)

"O.K., let's go!" I said.

And so, with the red cap pulled down almost to my eyes and hidden in the confines of a baby Fiat car, we set out to mingle with the excited crowds. Long before we reached the Polo ground we had to slow down to a snail's pace for there were hundreds of cars all travelling in the same direction and the people were so numerous and so excited that they simply ignored the stream of cars. It was no good hooting the horn for the noise of the crowds drowned it.

"Sorry, no parking here!" shouted a policeman as my driver hopefully pulled up for me to get a better look. But I had seen all I wanted. I had had the pleasure of being one of the crowd and sharing with them the thrill of Election Night. I was now quite happy to go home to bed.

I had only just got to sleep, it seemed, when I was awakened by jubilant shouting and banging on my door. Crowds of people suddenly burst in on me.

"You're in! You're in!" they yelled. It was a few minutes before I could wake myself up sufficiently to realize what it was all about. Then I found myself whisked off to the Polo Ground—without a disguise this time—where, I was told, the people were shouting for me. Amidst loud cheers I mounted the platform. The floodlights gave the proceedings a feeling of unreality and I had almost to pinch myself to make sure that it was not all an exciting dream. Kojo Botsio, Komla Gbedemah and many others who had been successful stood with me. It was a wonderful night!

When all the results had been declared we found that, in spite of the fact that I had to "sack" eighty-one people from the Party, we had won seventy-two out of the hundred and four seats in the Assembly. And in spite of the emergence of the N.P.P. at the eleventh hour, we managed to win nine of the twenty-one seats in the Northern Territories.

On the following day the Governor sent for me and, as leader of the majority party in the new Assembly, asked me to form a Government. I compared this meeting with the first time that I visited the Governor after the previous election in 1951, then as Leader of Government Business, now as Prime Minister. We both knew much more about each other; we had both had to weather pretty hectic storms, but we had managed each in our different way to survive.

The Ministers that I nominated this time were all, with the exception of Mr. Asafu-Adjaye, Party members and were as follows:

Kojo Botsio	—Minister of State (without portfolio)
K. A. Gbedemah	—Minister of Finance
I. Egala	—Minister of Health
J. H. Allassani	—Minister of Education
A. Casely-Hayford	—Minister of the Interior
A. E. Ofori-Atta	—Minister of Communications
Ako Adjei	—Minister of Trade and Labor
N. A. Welbeck	—Minister of Works
J. E. Jantuah	—Minister of Agriculture
E. O. Asafu-Adjaye	—Minister of Local Government

On the 28th of July all Members were sworn in at the new Legislative Assembly and the Speaker, Sir Emmanuel Quist, was re-elected.

On the following day the Assembly was ceremonially opened by His Excellency the Governor. The House was packed to capacity and presented a most colorful scene as all members were wearing national costumes. As we waited inside the House we heard a fanfare of trumpets outside, then the voice of the Governor's Aide-de-camp announced His Excellency's entry. We stood as the procession came in headed by the mace-bearer and the Speaker, and made its way to the dais where the Governor, impressive in dark blue ceremonial dress, took his seat on the Throne. It was then my duty to deliver to the Governor the Speech that we had prepared for him.

Before Sir Charles spoke, he delivered to the House two messages, one from the Queen and the other from the Secretary of State. In her message the Queen expressed deep satisfaction at the way the responsibilities undertaken by the Ministers and the Assembly three years previously had been so faithfully discharged and said that it had now been possible for the Gold Coast to take a further step towards assuming full responsibility within the Commonwealth. The opening of the present Assembly, which had been chosen wholly by direct election was intended to be the last step before the goal was reached. Her Majesty expressed confidence that the greater responsibilities undertaken by the members of the present Assembly would be carried out with energy and wisdom.

The Secretary of State, in his message that followed, expressed his satisfaction with the progress that had been made since the consultations had taken place between the governments of the two countries. He noted with warm satisfaction the confident relations that had grown up between the Governor and representative ministers and expressed the opinion that on those sure foundations further progress could be built. He hoped that with our new constitution even closer co-operation would exist between the peoples of the United Kingdom and of the Gold Coast.

After the Governor had delivered his Speech from the Throne, he left the House and the Assembly was adjourned until the following day.

The Convention People's Party, with seventy-two seats in the Legislative Assembly, formed the Government. On the opposite side of the House the largest anti-government party was the Northern People's Party which had twelve seats. The remaining twenty were held for the most part by Independents. Before long, however, these Independents began to attach themselves to either one party or another and by the middle of 1956 the strength of the C.P.P. had increased to seventy-nine seats.

When the leader of the Northern People's Party rose to introduce the members of the Opposition, I declared that I, as Leader of the Government, had something to say on the matter. I said that I was quite sure that in parliamentary democracies there could in certain cases be what might be called an "unofficial opposition," as was the case in the last Assembly, but that I understood that the ordinary parliamentary interpretation of Opposition was that, if the Government should be defeated, this party should be capable of forming the next Government without delay. This could not be achieved with the present composition of the so-called Opposition. I said that Government should be given time to make a further statement on this matter and the following day I did this. I began by reiterating that the Government would welcome an official Opposition, that we were fully conscious of the value of informed and constructive criticism and were determined to do everything possible to establish in the

Assembly the procedures and conventions of parliamentary democracy, which had to include a properly organized Opposition.

The position as it was, I said, did not encourage the Government to regard members on the opposite side of the House as being in the true sense an Opposition. There was, as I had pointed out, no group among them which could form an alternative Government. Also, the Government did not consider it desirable to recognize as an official opposition a party organized on a single regional basis. The Government would be prepared, however, to recognize and to support the payment of the appropriate salary to the leader of an opposition which was organized and known to be established on a *national* basis. Until such an organization emerged, the Government regretted that it could do no more than regard the members on the opposite side of the House as being an unofficial opposition—an unofficial body of critics of Government—and to accord to them recognition similar to that granted to the opposition during the early stages of the present Government.

As might be expected, this constitutional point aroused deep interest. My political enemies snapped it up at once as further proof that I was a dictator. "Kwame Nkrumah doesn't want any opposition at all!" they declared. They could not understand that I was fighting for the principle of the thing. In the long run, therefore, my Government gave in, but history has proved me to be correct.

Today all parties opposed to the C.P.P. are known throughout the country as "Domo." The word originated because of the difficulty that many of the people had in pronouncing the word "democracy" when the first of these opposition parties called itself the Democratic Party. The word "domo" proved very apt in describing the sudden mushroom-like appearance of these parties, for literally it means "mushroom" in the Twi language. Another nickname for the opposition is GOPA, which is an abbreviation of "Ghana Opposition Parties Amalgamated." The leaders of the opposition parties have always vied with one another for leadership and it was because of this that so many parties have emerged in the country. However, because these parties felt unable individually to stand up against the disciplined C.P.P., they amalgamated, and being unable to accept the leadership of one man, the amalgamation has become weaker and weaker. Other colonial territories are afflicted by this disease. A middle-class elite, without the battering-ram of the illiterate masses, can never hope to smash the forces of colonialism. Such a thing can be achieved only by a united people organized in a disciplined political party and led by that party.

In colonial countries where imperialism has succeeded in dividing the nationalist movement along tribal lines, the anti-imperialist struggle is invariably weakened and the main objectives of the nationalist movement—namely, unity and independence—is sacrificed on the altar of tribalism. An example is Nigeria where, until 1951, there was a united nationalist movement struggling for the unity and independence of Nigeria. The introduction of tribalism shattered the unity of the Nigerian nationalist movement and subsequently divided the country.

The Ashanti Problem

ABOUT THIS TIME IT BECAME CLEAR TO ME THAT FURTHER STEPS were necessary to control the price paid locally to the cocoa farmers, otherwise we would shortly be faced with inflation. Because the demand in the world market far exceeded the supply of cocoa, the price had risen to a record height. If a proportionately high price were paid locally to the farmers, there would be an immediate rise in prices of consumer goods followed by a demand for wage increases. The Development Plan that was under way would be affected because it would not be possible to keep within the limits of the finance agreed upon, and the Second Development Plan which was being drawn up would be impossible to carry out owing to the greatly increased costs that had not been reckoned upon.

Cocoa was, and still is the mainstay of our national economy. It accounted for 68 per cent of exports in 1955. It belongs to the country and it affects everyone, so we had to think of the general public as well as the cocoa farmers. I considered that it was not in the best interests of the country to be subjected to considerable or frequent fluctuations in the local price paid to the farmers and that the present price that was being paid to them was both fair and reasonable and offered an incentive for increased production. It was also in the interests of the cocoa farmers that they should receive a steady income over a period of years.

On August 10, 1954, therefore, the Cocoa Duty and Development Funds (Amendment) Bill was introduced into the Assembly and passed three days later with the blessing of the Opposition members. The effect of this Bill was that the price paid to the cocoa farmers should be pegged at seventy-two shillings a load (sixty pounds) for four years—that is, during the life of that Assembly. The Government guaranteed to pay this price irrespective of how low the world price of cocoa might fall during that period of time, and the funds that accrued to the Government would be used on expanding the economy of the country as a whole with special emphasis on agriculture. It was important to ensure that future generations should be spared the dangers of having to rely on cocoa as their only mainstay, as we had had to do. Also, by using cocoa funds for development and for providing amenities, it would be possible to improve the general standard of living in the country as a whole at an early date.

The cocoa farmers showed a favorable reaction to the Bill for, after experiencing the way the C.P.P. Government had kept their word over the "New Deal" for cocoa, they had faith that it would do so again in this case.

But other elements in the country, still laboring to find a chance of attacking the Government, picked on this Cocoa Bill as a heaven-sent opportunity to restart agitation. The result was that a month later all the remnants of various parties that had been formed at one time and another against the C.P.P. came together as the "Council for Higher Cocoa Prices."

The Council for Higher Cocoa Prices did not last long and was succeeded by the National Liberation Movement which put forward as its *raison d'etre* the demand for a federal form of government. Supporters of this movement endeavored at first to spread discontent with the Government throughout Ashanti by what they alleged to be the injustice of the Cocoa Bill to the Ashanti farmers and tried to convince the people of how much better off they would all be if they managed their own affairs. At this time allegations were made that the money which the cocoa growers were pouring into the Government coffers was being used in developing the Colony region of the country and that Ashanti, which should be deriving the most benefit from the money, was being neglected. Talk of this sort invites one to point to the gigantic hospital in Kumasi, the new library, the magnificent national bank building, and numerous other modern constructions that were appearing in the Ashanti region during this particular period. It didn't seem to count that first-class roads had been built from Kumasi and that the journey to Accra or elsewhere could now be made in a few hours in comfort, instead of having to spend one or two nights over the journey. Moreover, the N.L.M. did not seem to realize that the cocoa, which they felt so possessive about, would be worthless without the labor, which came mainly from the Northern Territories, and without the exportation, which was carried out in the South.

The National Liberation Movement and the Asanteman Council, headed by the Asantehene, joined together to form the opposition. As far as I could see, this was once again an unofficial opposition, for it could not successfully take over if the Government went out of office; it was in my view a movement on the part of the Asanteman Council to free themsleves and those of the Ashanti people who supported them from the influence of democracy as represented by the Convention People's Party.

With the failure of a purely political campaign, a campaign of violence developed in Ashanti where the situation became so desperate that hundreds of Ashanti C.P.P. men and women were forced to leave their homes and to seek refuge in other parts of the country.

My greatest difficulty at this time was to prevent party members from hitting back. Day by day delegations would plead with me to let them go up to Kumasi and fight back, but I refused to allow this. "We will not retaliate," I said, "be patient a little while and it will all blow over." One could hardly blame them, however, when they became almost mutinous after a sister of Krobo Edusei (who was then national propaganda secretary of the C.P.P.) had been shot in cold blood in Kumasi, and they insisted that they were going to restrain themselves no longer. I was unsympathetic but I was convinced that severe discipline was the only thing that would assure our final victory. To strike back would have caused serious civil disturbance, probably even civil war, which would have called for a state of emergency to be declared. This would have invited intervention from Britain and, in the eyes of the world, there would be no doubt whatever that a country in a state bordering on civil war was hardly in a fit condition to take charge of its own affairs. And this was during the transitional period when we had not got full control of defense. If the police and the army had been in the hands of my Government, the revolt, disobedience, and disregard of law, order and justice in Ashanti would never have happened.

As time went on I was dismayed to find that on the whole the British press appeared to be backing the Opposition and the stand which they were taking in Kumasi. One letter, which was published in a London newspaper about this time, forecast widespread bloodshed and accused me of possessing a private army! As a result of this and similar publications, thousands of readers in Britain and elsewhere were given an entirely false picture of domestic trouble in the Gold Coast. It was little wonder that I was forced to the conclusion that at the eleventh hour imperialist enemies were still trying to defeat my efforts towards independence.

A further cause for unrest in Ashanti occurred when the Bechemhene, the Juasohene, the Juabenhemaa, the Nimfahene of Kumasi and the Bamuhene of Kumasi, who were all supporters of the Government. were destooled by the Asanteman Council. Under the existing regulations, when a chief had been destooled by the State Council, he had no right of appeal. I realized that something would have to be done to stop this practice and, in November, 1955, an amendment to the State Council (Ashanti) Ordinance was introduced which permitted those chiefs who had been destooled the right of appeal to the Governor.

During this month, violence took a personal turn. On the 10th of November I had an exceptionally bad cold. As there was a lot of work that I wanted to do for the following day, I arranged for my private secretary, my personal accountant and several other people to come to my house in the evening. After we had finished most of the work, four of us were sitting out on the stoop chatting. It must have been nearly eight o'clock when we noticed a strong smell of sulphur. Nobody said anything for a while as we thought someone was burning refuse in the yard below where smoke had started to appear. Then my secretary said: "You know, it smells just like fireworks. It makes me think of Guy Fawkes' night at home—and it's only five days late, too!"

Suddenly my accountant jumped to his feet. "Fireworks!" he exclaimed. "Yes, you're right!" Without saying another word he and one of the party members who was with us jumped up and tore down the stairs. There was a great deal of commotion going on and I heard them asking for buckets of water. By this time the smoke was as dense as a London fog.

"What do you think it is?" my secretary asked me.

"I don't know," I said, "but this smoke is making my cold worse."

We were still sitting in our chairs when a bright orange glow suddenly lit up the whole of the back of the house and there was a violent explosion, followed within seconds by another. The house trembled, windows were blown in and we could hear the screams of women and children. I went downstairs to find my mother whose room was very near the explosion. The poor woman was speechless and there were tears in her eyes as she clutched hold of my arm. "Oh, you are safe!" she said with relief. I went into her room. There were no windows any more and the shattered glass was all over the place, even in her bed. When I got outside I found practically all my Ministers had arrived, worried and breathless. Then I became aware of an agitated buzz which was growing in intensity every minute.

"What's that?" I enquired of Botsio.

"The people," he said. "You can't move on the road outside."

The crowd gathered in their hundreds, shouting for me, wanting to see me to know that I was unharmed. Everybody was excited, shocked and disgusted. The following day—and for weeks afterwards—telegrams, cablegrams and letters poured into the office congratulating me on my lucky escape and condemning the dastardly act.

A few days later, the State Councils Bill was read for the second time and two days afterwards it became law. The disorder in Ashanti continued.

During these disturbances I always considered that the unhappy history of Ashanti, and the mystery regarding the Golden Stool, its symbol of feudal power, has made the acceptance and practice of democracy in that part of the country more difficult than elsewhere.

Dr. K. A. Busia in his book* points to certain practices he found there which could never exist in a democratic society:

* *The Position of the Chief in the Modern Political System of Ashanti* (London: Oxford University Press, 1951), pp. 189, 190, 193, 194.

"The most noticeable thing that struck me when I began my inquiries in Kumasi in 1942 was the considerable intrigue that went on regarding constitutional disputes that came before the Confederacy Council. Bribes were given and received in all such cases. It was so common that everybody knew about it, and everybody talked about it.

"When there is a constitutional dispute, both the chief concerned and his opponents, 'malcontents' as they are called, give bribes to the chiefs, registrars, secretaries, *Akyeame* (spokesmen), and others connected with the council to enlist their support. These sums of money are called 'presents.'

"Besides those who are officially connected with the courts, there are some residents in Kumasi who collect money from the parties to a constitutional dispute which they promise to take to one or other of the chiefs known to be sitting on the case, or to the Asantehene. These men make a living in this way, as besides the money they receive from others, they are paid for their services. Some influential chiefs have 'agents' who are known to have access to them, and who collect 'presents' for them in this way.

"I received and checked up information on a number of such cases.

". . . . . .The commoners are not consulted by the chiefs and elders, and they are not given a chance of expressing their views on the matters discussed. The educated commoners feel that they should be represented on the council. One of them, a trader in Kumasi, put the popular view in this way: 'Every day we see the chiefs going to the council. We have no say in what they discuss. When they come out they give us laws to obey. Most of these are in their own interest.' . . . ."

"It is not only the literate commoners who feel that the council is not sufficiently representative. An illiterate cocoa-farmer, sixty miles from Kumasi, put what is a general criticism most clearly when he said: 'All I know of the Confederacy Council is that whenever the chief comes back from Kumasi he brings a new law. We must not hold funeral celebrations. We must not plant cocoa. We must pay a levy. When

> you ask why, they say, "The Council says so," or "The Asantehene ruled it." Today we have too many masters, the District Commissioner, the chief, the Asantehene, and they all make laws for us!' . . . ."

If this is the case, then nobody—not even a chief—would dare to express publicly his own views on a subject if these were contrary to the wishes and ideas of the Asantehene and the Kumasi clan chiefs. If a chief did so he might be destooled and, until the passing of the State Councils Bill in 1956, he would have had no right of appeal against this.

It was the emergence of the C.P.P. in Ashanti that publicly exposed these practices, and not unnaturally those who have made their living this way feel that the Convention People's Party is their greatest enemy. But it is precisely because of what the Ashanti suffered under this autocracy that the C.P.P. got such a firm footing there when it first started. If any man in the whole of the country understands now the meaning of the word "Freedom," it is an Ashanti. I well remember a most touching sight at one of the rallies I held in Ashanti. After I had been holding forth at some length on the new order, an old man moved towards me, an amazed expression on his face and wonder in his eyes.

"Do you mean *me?*" he asked. "Do you mean that *I* can say whatever I like, that I can stand up in Kumasi and speak of the things that you have just told us? All this—in *Ashanti?*"

"Of course," I assured him as I laid my hand on his bent shoulders. "Why not? You are the same as the rest of us. If you believe in freedom then you say so!"

"If the C.P.P. can do this for me—then FREEDOM!" he yelled enthusiastically, as he stumped triumphantly back through the crowd.

In Search of Relaxation

IT WAS NEARING MIDNIGHT AND I HAD JUST DISMISSED THE CENTRAL Committee which met each Tuesday evening at my house to discuss party affairs and policy. Topsy, my black spaniel dog, who had been my companion now for the past twelve months, had shaken herself out of sleep to take on her adopted role of bodyguard and sentry. Standing at the top of the flight of steps, she made sure that everybody went down them. When she was satisfied, she pushed her way through the door that I was on the point of shutting and insisted on nosing around the various rooms to check that I was at last alone. Intending to get a glass of water, I followed her as she went into the dining room. Then on the table I noticed that my supper was still laid out for me.

"Good gracious!" I exclaimed to myself, "I have forgotten to eat anything!"

Remembering that I had had nothing to eat since I had taken the edge off my hunger with a couple of eggs early in the afternoon, I thought that I had better make an effort to eat something before I went to bed. I uncovered the dish and helped myself to some of the now cold and somewhat unappetizing fish stew. I noticed that the ants had already settled themselves into the pieces of bread that had been left for me and I sat and watched them as I ate. "Nothing will stop them," I thought, as I watched those minute creatures running purposefully backwards and forwards to the bread. "They will always succeed in their objective because they are disciplined and organized." There was not a single slacker among them.

Topsy shifted herself so that I would divert my attention to her.

I looked down into her mournful-looking eyes and smiled. Breaking my rule, I handed her a piece of fish from my plate which she swallowed like a pill.

I sat and thought over the events of the day and realized that I had been "on the go" for twenty hours out of the twenty-four. During that time I had held a Cabinet meeting, a meeting of Chief Regional Officers, a number of official interviews at the office and the day-to-day business there. I had advised on many problems for the men and women who were waiting for me at the Party headquarters and at my house and then, to round off the day, there had been the meeting of the Central Committee. And yet it had not been an exceptional day—each day of my life was like that now. Sometimes it was even worse.

I dragged myself to my feet and thanked God that I could now get to bed. Suddenly Topsy ran to the front door, barking furiously as she tried to get out. I had no need to wonder what the matter was. She had heard strange footsteps and it was my bet that there was a woman around somewhere. For some reason she could not bear a woman to come to my house unless she was very familiar with her. There was a knock at my door.

"Who on earth is here at this time of night?" I wondered as I undid the latch. The caller had already backed halfway down the steps on hearing Topsy's noisy objections to his knock, but I managed to quieten her. The man came up, took off his sandals and started to kneel before me.

"Put on your sandals," I said to him kindly. "Come and sit down here and tell me what the matter is." I indicated one of the chairs to him and sat myself in another opposite to him.

"It is about my wife, Kwame Nkrumah," he began.

(I am called Kwame Nkrumah by young and old alike. The words "Mister" and "Doctor" as a form of address are not a part of their vocabulary—and I like it this way, for it puts me on equal terms with them.)

"We have travelled a hundred and twenty miles to see you and maybe tomorrow will be too late. So we have come tonight."

"Where is your wife?" I asked him.

"She is down in the yard." He then said that she was expecting a child but that the time for her to have given birth had passed several weeks ago. They had come all that way to see me because they knew that I was the only person who could help her, he told me.

Wondering what was expected of me, I told him to go and bring his wife.

"Don't worry," I told her, placing my hand gently on her body. "Your child will be born very shortly and you will have no trouble. Have faith."

They went away grateful and happy. The following day I received word from the man that his wife had given birth to a male child that very morning and that they wanted to name him Kwame Nkrumah.

I wondered to myself how many Kwame Nkrumahs there must be in the country. None of them are any relation to me and most of them I have never set eyes on. If the history of the Gold Coast is not soon written, I feared, I shall go down on record as being a most prolific man.

I was truly glad to get to bed that night and sleep overtook me before I had even managed to get properly undressed. A couple of hours later I woke up sneezing. I had caught cold again from falling asleep in a state of half-undress. Apart from catching pneumonia in the United States, I had never had a day's illness that I could remember, but I can catch cold almost quicker than I draw breath.

At 4:00 A.M. I was awakened by the telephone ringing at my bedside. One of my ministers wanted to see me on a matter of urgency.

"O.K." I told him, "you can come now. I'll open the door for you."

By the time he left, it was getting on for five o'clock and I was preparing to read through the files and papers that I had brought from the office, when I was told that some people were sitting outside waiting to see me. I went out to find a young man and woman sitting some distance apart and rather obviously not on speaking terms. This time it was matrimonial trouble. Both of them had much to say against each other and they were both talking at once. I put my hand up to silence them and gave them the best and most sensible advice that a bachelor could be expected to have on such matters. Soon they quietened down and agreed to give things another try.

Then another figure appeared at the top of the stairs, an elderly woman. "Kwame Nkrumah, I give you myself, body and soul, only please give me some money for my *chop* (food)," she said. I laughed. "What do you think I want with you?" I chided her. "Here you are, this is all I have got."

I went back to my library and worked until about half-past seven and then went to have a bath and prepare myself to go to the office. As I was sitting in the bath scrubbing myself, a voice suddenly said at the bathroom door: "Excuse me . . . Excuse me . . ."

I was flabbergasted. "Has a man no privacy?" I thought, anger seething through my brain. But I managed to control my wrath somehow.

"Can you possibly wait outside until I have finished my bath?" I asked—too kindly it appeared.

"The matter is so urgent, Kwame Nkrumah." The man would not be put off. He stood where he was—though just out of sight, I was pleased to note—and poured out his troubles to the accompaniment of splashing water. I advised him on what I felt to be the best course of action and he departed. Hearing a buzz of conversation in the immediate vicinity, however, I called after him to kindly shut the front door behind him and to tell anybody else who was waiting to see me that I would be out in ten minutes.

After listening to problems on a variety of subjects, I eventually managed to tear myself away to keep my official appointments at the office. On the way I remembered that I had not had breakfast. On arrival at the office I asked my private secretary, Erica Powell, if she could get me a glass of water.

"Haven't you had any breakfast again, P.M.?" she asked.

"No, I was too busy. I forgot it."

"Then I'll get you some coffee and biscuits," she said, after reminding me once again of the important role that food plays in keeping body and soul together, "and it affects your mind, too" she added.

Somehow or other I did not feel my usual self these days. I was constantly feeling tired—not so much physically as mentally. My lack of regular meals and proper diet certainly may have had something to do with it, but apart from that I felt an almost urgent need to escape, to break away from the routine of my life and to be able to have a few hours to myself occasionally for reflection.

The Cabinet recess was due to take place in September and several of the Ministers had already left the country for various missions overseas or were planning a spot of leave. "Why shouldn't I take some leave?" I asked myself. The idea had several times occurred to me at one time and another but I had never allowed it to materialize. Just at that moment, however, Daniel Chapman, secretary to the Cabinet, came into my office.

"I was just thinking," I said, "why don't I take some leave?"

Daniel was most enthusiastic about the project. He was ready with his pad and pencil to make the necessary arrangements just as soon as I could make up my mind where I would go. I suggested some sea air and I thought it would be rather nice to cruise down the coast for a couple of weeks.

"Excellent idea!" said Daniel, as he made a note of it. "I will make enquiries at the various shipping companies straight away and find out whether there is a boat sailing for a round trip at the beginning of September." As he rushed out of the door I called him back. "By the way," I said, "I have much work that I shall want to get through—work that necessitates peaceful surroundings. I shall need both you and Erica on this trip, and I suggest that you take Efua (Mrs. Chapman) along with you. It will be a good change for her if she can manage to leave the children behind."

I could see that Daniel was as good as on board the boat and I noticed that he went in to Erica's office to tell her the news before he got down to making the arrangements.

And so it happened that the four of us, together with my nephew, Nyameke, who has been a necessary part of my household for some years now, arranged to board the Dutch merchant vessel *Nigerstroom* at Takoradi and travel as far as Douala in the French Cameroons and back, a trip of about two to three weeks.

I wanted to sneak quietly away, but it was pointed out to me that Prime Ministers just can't suddenly disappear without warning. I was reminded of the time when I "disappeared" the previous year for a week to a quiet spot about a hundred miles or so out of Accra in order to meditate. It was a personal matter and one from which I have always derived benefit, and I saw no reason to announce to the world where I was going. The only people who were told were the Governor and the Commissioner of Police. But the British press made such announcements as "Gold Coast Premier Disappears," "Kwame Nkrumah Vanishes," and gave wild and imaginative accounts of my probable visit to a *ju-ju* man.

"All right," I agreed, "you can issue a press release but it must not go out until I have set sail and no mention must be made of the name of the boat or its destination. You can just say that 'the Prime Minister has gone on a short sea trip.' "

I have often wondered why we bother to read newspapers—or, at any rate, why we bother to waste time on carefully worded statements to be printed in them. The ubiquitous "bush telegraph" system soon announced the details of my trip and by the time I arrived in Takoradi, the date and time of the departure of the *Nigerstroom* had already become a matter of importance to the Gold Coast people. Because of the crowds that were managing to leak into the dock area and were standing patiently on the quayside, it was arranged that I should board the boat from a launch which would come from the opposite side of the harbor. I said that I would arrive at eight-thirty in the evening of the day before the boat was due to sail.

A number of party members had come to me in Takoradi and were anxious to see me board the boat, so the Captain must have got something of a shock to see about thirty people following me out of the launch and up the gangway. To allay his fears I told him that a few of my friends had expressed the wish to see me on board and to take a look at my cabin.

"Of course, sir," he said with a smile as he shook my hand and welcomed me aboard. Then he called the chief steward and asked that my companions should be shown my cabin.

They all trooped down the long corridor to the last cabin. When they were shown inside I heard several gasps of admiration. Although it was a well appointed and very roomy cabin, I wondered at their enthusiasm until I got further inside. Then I saw the cause of it all. On the dressing table was an enormous bouquet of gay flowers attached to which was a note wishing me welcome and bon voyage from the shipping company, the Holland West-Afrika Lijn.

After this we all congregated in the lounge where drinks were served and we sat and chatted until the time came for the guests to leave the boat.

As soon as the engines started up around five o'clock the following morning, I was up and dressed and wandering around the deck. A voice called to me from somewhere overhead: "Mr. Prime Minister—come up here if you like. You can get a good view of Takoradi harbor and see how we pilot the boat out to sea." It was the Captain. A few seconds later I was standing with him on the bridge and learning everything that a novice could expect to know about piloting and steering a ship. As soon as we were under way the Captain took me into his cabin where we sat and chatted about boats until a bell sounded.

"What is that?" I asked when I heard the bell.

"That's for breakfast, sir. I'm afraid I am not always very good company first thing in the morning so I have formed the habit of having my breakfast up here on a tray," the Captain remarked, somewhat apologetically.

"You are lucky!" I declared. "I very rarely get any at all. A prime minister has to work hard. I've just realized that this is the first vacation I have ever taken."

The Captain raised his eyebrows. "Well, you must take things easy while you are aboard my ship," he said. Then, with a twinkle in his eye but in a commanding voice, he declared: "And as Captain of this ship, I'll make darned sure you do!"

The steward brought in the Captain's breakfast and I got to my feet and went to join the others. The dining room was just next to my cabin. Daniel, Efua and Erica were all seated round a table surrounded by food.

"What's all this?" I inquired, pointing at a plate of smoked meats, some queer looking fish and an assortment of other strange looking fare. "And where's Nyameke?"

"He's discovered a Gold Coast boy on board and wants to have his meals with him somewhere else," Daniel informed me.

There was so much for breakfast that I thought it would keep me going for the rest of the trip. Luckily I had managed to work up a bit of an appetite with the fresh air and sea breeze on the bridge. I noticed that Efua was very quiet and asked her what was the matter. She smiled—not a happy smile but a brave attempt—then she suddenly jumped up from the table and rushed to her cabin.

"Poor Efua!" we chorused.

"But it's so calm!" I declared in amazement. We learned, however, that just as soon as the boat left the dockside, however still the water might be, Efua felt the ripples of it and there was nothing anyone could do about it.

After breakfast I roamed the decks again. I couldn't accustom myself to the idea that I had simply nothing to do all day, nobody to worry me with problems, and no telephone bells to distract me. I had brought a couple of books along with me and I also intended doing something about writing my autobiography, but I felt they could wait. Just then I was determined to try and enjoy this relaxation that I had heard so much about. After I had circled the decks about half a dozen times, leaned on the rails and examined the sea, scanned the horizon for a glimpse of my native land and peered inquisitively into various doorways leading off from the deck, each of which seemed to house some officer or other, I must say I felt that I had done pretty well all that there was to be done on the *Nigerstroom* and I was beginning to have my doubts about being able to amuse myself for another fourteen days or so. Suddenly Erica appeared round the corner looking, I thought, also at a loose end.

"Hello P.M., we wondered where you had got to."

"I've been walking round the deck. I think I'll go and lie down in my cabin and read."

"You can't very well go now," she said, "because they're cleaning it. Why don't you read your book up here or in the lounge?"

She went off to get my book while I arranged a chair for myself. The morning slipped by and around midday the Captain came along. "How's the relaxation going?" he asked.

"I don't know, Captain. I'm not used to lying around like this all day. I think you'll have to find me a job before the trip is over."

"Can you play darts?" he asked.

"I've never tried."

"Well come along and have a game. I always play against the First Officer before lunch. It's my daily exercise."

And so each noon the Captain and I, with the First Officer, the Dutch consul in Nigeria, who had been asked by the Dutch authorities to accompany me on the trip, Daniel or Erica, or whoever else happened to be around when we needed a fourth player, paired up and played against each other.

"Losers buy the beer!" the Captain would announce.

These gatherings round the dart board each lunchtime are quite my happiest memories of the trip.

The following morning the boat docked at Lagos. Again I went up to the bridge and watched the pilot come aboard at the entrance of the harbor mouth and pilot the boat safely through the tricky mudbanks and shallow waters.

Soon after we docked, the A.D.C. to the Governor-General of Nigeria and the Chief Secretary came aboard to extend a welcome on behalf of Sir James Robertson and asked if I would care to have tea at Government House that afternoon. I accepted and on the return trip to Lagos I had lunch there and had a long and useful chat with the Governor-General on current affairs of mutual interest. On each occasion I was transported by the Government House launch.

Word soon got round that I was on board, and day and night people were lining the quayside expecting me to come ashore. Because so many tried to come aboard to speak to me, a policeman had to be stationed at the top of the gangway to keep people away. I wanted very much to go ashore and say a few words to the expectant crowds, but I realized that this might cause embarrassment to the Government of Nigeria since I was on an unofficial visit. I hoped that the people would understand and I asked that the facts should be explained to them in the local newspapers.

But I had to find a way to visit my relative, the same one who had done so much to help me with my passage money to the United States about twenty years earlier. So one night his son came and collected the four of us and took us out to Yaba where he lived. He was now an old man and was not in very good health, but he was delighted to see me again and we had a long chat together. He had a private zoo in his garden and I was most amused to find a large chimpanzee sitting under the house smoking a cigarette like an old man and obviously enjoying every puff. On my return to Lagos I paid another visit to the house and this time a number of his friends, who were all known to me, were invited. It was a happy gathering and the old man seemed to be filled with new life as he watched us dancing the Gold Coast "Highlife" to the music of his radio-phonograph.

The Nigerian port authority representatives took me on a tour of inspection of the wharves and warehouses and then by launch round the harbor to watch the dredgers at work and to see the dry dock. I noticed that there was a Japanese boat in the harbor and expressed the wish to see over it. The Japanese were very happy to show me around. The thing that impressed me most about the ship was that at five feet nine inches, I had suddenly become too big to be comfortable. Every time I passed through a door, if I forgot to stoop I was nearly decapitated.

There was, of course, plenty of activity on board the *Nigerstroom,* too, and I spent a lot of time watching the cranes hauling up the cargo out of the hold. It took five days to unload all there was and at five o'clock in the afternoon we set sail for Douala. Crowds waved good-by from the dockside and there were many shouts of "Freedom!" and hands raised in the C.P.P. "Freedom" salute. There were no doubt many Gold Coast people among them.

Before we reached Douala a cable arrived from the Governor asking me and my party to lunch. I replied that we would be pleased to accept the following day. Early in the morning of the 12th of September we passed the island of Fernando Po.

"That is a very important island to us," I told the Captain.

"Fernando Po? But it's Spanish!" he retorted.

"I don't care about that. It was from there that our cocoa originated.

"Really?" the Captain said with interest.

"Yes, in 1879 a Gold Coast man from Christianborg, Accra, called Teeteh Quarshie returned home from Sao Tome in Fernando Po and brought with him a cocoa seed which he planted in Mampong. From that seed our cocoa crop developed and has become our most important export. I hope I don't sound like a walking *Ency-*

clopaedia Britannica," I added, "but that is something that I happen to know."

Two hours later we arrived in Douala and I was most impressed to see the mechanically driven trolleys and cranes that were used to discharge cargo. I mentioned this to the French harbor official who took us in a launch on a tour of the harbor later in the day, and he declared proudly that Douala boasted the quickest turn-round of any port on the west coast of Africa. I could believe it, too, for they got into action as soon as the boat docked and appeared to be hard at it all day and night. It was difficult to ignore them, in fact, for the whirring of engines and clanking of gears made this impossible.

The British Consul came aboard to pay his respects and I asked him tactfully about the political situation in the country, for I had received from time to time disturbing accounts and petitions from various political movements in the French Cameroons. He was unable to tell me very much because he said he had not been in the country very long. I gathered from the French harbor official, who was otherwise noncommital on the subject, that there existed strong tribal hatred. He said that this was so prevalent that a few days previously one of the dock workers had fallen into the water and was unable to swim. He was screaming for assistance but the rest of the men, because they were not of his tribe and were not sympathetic towards him, never moved a muscle to help him. In the end the Frenchman forced one of the men to dive in and save him. I felt that this was a most distressing and unsatisfactory state of affairs in any country and hoped that I might be able to find out more from the Governor at lunchtime.

Rain was pouring down when two carloads of French officials arrived at the docks to escort us to the Governor's residence. The driver of our car seemed to be tearing at breakneck speed and, after he had missed several pedestrians and cyclists by mere centimeters, I felt I could bear it no longer and called out: "Not so fast, driver." He took not the slightest notice, so, thinking that he might be a little deaf, I shouted louder. At this he just turned his head at a complete right-angle and stared at me, and then returned his wandering gaze to the road again—mercifully.

Daniel suddenly laughed. "Of course, he can't understand you. He's French!"

By the time we had thought up what we wanted to say and how to say it in French, the race was over and our tires screeched once more as we turned into the gates of the Governor's residence. In spite of the torrential rain, a guard or honor had been posted at the gates and we crawled past to acknowledge their salute. I was most impressed.

The Governor and his wife were at the steps to meet us and were very charming and welcoming. Fortunately they both spoke good English and I managed to have long conversations with them. Both of them appeared to be very fond of the people and to have their cause at heart, but they carefully avoided answering any questions I asked about the political situation. I felt by this time that it was a matter which was simply not discussed.

The lunch was first class. Having had over a week on board the *Nigerstroom* encouraged by the Captain and the Chief Steward to sample all the appetizing Dutch dishes, I was becoming quite food conscious—almost a gourmet, in fact—and for the first time in my life eating was becoming quite an enjoyable pastime. I have never tasted such a wonderful fish as was served for one of the courses. I had two helpings in spite of the threatening array of knives and forks before me, which promised more to follow than I would ever be able to cope with.

That night two newspaper reporters managed to get on board. They approached Erica first and she said that I was not available but passed them on to Daniel. Dan, because he felt sorry for them, took them into the lounge and gave them a few drinks. In the meantime Erica warned me that they were there and managed to smuggle me past the lounge door and up onto the deck where I had to stay until they had gone. Even though I would like to have seen them—indeed I wanted to see them, for I knew that I would be able to find out what was going on in the country from them—I had to remember all the time that I was an unofficial visitor to the country and that I had to be cautious. It would have been embarrassing if I had been reported in the local papers giving my democratic views to a reporter and it would probably have been misinterpreted by the French and British Governments.

The following morning we took the Captain, the chief engineer and the Dutch Consul up country to inspect a hydroelectric power station that was being built. I was especially interested to see this because of our own Volta River Project. The journey took about two hours each way. It was a very humid day with intermittent showers and the French were tireless in showing us all there was to see. We followed them round power stations, to the top of the dam and over rough soil where new projects were being started. It was most interesting but as we grew hotter and thirstier, I sensed a feeling of unrest among some of the party. Then I heard the Captain say to somebody, as he looked at his watch, "I could certainly do with one myself."

"So could I, Captain," I said smiling.

Then the Dutch Consul, being the most diplomatic and speaking the most impeccable French, asked one of our hosts whether it was possible to buy some beer to refresh the party. The Frenchman looked quite taken aback and said that he doubted whether we would be able to get any around there. As I saw that the interest of my parched and weary party was dwindling in technical subjects, I said that I thought we had better make a move as we had a long journey before us.

One thing that I remember very vividly about the occasion—probably because it was first time that I have ever seen it happen in any colony—was the way all the workers, both European and African, climbed into the waiting trucks when the lunch buzzer sounded. This complete disregard of color on the part of the European workers greatly impressed me.

It seemed no time at all before we were on our way back to Takoradi. Luckily there was a lot of cocoa to be loaded at Accra so I had the opportunity of watching my countrymen paddling out in the surf to the boats anchored off Accra—a distance of about a mile and extremely hard-going in heavy surf—to load great bags of cocoa. Sometimes bags would drop into the sea and I became concerned at our loss of revenue, but the Captain assured me that every bag was picked up by the surf boats, which was true. One man in each boat would climb up the side of the ship with the aid of a rope and get his consignment note signed by the officer supervising the loading. It was remarkable to watch the agility of these men but more remarkable than ever to see how little they ate—a handful of rice or gari. It was a miracle that they had such strength to carry out such an arduous job.

"These men should have an issue of vitamins," I said to Daniel, who was also watching over the rail.

"You're quite right," he said. "According to a doctor friend of mine, although they have such strength and appear to be vigorous and healthy, they have no resistance at all against disease."

"Something must be done about it as soon as possible," I said. Schools, hospitals, child welfare, libraries—yes, all of vital importance, but how many people gave a thought to men such as these, developing huge muscles through the weights they carry and the surf that they battle against, appearing on the face of it as strong and healthy men. And yet they died young, as soon as disease overtook them. Their place was taken by others and so it would go on, year after year. Had anyone given the matter a thought? I felt once again the urgent need to implement my party's social policy to improve economic standards and working conditions such as these.

If things had gone according to schedule, we should have landed in Takoradi on my birthday. However, in the early morning of the previous day it rained and the surf was apparently too bad for the boats to load the *Nigerstroom*. At about midday the fishing boats set out, a most picturesque sight with their white sails almost dazzling in the bright sun. They would be out all night fishing in the deep waters.

"Nkrumah's fleet," said the Captain who came up beside me and must have been reading my thoughts.

"Yes, my fleet," I answered proudly. "Good luck to them!"

"That is the foundation of a navy, you know," the Captain said as we watched them disappearing over the horizon.

The following day the surf boats were at work again and the Captain told us that, all being well, we would be sailing for Takoradi that evening. As it was my birthday, I invited the Captain and his officers to drink champagne before lunch. There was a touch of sadness about the gathering in the lounge that day which even the champagne failed to dispel. I played my last darts match with a somewhat heavy heart.

When dinner time came I decided that, because it was my birthday and because it was the last night of my holiday, I would wear my dinner jacket. It was a last minute idea and when I poked my nose into Dan's cabin to tell him his face fell for he said that he had already packed his. I had no idea of what was in store for me, but as things turned out I was very pleased that I had decided to dress for the occasion.

When I entered the dining room the first thing I noticed was that our usual table was no longer there. Then I saw that there was only one table in the room, one long table down the center, most beautifully decorated. The chief steward, always full of wit and humor, met me as I entered and ushered me to the place of honor at one end of the table with the Captain at the other end. The meal was superb and every dish presented was so colorful and so beautifully arranged that it seemed sheer sacrilege to disturb it. The crowning glory was a magnificent birthday cake which I had to cut.

At the end of the meal the Captain rose to his feet and said that he would like to say a few words. "Mr. Prime Minister," he began, "I am going to be quite frank with you. When we heard that we were going to have a Prime Minister and his party on board, we didn't like it! We didn't like it at all! But all I can say, Dr. Nkrumah, is that we have all—every one of us—been genuinely happy to have had you with us; we are glad and honored to have met you and to have got to know you, and we hope that whenever you take another sea trip, you will choose to travel again with the *Nigerstroom*. Here's to your success and to our next meeting!" he said as he raised his glass.

There was sincerity in these words. Everyone had indeed been more than kind to us and I was so conscious of this fact that I wanted to give them each something to remember us by. I had sent Efua and Erica to shop when we were in Lagos and they returned with a silver tankard for each of them. I felt that this was something that I could not have chosen better, for they could use them during that pleasurable hour before lunch around the dart board, the hour that I had grown to love. And so, after the Captain had finished his speech, I stood up and said a few words of thanks and then presented a tankard to him and one to each of his officers. My only regret was that it had not been possible to get them inscribed in the short space of time.

We arrived at Takoradi at two in the morning and we stayed on the bridge with the Captain until the boat had been safely anchored outside the harbor entrance.

The following day, after I had made a tour of inspection of the harbor, I bade farewell to the Captain and his officers and stepped into the launch that was to take me ashore. I certainly weighed a good many pounds more than when I embarked two weeks previously! As we moved away and sorrowfully waved our farewells to the *Nigerstroom* and her crew, three blasts sounded from the ship. I was deeply touched and turned my head away towards the shore.

The whole of the quayside was thick with people, so that it was a job to get a foothold beyond the stone steps leading up from the launch. When I eventually reached my car it was almost as if it was carried by the people through the streets of Takoradi, so close were they. Then the people kept struggling to see me, so I decided to get out of the car and continue the journey standing in an open jeep where I could acknowledge their welcome more easily. The people had arranged reception committees and a mass meeting in the afternoon, followed by a grand reception at night, but as I was anxious to return to Accra the same day, I addressed the crowd from a balcony and explained to them my disappointment at not being able to be present throughout the celebrations that they had arranged for me. Then I left for Accra early in the afternoon. I travelled back with Kojo Botsio who had come to meet me, and during the journey he told me all that had been happening while I had been away.

How different I felt! My old enthusiasm had returned and I had more energy than I knew how to expend.

"You know, Kojo," I said, as I interrupted his discourse, "we *must* do something about getting a yacht."

The "Federation" Issue

AS SOON AS THE 1954 GENERAL ELECTION WAS OVER, THE OPPOsition parties began agitating for another election. When the cocoa price was pegged they really felt they were getting somewhere, that they had got something concrete to criticize, and they began their drive for a federal form of government, a subject which they could certainly not have studied in any great detail, for they would have been the first to campaign against the cost of operating such a system in a country of just under 92,000 square miles with a population of five million people. But the word "federation" was to become almost an obsession with them.

In an attempt to talk matters over and to smooth out some of the differences that had arisen, four members of the Legislative Assembly on the Government benches (two of whom came from constituencies in Kumasi) invited the leaders of the N.L.M. to a round-table conference. The reply was that they were unable to accept such an invitation since this did not come directly from the Government. So I sent another invitation to them myself on behalf of the Government and, when this was refused, yet another. This, too, was turned down flat.

In a further attempt to bring about an understanding and at the same time to prove to them the sincerity of the Government's desire to give full consideration to their demand for a federal form of government, I moved a Motion in the Assembly on April 5, 1955, seeking the approval of the House for the appointment of a Select Committee "to examine the question of a federal system of government for the Gold Coast, and the question of a Second Chamber, which have been raised in certain quarters, and, after consultation with responsible bodies or individuals, to make recommendations for the consideration of the Legislative Assembly." I pointed out to the House, in a lengthy speech, that my task lay in leading into independence "a Gold Coast with a people which is united and in harmony" and that I had to ensure that there would be stable and effective government, especially during the period which immediately followed independence.

I had previously arranged to meet the Leader of the Opposition and he informed me that he intended proposing an amendment to the Motion in support of "the general demand for a Constituent Assembly." Although under the existing standing orders, the Opposition was entitled to have only two members on the Committee, as against seven from the Government benches, I agreed at this meeting to allow the Leader of the Opposition to nominate five members.

After my Motion had been seconded, the Leader of the Opposition surprised the House by withdrawing his amendment saying that as the Opposition supported the general demand for a Constituent Assembly, they felt it was their "duty in the highest interest of the country to refrain from participating in the farcical drama about to be enacted."

Having got this off his chest, he and his twenty supporters rose to their feet and, amidst loud cheers and jeers from other members of the House, walked out. A few minutes later there was an even louder burst of laughter as the Leader of the Opposition suddenly returned to collect his bundle of papers which, in his haste and confusion, he had left behind. Government backbenchers hastily filled the seats vacated by the Opposition members and, there being a quorum, the debate continued and a Select Committee was set up in accordance with the terms of my Motion.

When the Speaker announced on the following day the names of the members of the House who had been appointed to serve on the Select Committee, he mentiond that as five of the names submitted were those of Opposition members who had dissociated themselves from the Motion, he saw no object in appointing them against their will. He then proceeded to announce the names of twelve members, including the Chairman, Mr. C. H. Chapman, and the Deputy Speaker.

The Select Committee, after holding twenty-two meetings and considering two hundred and seventy-nine memoranda and sixty other written communications, issued its report on July 26, 1955, in which it declared its decision not to recommend a federal form of Government. It recommended that regional councils should be set up to which certain powers and functions of the central Government should be delegated "to ensure full consultation and collaboration between itself and the various regions in the planning of development." With regard to the creation of a Second Chamber, the Committee suggested that this should be examined again at some future time after the attainment of independence.

The N.L.M. and its allies gave as their reason for boycotting the Select Committee the fact that they did not consider that the Committee was competent to deal with national matters, in spite of the fact that it was composed entirely of members of the National Legislative Assembly. Because of the way they interpreted a statement made by the Secretary of State—that until there was a more settled atmosphere in the Gold Coast the transfer of power would be delayed—they had got it firmly fixed in their heads that as long as they disagreed with everything the Government proposed, they would be assured of delaying independence indefinitely. Every time the constitution issue was raised in our new Assembly, the Opposition members gathered up their things and marched out. Violence and intimidation in Kumasi were as rife as ever and, this was being extended to other areas in the country.

The British Government was the only body which could have forced these obstructionists to see sense, but they remained aloof, apart from giving publicity to the Ashanti situation in both Houses of Parliament and, because of this, through the press. Thus its actions actually served as a stimulant to the unrest in Kumasi. Unless the lawless element felt fully confident of such a backing, they would never have dared to persist in their actions.

But in spite of all this—and it was depressing, to say the least—I would not give up. A month later I sought a mandate from the Legislature to request Her Majesty's Government to send to the

Gold Coast a Constitutional Adviser to help formulate an acceptable constitution for the country and also to advise on the devolution of powers and functions to the regions.

On the 26th of September, therefore, Sir Frederick Bourne arrived in the country for this purpose, and all parties and organizations concerned were invited to avail themselves of his services. Sir Frederick had had many years experience of constitutional matters in India and Pakistan and, at first, because of his connection with Pakistan, some people were a little worried as to whether he would not advocate a partition of the Gold Coast. But they need have had no fears, as it turned out, for he was not only highly intelligent but conscientious and sincere in the mission he had undertaken. He also acquired, after a short while in the country, a true affection for and understanding of the people whose cause he took very deeply to heart. He visited all the regions and met and had discussions with a great number of bodies and individuals. When he went to Kumasi, however, to meet the leaders of the N.L.M. and its allies, they preferred not to see him, making as their excuse that the Government, by passing the State Councils (Ashanti) Amendment Bill had "prejudiced his work and had shown that they were neither sincere nor serious in their attitude to him." Because of the passing of that bill, the Opposition were unwilling to take part in any discussions regarding future constitutional developments.

Sir Frederick, along with many others, felt that the State Councils Ordinance was ill-timed and that it should have been postponed until a later date. But it should be appreciated that the circumstances in the country at that particular time warranted passing into law an ordinance of that nature, when chiefs were being unjustly destooled for not supporting the federalist idea and were being intimidated into joining the N.L.M. They had no right of appeal and it was high time that the Government took measures to protect them from such unfair treatment. If the bill had been withdrawn, it would not only have weakened the Assembly but the chiefs for whose benefit it was being put through, and would have suffered at the hands of those who dealt in corruption, violence and injustice.

The Constitutional Adviser completed his work and reported to the Governor on the 17th of December. In this report he recommended the devolution of certain powers and functions to Regional Assemblies which would be empowered to plan their own developments and to apply for grants-in-aid from the Government. They would be consultative and deliberative, but all legislation would be enacted by the central legislature. The Regional Assemblies would have no power to levy taxation and on all constitutional and traditional matters which concerned a particular region, the traditional Council and the appropriate Regional Assembly would be consulted.

When I returned to Accra from my sea trip towards the end of September, the Secretary of State for the Colonies, Mr. A. T. Lennox-Boyd, extended an invitation to me through the Governor to visit him in London in order to discuss Gold Coast affairs with special reference to the timetable for the granting of independence. I had already met Mr. Lennox-Boyd when I passed through London in 1951 on my way back from America, and I would have welcomed another meeting with him and an opportunity to work out a mutually agreeable program for the transfer of power from the British Government to the Government, chiefs and people of the Gold Coast. But it was not as easy as that. The year 1956 had been widely regarded in the country as being the year of our independence; the whole country, including the Legislative Assembly and its Ashanti members, were firmly behind me and my Government in this demand. The present transitional period had already given rise to difficulties: there had been divided authority at high level, divided loyalties in the civil service, criticism against the Government for not doing things which it was, in fact, not able to do, and a feeling by some that the Government had no power at all and could therefore be ignored. The uncertainty of this transitional period was having its repercussions in commerce where it discouraged trade and foreign investment; it was also having an effect in the United Nations, for some delegates had already expressed their fears that the U. K. government might now put forward a claim to annex the Trust Territory of Togoland, a question which was before the United Nations. If a definite date could be fixed for the transfer of power by the British Government, the leaders of the opposition parties would act in a more responsible and co-operative manner.

Although the Government and the Party had now decided in favor of regional devolution, and although we would never be able to agree with those who talked of "federation or nothing," such disagreement, I felt, should not hinder or delay the fixing of a date for independence and the form of government to be adopted thereafter should be left for the people to decide.

I therefore replied to the Secretary of State that, much as I welcomed his invitation and much as I hoped I would be able to accept, if such preliminary discussions took place between us it was imperative that I returned to the Gold Coast with something positive to tell my people regarding the date for the final transfer of power. If this could not be assured, then any meeting between us in London would do nothing but create confusion, bitterness and ill-will in this country.

The people were expecting me to make a journey to London certainly, but they were banking on my returning with independence in my brief case. I could not and I would not disappoint them.

The Secretary of State intimated that the United Kingdom Government would hesitate to grant Independence to the Gold Coast until a substantial majority of the people had shown that they wanted Independence in the very near future and had agreed upon a workable constitution for the country. If the Constitutional Adviser succeeded in recommending proposals which were generally acceptable to the majority, all well and good. If he failed, then there appeared to be no alternative but to call a general election in order to seek the views of the people.

I was equally hopeful that, as a result of Sir Frederick Bourne's mission, it would be possible for the Gold Coast Government to put forward its proposals for the form of the constitution after Independence, confident of the support of the majority of the people of the country.

"I should like to emphasize," I wrote in reply, "that nothing must be done to weaken the cause of democracy by reducing the status of our freely-elected Legislative Assembly through giving greater weight to the words of a minority as opposed to the decisions of the Assembly. I am ready to go to a general election when circumstances demand one."

The Governor went on leave in February, 1956, and before he left the country, I had several discussions with him in which I put forward the views and proposals I wished him to convey to the Secretary of State.

I told him that in an endeavor to satisfy the two conditions laid down by the Secretary of State—that a substantial majority of the people should show their desire for Independence in the very near future and should agree upon a constitution which not only met their needs but was also workable—I had convened a conference of all the principal representative bodies and organizations in the country to meet under the chairmanship of Mr. C. W. Tachie-Manson (a member of the Gold Coast Public Service Commission), to discuss not only Sir Frederick Bourne's Report, but also any other matters affecting the form of the constitution.

If general agreement on the form of the constitution was reached at that conference, then the Government would perpare a White Paper setting out its constitutional proposals based on that agreement and, after due consideration had been given to this throughout the country, it would introduce a resolution adopting these proposals at the Budget meeting of the Assembly which was then due to take place. If this resolution were adopted, then I would approach the U.K. Government in order to have the necessary legislative enactments made to give the Gold Coast its independence under the constitution adopted by the Assembly.

If the Conference failed, then I would prepare a White Paper setting out my constitutional proposals and have it debated at the Budget session of the Assembly. If circumstances then demand a general election, I would go to the people for their verdict.

"But," I added, "if I go to a general election to seek a mandate from the people that my constitutional proposals are acceptable, and if the people desire to enter upon Independence under that form of constitution immediately, and if I am returned to power with that mandate—even though it be with the smallest of majorities and irrespective of the fact that the winning party might be in the minority in one or more of the regions of the country—I want assurance that British Government would, after a resolution has been duly passed by the new Assembly, declare a firm date for Independence and take immediate steps to enact the necessary legislation for the transfer of power to the Gold Coast Government."

I had invited Sir Frederick Bourne to return to the Gold Coast as Constitutional Adviser to the Conference that I had called and which opened at Achimota on the 16th of February. It was attended by delegations from the Brong-Kyempem Council, the C.P.P., the Ex-Servicemen's Union, the Muslin Council, the Joint Provincial Council of Chiefs, the Trades Union Congress, the Trans-Volta Togoland Council and Local Government Councils in the Northern Territories. The N.L.M. and its allies had, as was expected, refused to associate themselves with the Conference. At the second meeting the Joint Provincial Council delegates asked permission to use what persuasion they could to bring about a change of heart in the Asanteman Council and the National Liberation Movement and its allies and to see if they would not send representatives to the Conference. And so the Conference was adjourned for a week to enable the J.P.C. delegates to contact these bodies. But it was all in vain and their mission was unsuccessful.

On the 8th of March two of the four J.P.C. delegates made yet another effort on behalf of the Conference to persuade these obstructionists to take part in the proceedings, but they returned after four days, unsuccessful once more.

The Conference came to an end on the 16th of March and issued its Report forthwith. Almost all the recommendations of Sir Frederick Bourne were agreed upon and in addition it recommended that there should be a House of Chiefs in each Region to discuss social and cultural legislation.

The Achimota Conference due to the continued absence of the N.L.M. had failed to meet the terms required by the Secretary of State. I therefore set to work to produce my own constitutional proposals for Gold Coast Independence in order that they could be circulated before I introduced my motion on the White Paper resulting therefrom at the Budget session of the Assembly in the middle of May.

I was, however, far from happy. Apart from the continued and deliberate refusals of the N.L.M. and its supporters to co-operate in any way whatever, violence was still common in Kumasi and nothing appeared to be done to check this. Then arms and ammunition were found in both camps and those responsible for their possession were hauled before the court. Because of this, I felt that if a general election were held in the near future it appeared extremely doubtful that it would be conducted without violence and intimidation of peaceful citizens by the supporters of the N.L.M. What guarantee was there, also, that the N.L.M.—who must know from the outset that they could not hope to win a majority in a general election—would change their present attitude even after a general election had been held? My Party Executive Members were almost unanimous in voting against a general election and even to mention the subject was like waving a red rag before a bull.

And so I asked Sir Gordon Hadow, the Officer Administering the Government in the absence of the Governor, to convey my decision against going to a general election, and my reasons for this decision to the Governor so that he could bring this before the Secretary of State during their forthcoming discussions.

Constitutionally and politically I did not see any necessity for going to a general election before Independence. I assumed that the British Government would grant us independence at the date we had in mind without having to plunge the country into a general election, because I feared that an election campaign might be used in some quarters to cause riot, bloodshed and general confusion in the country.

The Secretary of State, while sympathizing with my point of view, intimated that as the Achimota Conference had failed in providing the requisite agreement, there appeared to him to be no alternative but to hold a general election.

I sent for Kojo Botsio.

"There is only one thing for it," I told him. "You will have to fly to London on my behalf and put over my views to the Secretary of State and the Governor. I wish I could go myself but you know as well as I do that this would be impossible at the present time."

Kojo nodded his head in agreement. I sent for Daniel Chapman and told him to book a passage on the London plane the following day. "And tell Erica," I called out to him as he was half out of the door, "that I do not want to be disturbed by anyone for the next couple of hours."

I turned to Botsio. "This is a vital mission, Kojo, and you must be sure to put over all the facts. Make it clear from the outset that neither I, my Party nor, indeed, the overwhelming majority of the people of the Gold Coast can accept the proposal to go to a general election before Independence. Explain how this would lead to confusion and would tend to destroy the confidence that the people have in the Government; it would completely ignore the developments of the past few years and would set the clock back.

"I brought my Party into power with a mandate to negotiate for 'self-government *now*'; we still have a great—and an increasing—majority in the Assembly. The Government has never been defeated on a vote of confidence and I am expected to fulfill my promise to the country. Point out to them, Kojo, that there is no need whatever to go back again to the country to seek anew a mandate which was renewed only as recently as June, 1954. I feel very strongly that to ignore the established and confirmed will of the people of the Gold Coast for Independence and to impose new conditions on them at this final stage would defeat the very essence of parliamentary democracy.

"In my opinion," I went on, "the essential issue between the British Government and ours at the present time is the fixing of a firm date for Independence. Constitutionally I cannot accept another general election as a prerequisite to independence. By forcing it upon us the British Government will give the impression that they are condoning the anti-constitutional attitude of the N.L.M. and will thereby undermine the fundamental principles of the British parliamentary system. It appears to me—and don't forget this point, Kojo—that the Secretary of State is willing to use the refusal of the N.L.M. and its allies to participate in the discussions on the Bourne Report as a reason for pressure for another general election. This would be a very dangerous precedent to set.

"A general election could not, in my opinion, be held under the present conditions existing in Ashanti without causing riots and bloodshed, intimidation and disorder. By imposing a general election on us as a prerequisite for the transfer of power, the N.L.M.

will be offered the chance of exploiting the situation to bring about a state of general unrest and violence which would give Her Majesty's Government the opportunity to intervene. And what would the world feel about British sincerity then? What effect will it have on those territories who are also aspiring to independence and also on the members of the United Nations?"

Daniel Chapman appeared at the door and interrupted me.

"The London flights are all booked up for the next three days," he informed us.

"*What?*" I almost yelled at him. "Didn't you say that this was priority, that a minister was travelling on urgent business?"

"Yes, but they say that they simply have no space."

"You had better go up to the airport yourself," I said to Kojo. "See the airport manager and ask him what he can do for you. Come straight back."

After a good deal of trouble Kojo succeeded in getting a seat on the plane leaving in two days time. "It was the best they could do," he explained.

I returned to the matter on hand. "Emphasize the fact that the majority of the people of this country want self-government now, not another general election. And make this point clear, too, Kojo. Tell them at the Colonial Office that my opposition to a general election is not based on any fear that we might not win it—far from it. My only concern is to avoid disorder and bloodshed. To give in to the N.L.M., would only encourage their wilful defiance of the constitution, and would go against the will of the majority. God knows that I have always advocated the need for a strong Opposition and I am content that political disagreement is just as it should be under a system of parliamentary democracy.

"And you might add, Kojo, that as far as I am aware the Secretary of State has never made any public statement either inside or outside Parliament condemning the violence being perpetrated in Ashanti; in fact nothing has encouraged the N.L.M. more than that statement he made saying that there would have to be a 'general agreement'—whatever that might mean—before self-government was granted. You might also add that I was very surprised that no apology was demanded from the N.L.M. when they stoned the Governor's car in Kumasi."

I then detailed my plans, to present my White Paper at the forthcoming Budget session of the Assembly, and a second White Paper indicating the amendments to be made to our existing Constitutional Instruments to enable the Gold Coast to become a sovereign and independent state within the Commonwealth, and, after a debate on these, to make a formal motion for independence. I would then expect the British Government to proceed with the enactment of the necessary legislation to grant us our independence. I stressed the ill-effects that the uncertainty of this transitional period was having on the country and ended by saying that it was my firm resolve not to weaken the cause of democracy in the Gold Coast by setting at naught the provisions of the Constitution and the powers of our Legislative Assembly.

On the 23rd of March Kojo Botsio took off from the Accra airport. I did not want to cause comment by seeing him off and had to content myself with waving to the plane as it roared over my house. It was an anxious mission for him and I knew that he felt deeply the responsibility with which he had been entrusted. But I don't think I could have relied on any better man for putting over my views.

Both the Governor and Botsio returned to Accra a week later. It was Good Friday and I had arranged to tour the three hospitals in Accra. I had not known at the time I made arrangements for this that Kojo would be returning on that day, for I had had no word from him apart from a cable to say that he had arrived safely. Anyhow, we managed to have a short chat before I set out and he assured me that things had gone well, though perhaps not exactly as I had planned. He had been impressed, he said, by the sincerity of Mr. Lennox-Boyd and he felt sure that he was genuinely out to help the Gold Coast gain its independence. "But it looks as if a general election is the only answer," he said.

The following day I met the Governor and after the discussions I had with both him and with Kojo Botsio and after studying the views of the Secretary of State in a letter I received from him a few days later, I realized that there were three possible courses of action that I could take. Firstly, to make a unilateral Declaration of Independence, which would be a revolutionary step and one which I would hesitate to take unless I was forced; secondly, to let the present constitution run its course until 1958, which would mean delaying Independence and throwing the country into a state of confusion, distrust and discontentment; and thirdly, to hold a general election in the near future.

My main concern was that a general election might give rise to more violence in Ashanti. However, the Governor assured me that he would be prepared to take all possible measures to ensure that a general election would be held in a free and fair manner and the Secretary of State in his letter assured me that Her Majesty's Government would fully support the Governor in this. In view of this I said that I would be willing to declare a general election during the forthcoming session of the Legislative Assembly, the date of the election being in all probability towards the middle of July.

On the 11th of May the Secretary of State made a statement in the House of Commons. It had always been the wish of Her Majesty's Government, he declared, that the Gold Coast should achieve its independence within the Commonwealth. The present Constitution marked the last stage before the assumption by the Gold Coast of full responsibility for its own affairs, but since its introduction a dispute had arisen within the country about the form of constitution which the Gold Coast should have when it achieved that independence. All efforts to bring about a reconciliation between the major parties had so far been unsuccessful.

"I have been in close touch with the Prime Minister of the Gold Coast on these matters," he said. "It is the considered view of his Government that the time has now come for the Gold Coast to assume full responsibility within the Commonwealth for its own affairs. I have made my view clear to him that because of the failure to resolve the constitutional dispute we can only achieve our common aim of the early independence of that country within the Commonwealth in one way and in one way alone; that is, to demonstrate to the world that the peoples of the Gold Coast have had a full and free opportunity to consider their Constitution and to express their views on it in a general election.

"I have told Dr. Nkrumah that if a general election is held Her Majesty's Government will be ready to accept a motion calling for independence with the Commonwealth passed by a reasonable majority in a newly elected Legislature and then to declare a firm date for this purpose.

"Full membership of the Commonwealth is, of course, a different question and is a matter of consultation between all existing members of the Commonwealth."

Two days later I called a meeting of the National Executive of my Party. Whilst they agreed to the Secretary of State's request for a general election, there were certain points that they were concerned about and they asked me to convey these to the Governor. They felt that the Governor should contact the political leaders of every party, including the Asantehene, and warn the people against violence and at the same time make it clear that he was personally responsible for the security and defense forces which would be used in maintaining law and order during this period; that, if there should be violence during the election period, the British Government would not use this as an excuse to delay Independence and that the French Consul-General should be asked to warn all French citizens that they must not in any way interfere with the general election.

Now that the decision had been made, the C.P.P. supporters welcomed this challenge wholeheartedly. The supporters of the N.L.M. and its allies, however, now that their cry for a general election had been answered, were so baffled that they made no mention of it. In fact several reports came in from Kumasi that a general election was the last thing that they expected and the last thing they wanted.

Commissions of Enquiry

BEFORE WE TOOK OUR PLACE AMONG THE FREE COUNTRIES OF the world, there was the matter of the Cocoa Purchasing Company to be cleared up, for I insisted that my Party should enter upon Independence with a clean sheet and that it should be publicly absolved of the allegations that were being levelled against it.

When I first began my country-wide political organizing in 1948, I had been surprised and concerned to discover the number of cocoa farmers who had become so indebted to foreign-owned cocoa buying firms and African middlemen and brokers that their farms had been confiscated. These farmers were constantly appealing to me to do something about this, but at that time it was not so easy. Most of the retail trade, as well as industrial enterprises of the country, was in the hands of non-Africans, a state of affairs which had arisen firstly on account of the lack of adequate capital on the part of the Africans and, secondly, because of the absence of training facilities for Africans to become really successful business men. It is true that the various mercantile firms of the country had for years recruited young Africans, some of whom rendered very valuable service to their employers, but neither the training they received nor the money they earned was sufficient to equip them for private enterprise.

There was no doubt in my mind that if capital were available, a number of Africans would quickly gain the necessary experience to be able to manage fairly large business concerns. But I realized, too, that it was not easy for Africans themselves to raise loans from the banks because of the lack, in most cases, of adequate security or suitable guarantors, and that if this relief from indebtedness was to be brought about and the African was to be encouraged to manage his own affairs, the problem would have to be tackled by the Government itself.

I was not alone in recognizing this unwholesome state of affairs in the country, for several reports issued from time to time by various commissions referred to the question of the indebtedness of farmers in this country. Professor Shepherd in the report which he made as early as 1936 recommended strongly the establishment of an organization of farmers, both for the marketing of cocoa and for the issuing of loans to meet the indebtedness of farmers. Under Gold Coast conditions, however, it seemed clear to me that such loans would have to be issued through organizations rather than direct to farmers, for in this country it is generally difficult to secure title to property which would be acceptable as a basis for granting loans. If loans were given through organizations, I felt that such organizations—having some control over their members—would be better equipped to ensure redemption of loans than would lenders making loans direct to individual farmers. With this in view, the Cocoa Purchasing Company was set up as a subsidiary of the Cocoa Marketing Board.

Within a year of the formation of the Cocoa Purchasing Company, thousands of farms had been redeemed by the original owners and within three years this Company had become the primary local cocoa buying agent in the country—and this in face of severe competition from European firms long established in the cocoa trade in the Gold Coast.

Before long, however, rumors began to spread concerning the Company. In 1953 the then Chairman of the Cocoa Marketing Board made a report to the Board pointing out some irregularities in the C.P.C. When I received a copy of this report, I discussed it with the Central Committee of my Party and I also referred the matter to the Minister responsible for the broad policy of the Cocoa Marketing Board. When this Board appeared to do nothing to implement the report of its Chairman, however, I decided that it was necessary for me to see what influence I could exert on the Cocoa Purchasing Company, through the Cocoa Marketing Board, to put its house in order. I could not stand by and watch something that I had created and which had flourished so rapidly suddenly wither away through the machinations of people who sought its destruction.

Towards the end of 1955, I ordered an enquiry by the police into the affairs of the Company. After this, petition after petition began to flow into Government House for onward transmission to the Secretary of State for the Colonies, asking for a commission of enquiry to be set up to investigate the affairs of the C.P.C. The Government, through the police, tried to prove the truth of these allegations in order that they could be brought before the court, but there was no evidence on which to initiate criminal proceedings against anyone in authority.

Eventually I appointed a committee of two to investigate the affairs of the Company and, later, on the advice of the Chairman of the Committee, the Cabinet decided to appoint a Commission of Enquiry, for under a Commission of Enquiry witnesses could be examined on oath.

The Report of the Commission, issued at the end of August, 1956, proposed, among other things, that the Cocoa Purchasing Company should be reconstituted and that it should be run by a board of directors composed of three members nominated by the Opposition, three members nominated by the Government and a Chairman nominated by the Governor. This was in fact the only recommendation of the Commission which the Government was unable to accept, as the appointment of a Board on this basis would weaken materially the power of the Government over the Board and render the Government powerless to carry out satisfactorily even the limited direct responsibilities it has under the Ordinance.

In its findings the Commission alleged that the Cocoa Purchasing Company was controlled by the Convention People's Party, basing such allegation mainly on the fact that the affairs of the Cocoa Purchasing Company were discussed at the Central Committee of my Party. It seemed to me that it was perfectly in order for Party members to discuss a matter with which they were being publicly associated at the Central Committee meetings of their Party.

It was also stated by the Commission that the Government knew all about the shortcomings of the Cocoa Purchasing Company, but in spite of this took no steps to rectify them. They had overlooked the fact that it was I, as Prime Minister, who ordered an enquiry to be made into the affairs of the C.P.C. by the police, and also that it was the Government which appointed the Commission of Enquiry. Time and time again, Government spokesmen, both in the Assembly and outside, have stated that reports of any charges of irregularities in the Cocoa Purchasing Company should be made to the police for, so far as criminal proceedings were concerned, this was a matter entirely for the Attorney General, over whom my Government had no jurisdiction.

The main cause of the shortcomings in the conduct of the Cocoa Purchasing Company reported upon by the Commission is the absence of sufficiently effective control over statutory authorities by either the Assembly or the Government. The proper constitutional position is for the Government of the day to accept ultimate political responsibility for the disposal of public funds and for the conduct of statutory authorities which are entrusted with such funds.

In the light of the Report, I not only proposed changes in the organization and administration of the Cocoa Purchasing Company, but also decided to review the position of all statutory boards and corporations, my purpose being to increase the degree of public accountability of all statutory boards.

The Report of this Commission put me in mind of a previous enquiry in December, 1953, when an attempt was made to discredit me and the Government by allegations of bribery and corruption.

I was not blind to the existence or the possibility of bribery and corruption in the country among both Europeans and Africans. Things had moved fast, the feeling of power was a new thing; the desire to possess cars, houses, and other commodities that were regarded as necessities by the European population in the country, was not unnatural in people who were suddenly made to feel that they were being prepared to take over from those Europeans; and money, the wherewithal to obtain these luxuries was tempting.

In any event, this enquiry centered around Mr. J. A. Braimah, who was at that time my Minister of Communications and Works. The story that he told was that an Armenian contractor had promised to give him £2,000 as a gift, after the contract for a training college in the Northern Territories, which had been awarded to him, had been signed. According to Mr. Braimah's statement, he eventually accepted this gift which was made to him in instalments of £500 in £1 notes on four occasions. Braimah said that he had for some months past heard stories of bribery and corruption and had suddenly realized that by accepting these brown paper parcels of pound notes he was committing a serious offense. In due course the Commission of Enquiry found him guilty of accepting the £2,000. Under the Gold Coast constitution the responsibility for prosecutions rested entirely with the Attorney General. Mr. Braimah was not prosecuted.

The Commission was in no doubt that the contractor had given Mr. Braimah the sum of £2,000 for the purpose of influencing him to use his position in his favour. This man was tried on charges of corruption and convicted, but he successfully appealed.

It seemed to me that behind this case was a clear attempt to implicate me. When the Commission of Enquiry began its work I was busy preparing for the forthcoming election and was campaigning in Togoland. One morning my attention was drawn to a report of the proceedings in the daily newspaper in which it was stated that Braimah, in his statement to the Commission, had mentioned my name in connection with rumors of bribes. I was completely taken aback and issued a denial at once which was published in the same newspaper.

When I returned to Accra, however, I decided that the allegations made against me were too serious to be dismissed by a mere denial in the daily paper. I therefore appeared before the Commission and was completely exonerated. To quote from their official report:

> "Allegations were made in respect of acceptance of bribes or improper conduct by the Prime Minister in connection with four government contracts. In each of these cases we find that there was no justification for the allegation."

Such were the findings of the Commission. But to me the whole thing went far deeper. It was my view that Braimah was only the dupe, and I was quite convinced that the affair was a calculated attempt to bring my Government into disrepute by suggesting that bribery and corruption was rife among those in power.

Togoland under Trusteeship

THE QUESTION OF A GENERAL ELECTION WAS NOT, HOWEVER, THE only matter that was exercising my mind at that particular time. The moment had arrived for the people of Togoland under United Kingdom Administration to decide their future, and to indicate whether they wanted to unite with an independent Gold Coast or remain under British administration until such time as their political future could be determined.

This stretch of land of 13,041 square miles lies between the Gold Coast and French Togoland. From 1884 until the outbreak of war in 1914, the whole of this area, together with French Togoland, was a German Protectorate. For the next six years the western portion of the Protectorate, including most of the Ewe country now forming southern French Togoland, came under British administration and, had it remained so, it is doubtful whether the Togoland problem would ever have arisen. However, in 1920 Britain divided the spoils with her neighboring colonizer, France, irrespective of the fact that both the boundaries—that dividing French from British Togoland and that dividing British Togoland from the Gold Coast (although the latter was superficial as long as the Gold Coast remained a dependent country)—split up the various tribes in the area.

It was the Ewe people inhabiting the south who really started the agitation. They were in the unfortunate position of falling into three separate divisions: the Gold Coast, British Togoland and French Togoland. And so they formed the All-Ewe Conference with the object of agitating for the removal of all international frontiers that separated the Ewe people.

When the Ewe question was brought up before the United Nations the Governments of France and of the United Kingdom both admitted "that there was good reason to believe that the objects and views expressed by all the All-Ewe Conference were those of the mass of the Ewe people, whether educated or not." But the cause of Ewe unification suffered a severe blow when the British delegation announced in the United Nations that it would not allow the question of the Ewes of the Gold Coast to be discussed together with the question of the Ewes in the Trust Territories, because the Gold Coast is not a Trust Territory.

The Ewe demand for the unification of their people was purely a matter between the African peoples concerned, on the one hand, and the colonial powers on the other. It must be obvious to the whole world that one cannot hope to meet with success and agreement by splitting up homogeneous tribes by international frontiers as if one were cutting a cake. Most members of the United Nations, including some of the colonial powers, were sympathetic with the Ewe cause, but the only searching of heart was among the British and the French, both of whom were, after all, primarily concerned in this particular problem. As is well known, if a plebiscite had taken place on the Ewe question alone, the people would have voted solidly for union with their kinsmen in British Togoland and the Gold Coast under British administration. But this would have angered the French and embarrassed the British and it was for this reason that Ewe unification was opposed by these two powers and everything was done to delay a decision on the matter.

This refusal to allow the Ewe people to have a plebiscite to decide their own problem gave time for opposition parties to emerge—and this is where the complications set in.

At this point my interest in the Togoland issue began to grow. I had never for one minute contemplated excluding that part of Togoland under United Kingdom administration from my political organization of the Gold Coast, for it was my aim to bring about a united country embracing all four regions—the Northern Territories, Ashanti, the Colony and Trans-Volta/Togoland. I realized at this juncture that at all costs emphasis had to be placed on Independence and that the whole question should be viewed from the angle of freedom and independence for the people of both the Gold Coast and British Togoland.

I therefore impressed upon the British Government the necessity for making a statement in the United Nations that the Independence of the Gold Coast was imminent and that the Togoland question should be solved in the light of this. When this fact was made plain, the attitude of many of the anti-colonial delegates changed and, instead of supporting the African nationalists who were in opposition to the colonial powers and were supporting the unification of the two Togolands (i.e. the reconstitution of the former German Togoland), they felt that if the Gold Coast was going to be independent, then this was a great opportunity for British Togoland to also achieve Independence at the same time.

The British statement on the future of British Togoland was submitted to the United Nations Trusteeship Council in 1954. In this statement the British Government pointed out that when the Gold Coast achieved Independence, Her Majesty's Government would no longer be in a position to continue to administer Togoland under United Kingdom administration as an integral part of the Gold Coast. Indeed, the British Government suggested that the objectives of the Trusteeship agreement would be achieved if Togoland attained self-government as an integral part of an independent Gold Coast.

As a result of the British statement, the United Nations decided to dispatch a visiting mission to British Togoland in August, 1955, to put forward proposals as to how the wishes of the inhabitants about their future status could best be ascertained.

The report of the visiting mission evoked in the United Nations a great deal of discussion, some of it acrimonious. They finally decided, however, that a plebiscite should be held in Togoland under British administration as soon as possible in order that the people themselves should decide whether they wanted to unite with the Gold Coast at the time of Gold Coast independence or whether the territory should be separated from the Gold Coast and continue under Trusteeship.

The United Nations appointed as its Plebiscite Commissioner Eduardo Espinoza y Prieto, assisted by a team of United Nations observers drawn from a number of different nationalities, and the Colonial Office in London seconded Sir John Dring as Plebiscite Administrator. Much organization was needed not only in the arrangements for the actual plebiscite, but in preparing the people and in making sure that they understood the issues at stake. It was important that I impress upon my party organizers in Togoland that the plebiscite was not just a temporary affair, like a general election, but that they were making history and that whatever they decided would seal the fate of generations of their people to come.

There were two opposing parties contesting the plebiscite: my party—the Convention People's Party, standing for unification of the Trust Territory with an independent Gold Coast, and the Togoland Congress, which was supported by all anti-C.P.P. Government parties and agitated for the separation of British Togoland from the Gold Coast. I refrained from visiting British Togoland during the period of the plebiscite because I did not want it to be said that I had in any way used my personal influence to sway the people to vote other than by their own free will.

In spite of the fear on account of threats of violence and intimidation that was strong in some quarters, the day of the plebiscite, May 9, 1956, could not have been more peaceful. Of eighty-two per cent of the registered voters who cast their votes, fifty-eight per cent voted for union with the Gold Coast. The results were 93,095 in favor of union and 67,492 in favor of separation.

It was indeed a complex problem. I would like to say that in my opinion the Government of India deserves the highest praise for the way it helped to sort out the tangles created in the minds of members of the United Nations by the diverse and conflicting opinions of the numerous petitioners who appeared before them on the Ewe and Togoland question. It appeared that to the Indian delegation the most important thing was that no opportuntity for achieving real independence for any colonial territory should be missed. For this reason they supported very strongly the early independence of the Gold Coast and British Togoland as implied in the British statement of 1954.

To other delegations, particularly those of Latin America and certain parts of Asia, the important thing was the maintenance of the separate existence of the Trust Territories. In this they appeared to overlook the fact that the peoples of British Togoland and the Gold Coast are kinfolk arbitrarily divided by an international frontier in the same way that the peoples of French Togoland are arbitrarily separated from their kinsmen in British Togoland and the Gold Coast respectively. Little did they realize that it is impossible to draw a satisfactory frontier between the river Volta and the river Mono without cutting across some of the tribes who inhabit the region. With the administration of British Togoland as an integral part of the Gold Coast, the tribes formerly divided by the common frontier in effect became reunited. The close association of British Togoland and the Gold Coast should, therefore, be left undisturbed.

But the real problem now awaiting solution is what is to be done about the peoples split in two by the present Anglo-French frontier dividing French Togoland from the Gold Coast near the coast, and French Togoland from British Togoland further north? Similarly, what is to be done about the Nzima tribes who, in the west of the country, have been split up by the boundary separating the French Ivory Coast and the Gold Coast?

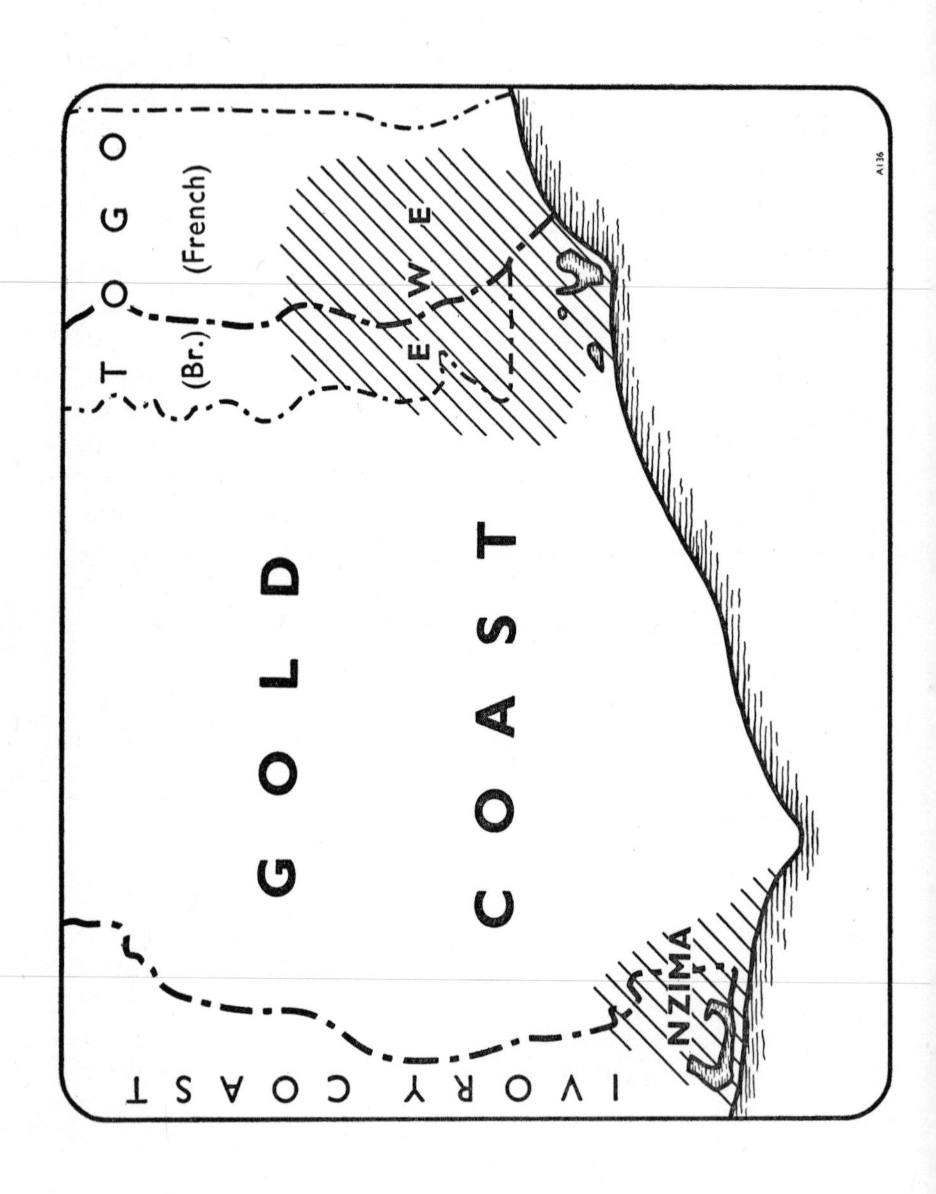
TOGO
(French)
(Br.)
EWE
GOLD COAST
NZIMA
IVORY COAST
A136

The Final Test

SIX DAYS AFTER THE PLEBISCITE IN BRITISH TOGOLAND, ON THE 15th of May, the ceremonial opening of the Legislative Assembly took place. In his Speech from the Throne, the Governor referred to the message from Her Majesty the Queen which he had read to the Assembly two years previously in which she had expressed her deep satisfaction that the Gold Coast had reached a step which was intended to be the last one before the goal of independence had been reached. The Governor explained to the House that when the Queen's Message was delivered, it had not been apparent that differences would arise in the country regarding the basic form of the constitution under which the Gold Coast should attain independence. He went on to enumerate the number of attempts that had been made to settle these differences, without success. He then referred to the Secretary of State's statement in the House of Commons the previous week. As it did not appear to the Government that any useful purpose would be served by attempting to arrange further conferences on the constitutional issue, in fulfillment of its aim to achieve independence for the country as soon as possible, it would submit its constitutional proposals for Gold Coast Independence to be debated at the present meeting of the Assembly and, when these had been debated, it would go to the country.

"It will seek a mandate from the people," he said, "that they desire the immediate grant of Independence and wish these proposals, in the form finally approved by this House, to form the basis of the self-governing constitution." He informed the House that he proposed to dissolve the Assembly in due course and that a general election would then be held.

Three days later I moved that the Assembly should adopt the Government's White Paper containing its constitutional proposals for a sovereign and independent Gold Coast and its statement on the Report of the Constitutional Adviser and the Report of the Achimota Conference.

The White Paper proposed that upon Independence the country should be renamed Ghana and should be a member state of the Commonwealth. In spite of the fact that various members of the opposition parties had for many years associated themselves with the name of Ghana and that many of their short-lived parties had included this name in the titles, they had recently attacked the idea. In my speech I pointed out to the House that the name Ghana was deeply rooted in ancient African history, especially that of the western portion of Africa known as the Western Sudan. It kindled in the imagination of modern West African youth, I told them, the grandeur and the achievements of a great medieval civilization which our ancestors developed many centuries before the European penetration and subsequent domination of Africa began. According to tradition, the various peoples of tribal groups in the Gold Coast were originally members of this great empire.

I pointed out that it was from this rich historical background that the name of Ghana had been proposed as the new name of the Gold Coast upon the attainment of Independence and that we took pride in the name, not out of romanticism, but as an inspiration for the future.

Other points proposed in the White Paper were that there should be a Governor-General appointed by the Queen on the advice of the Ghana Government; that supreme legislative power would be vested in the Ghana Parliament whose laws would be Acts of Parliament; the life of Parliament would be five years, though that of the present Assembly would remain four years; Ghana would become an independent sovereign state and would have full responsibility for defense and external affairs. It was proposed to set up the following regions: Eastern, Western, Ashanti, Brong, Northern and Trans-Volta/Togoland and also an independent Accra/Tema district. A Regional Assembly could be established by an Act of Parliament in any region completely covered by district councils, where a majority of the district councils desired it, and in any other region where a majority of local councils desired it. Except with the consent of a majority of two-thirds of the members of Parliament, no Regional Assembly should be abolished or suspended and no changes should be made in the composition or powers of a Regional Assembly.

My motion was debated upon and passed, and on the 5th of June the Governor issued two Proclamations, one dissolving the Legislative Assembly and the second declaring a general election to take place on the 12th and 17th of July in the Northern Territories (two days were essential owing to the inaccessibility of some districts), and on the 17th of July in the rest of the country.

Now that the final test in the form of a general election was about to be played out, I experienced a deep sense of satisfaction and happiness. The years of my long struggle were almost at an end, one way or the other. I felt that I had done all I could to lead the country to the freedom that I had always believed they wanted. It was now up to the chiefs and people to say whether they desired that freedom or not.

The manifesto which I issued was brief and simple. I pointed out in the introduction that it was an historic document, for according to the way the country voted, history would be made or marred. There were, I said, only two questions to ask oneself: "Do I want Independence in my life time?" or "Do I want to revert to feudalism and imperialism?" I was determined not to allow the election campaign to drift away from the issue which had provoked it, that is, a unitary versus a federal structure of government. The election was decisive in our struggle for final political freedom for Ghana and that point must be made clear to the people. The pledge of the Secretary of State for the Colonies was so absolute that he could not go back on it, and I had no doubt whatever that that pledge had been sincerely given.

Yet, in spite of the decisive nature of the forthcoming general election, and the urgent need for discipline, co-operation and eagerness within the C.P.P., I experienced the same old trouble with Party members trying to stand independently against the official candidates. I began to feel, however, that much of this confusion was caused through misunderstanding, for I found that as soon as I went in person to speak to those concerned, they immediately showed their willingness to step down in favor of the official candidates. The trouble was that this entailed so much extra travelling. On two occasions in particular I never went to bed at all for forty-eight hours and I began to wonder just how far a man of forty-six could stretch his strength and energy. I began to get splitting headaches, something that I have never suffered from before, and my stomach became upset. I had addressed so many rallies and gatherings that my voice had almost gone. But then the sun came out—as it always does in the end—and by the 20th of June, the final date for the registration of candidates, party members had been nominated to contest each of the 104 seats for the next Assembly. By the 2nd of July, five of these seats were already secured for us unopposed.

The Party entered the campaign in high spirits and the election machine was soon working efficiently. There could only be one place to launch this momentous election campaign, that same Arena in Accra which had witnessed the birth of my Party and so many decisive rallies in our long and arduous struggle. Long before my car reached the Arena, dense crowds had brought it to a standstill. As soon as I was recognized there was one deafening yell of "Freedom!" as every arm was raised in the "Freedom" salute. Before I knew what was happening I was seized bodily and hoisted like a flag to be carried triumphantly through the excited masses until I was lowered onto the platform to join my ministerial and other Party colleagues.

In my speech I emphasized the clear cut issue which was involved in the election and warned the people not to be misled or intimidated by opposition election stunts. I mentioned in particular the reports that had lately come from Ashanti that the ballot would not really be secret and that by means of a photographic device, a record would be made of all those who dared to put their voting papers in the box of the Red Cockerel—the symbol of the Convention People's Party.

"Now, you are intelligent people," I cried amid the storm of indignation. "It is an insult to your intelligence to spread such ridiculous stories!"

I then urged all those C.P.P. supporters who had fled from Ashanti not to be afraid to return there to cast their votes. I reminded them that the Governor, in a recent broadcast speech, had made it clear to the country that he was responsible for the maintenance of law and order during the election period, and that he would see that all forms of violence and intimidation at that time were kept in check.

"This is the end of the road," I concluded. "Whether we go through the golden gate to freedom, or whether we remain behind is now a matter for you to decide. You, you, you and you!" I shouted, as I pointed to all corners of the crowd.

Arms suddenly appeared, there was a roar of voices, and within seconds I was snatched from the platform and placed in an improvised sedan chair, well cushioned and shaded by a large umbrella. I experienced a slight flutter in my stomach as I took off, but once I was airborne I discovered that it provided about the most comfortable form of transport that I had yet experienced. On one or two occasions, however, when my bearers took it into their heads to trot or to join in the rhythm of the dancers, I would have welcomed the secure embrace of a safety belt!

The weeks that followed were completely taken up with electioneering in all parts of the country. Just as soon as I returned to Accra after an extensive campaign in one part of the country, I would receive an urgent summons to support one of my candidates in another area. Some pepole registered their objection to the official Party candidate and wanted to put up others of their choice. Time and time again I pointed out to the people that this was no ordinary election, it was no time to spend bickering about personal preferences for individuals when the whole interest of the country was at stake.

The outcome of the general election became the main topic of conversation at cocktail parties and social gatherings throughout the country. Although I had no time myself to attend such functions, I heard that the figure being quoted in these semi-official circles was, C.P.P. 56; N.L.M. 48. As time went on, however, the enthusiasm with which I was received throughout the country couldn't fail to leave its mark on the speculators, and one evening a friend of mine called in to see me after he had attended a large cocktail party and told me that one man in particular, who had previously forecasted a substantially reduced majority for the C.P.P., was now convinced that my Party would be returned with at least the same majority that we had in the last Assembly.

Up till now, however, our campaign had been largely concentrated in the areas where we knew we had the strongest support. It now became imperative that we should penetrate into Ashanti where, for nearly eighteen months, violence and other forms of intimidation had driven the C.P.P. into becoming virtually an underground movement. Because of the attacks on Party members and supporters which had been made in Kumasi, it had not been considered good policy for leading Party members to visit the town. This was not because we feared personally for our safety, but because we did not wish to do anything which might encourage more riots and bloodshed and invite imperialist intervention which would only postpone our independence. But this abstinence from democratic right and duty could not continue during a general election.

"Now on Sunday, the First of July," I announced to my Party Executive, "we will hold a monster rally in Kumasi."

My words were drowned in cries of jubilation. "At last!" they cried. "At last we can show them."

The enthusiasm with which my announcement was greeted throughout the rest of the country was unbounded. Reports reached me two days before the rally was due to be held that truck load after truck load of people were arriving in Kumasi for the rally. It was then that I began to doubt the wisdom of a personal appearance in the capital of Ashanti at such a time. I knew well enough the reception I would receive. The people would be almost mad with excitement and would be capable of demonstrating their jubilation in a variety of ways that might cause friction with the supporters of the opposition parties. I discussed the matter with the Central Committee of my Party and, after a great struggle of heads against hearts, it was decided that I should not go.

We chartered a plane to take the rest of the party members to the rally and they were due to take off from Accra at 10 A.M. At about

10:30 A. M. they all arrived back at my house seething with rage.

"They refuse to take us! They say that there is a leak in one of the gas tanks!"

"Is that the only plane available, then?" I asked, deeply disappointed.

"So they say."

"Well, you'll have to go by road. If you start now, you should arrive somewhere around two-thirty or three this afternoon."

Without another word they scrambled into two cars and were on the road. I waited anxiously for news and prayed that they would not have an accident on the way for they were in such a hurry to arrive at Kumasi in time that I knew they would be driving at breakneck speed.

They returned at about 9:30 P.M. that evening and excitedly recounted what was obviously a most successful rally. Thousands had attended and the way things had gone left no doubt in any of their minds as to the strength of support our Party still had there.

Krobo Edusei, one of the members who had taken part in the rally (now one of the Ministers without Portfolio in the present Government), came to me the following day at the Party Headquarters and said, "Tell me, Kwame—what sort of a man *are* you?"

I was a bit taken aback and asked him what he meant.

"I admit," he said, "that the rally in Kumasi was a huge success. But at the same time there was something sadly lacking. When you are there it makes so much difference both to the crowds and to us. Yesterday your absence made a vacuum."

I was deeply touched by what he said and by the sincerity with which he spoke.

"But one should not wonder at that," he added, more brightly, "for after all Kwame Nkrumah is the C.P.P. and the C.P.P. is Kwame Nkrumah!"

I have wondered since whether in fact my non-appearance in Kumasi did have an effect on the results there. Could my presence have secured, for instance, the seat of that promising young man, J. E. Jantuah, Minister of Agriculture in my last Government? On the whole, however, I feel that the risks involved would not have justified it. As it was there were a number of minor skirmishes during the day between the police and gangs of opposition hooligans, and two explosions and a number of gun shots during the morning were indications in themselves of the tenseness of the atmosphere in Kumasi.

As the election campaign worked towards its climax, the opposition became more and more reckless in their statements of confidence in winning the election, and equally at pains to impress upon their audiences that the defeat of the C.P.P. was already assured. In a letter to the Governor, which was released for publication on the day of the election and appeared in the press the day after, Dr. Busia began by listing in detail the organizations forming the National Liberation Movement and its allies and the names of seventeen independent candidates who, he said, had agreed to support these groups and to accept him as their Parliamentary Leader. Then he went on to state: "In accordance with constitutional practice in the United Kingdom, the National Liberation Movement and its Allies will expect Your Excellency to call upon Doctor K. A. Busia, their Parliamentary Leader, to form a Government should they (together with the independents supporting them) win more than 52 seats at the election." By the time this appeared in the newspapers on July 18th, it was already apparent from the results so far declared that the opposition had lost the election. Never can a tactical move have rebounded so woefully upon its initiators!

"Well!" I exclaimed to a small gathering of Party members who were seated around me on the verandah. "Have you read this? It is good news! It is as I have always said—these people are really with us all the time, if they would only admit it."

"How do you mean, Kwame?" somebody asked.

"Well—read it yourself. Dr. Busia says that he is prepared to form a government with anything over 52 members. That means that he recognizes the fact that a simple over-all majority—even of one seat, mind you!—constitutes a democratic verdict."

There were loud cheers. "If he is sincere," I continued, "we have nothing more to worry about—it will all be plain sailing from now on, for we are all talking the same language at last."

In the election the C.P.P. won 71 seats, increased later by the support of one of the Independents, which gave us a majority of

40 in the Legislative Assembly of 104. This was surely more than sufficient to meet the requirements of the Secretary of State that we should have a "reasonable majority."

Though my Party lost some seats in Ashanti, it made gains elsewhere and its support was so distributed throughout the country as a whole that, quite apart from our large parliamentary representation, we could claim to be the only party able to speak in a national sense. We won every seat in the two regions of the Colony and in the Accra municipality, obtaining 82 per cent of the total votes cast. In Trans-Volta/Togoland we won eight seats out of thirteen and also polled a clear majority of the total votes. In the Northern Territories we won eleven seats out of twenty-six (increasing our representation from there but losing, unfortunately, my former Minister of Health, Imoru Egala). Even in Ashanti, where the N.L.M. had anticipated an absolute victory, we won eight of the twenty-one seats and, with 43 per cent of the total votes cast, actually increased our poll as compared with the previous election.

The following day I was invited by the Governor to form a government. Having lost two of my former ministers in the election, and because of the resignation of the Minister of Trade and Labor, Mr. E. O. Asafu-Adjaye, it took three days before I was satisfied that the men I had selected were the right ones for the task that lay ahead of us. In particular I tried to choose my ministers to some extent according to the regions. Eventually the names I selected were as follows:

A. Casely-Hayford—Minister of Communications
Kojo Botsio—Minister of Trade & Labor
K. A. Gbedemah—Minister of Finance
A. E. Inkumsah—Minister of Housing
A. E. A. Ofori-Atta—Minister of Local Government
J. H. Allassani—Minister of Health
Ako Adjei—Minister of the Interior
N. A. Welbeck—Minister of Works
J. B. Erzuah—Minister of Education
B. Yeboah-Afari—Minister of Agriculture

Krobo Edusei—Minister without Portfolio
L. R. Abavana—Minister without Portfolio

Kofi Baako was once again my Ministerial Secretary and the Government Chief Whip.

There was no doubt that we had won the election with a clear majority, but even these indisputable figures did not satisfy the opposition. As soon as the final position was known, Dr. Busia called a press conference in Kumasi and made the astonishing announcement that the election results had established the case of the Opposition for a federal form of government. He acknowledged the fact that the election had been fought on this issue, but he maintained that because the C.P.P. had not won over-all majorities in Ashanti and in the Northern Territories, this proved the case for federalism. He sought to support this extraordinary case by inventing a further region which he called "the Southern part of the Trust Territory of Togoland." Of the six seats forming this area, he said, the C.P.P. had won only three which, according to his theory, showed that the people there were not in favor of a unitary constitution. He had to admit that the Colony was overwhelmingly in favor of the C.P.P., but in spite of this, he concluded by saying: "This picture quite clearly resolves the constitutional dispute in favor of those who advocate a federal form of government."

On the day of the formal opening of the Assembly the Opposition benches were completely deserted. As the time drew near for the arrival of the Governor those on the Government benches became restless and concerned.

"Surely the Opposition is not going to boycott the Assembly on today of all days?" somebody asked me.

I shrugged my shoulders.

"But," said another, in disgust, "such behavior is contemptuous of the dignity and authority of the Legislative Assembly and the democratic institutions vested in it."

"Not only that," interrupted another, "it is an insult to His Excellency and, through him, to the Queen of England."

There was sudden silence as the Governor's A.D.C. announced to the House the arrival of His Excellency. Shortly before the Governor had finished his speech from the Throne, two Opposition members from Togoland arrived, but they were the only ones on the Opposition benches who were present during the whole of the proceedings.

Perhaps the Opposition realized later that such behavior was hardly likely to commend them to the Government in Great Britain as statesmanlike and responsible politicians. At any rate, they issued a statement to explain the reasons for the absence of the Opposition. It said that they had held a meeting that morning and that by the time they reached the Assembly, the crowd there was so dense that the police would not let them take their cars through. A policeman, they said, had suggested that they should get out and walk, but they were afraid to do so as they had been given a rough reception by the crowd on the previous day when Members had been formally sworn in. Apparently there had been booing by part of the crowd, mostly from a number of market women.

The highlight of the Governor's Speech was the statement that the Government would that week introduce a motion calling on the British Government to pass a Bill declaring the Gold Coast a sovereign and independent State within the Commonwealth. The following day, the Opposition tabled an amendment criticizing this proposal on the grounds that it was premature until a further effort had been made to produce what they called "an agreed Constitution," until action had been taken on the publication of the Commission's Report regarding the affairs of the Cocoa Purchasing Company, and until action had been taken against what they alleged was "widespread corruption in public corporations." In their speeches which followed, the Opposition gave no evidence in support of these allegations, and the Assembly rejected the amendment by a majority of thirty-seven. The evening following this defeat, the Opposition issued yet another statement saying that they would not attend the Assembly when the Independence Motion came before the House.

I deeply regretted this attitude which was so unbecoming to the dignity of the Assembly and such an ugly blot on the record of our country's struggle to independent nationhood. This moment was the culmination of hard years of effort during which so many of our people had sacrificed selflessly for our cause. It was a moment of tremendous drama when all should have experienced a profound sense of history and dedicated themselves afresh to the cause.

In my speech introducing the Motion for Independence, I tried to express something of the momentousness of the occasion and, although I was bound to deal in detail with the challenge which the Opposition had made, I tried to avoid rancor and to lift the question to a national level above the conflict of party politics. At the same time I had to remember that my speech was, in effect, the statement of my Government's case in support of the Motion.

After recalling once more the suffering and sacrifice which we had endured on the road to independence, I went on to remind the House that when the Assembly approved my Motion for the adoption of the White Paper containing Constitutional Proposals for an Independent Gold Coast on May 22, 1956, the country was, even at that time, ready to take over its own affairs. However, even as we were moving into those final stages, "there arose in the country a point of view, advocated with a persistence which," I said, "I feel frequently went outside the bounds of legitimate political activity, that our future constitutional development should be upon the basis of a federal instead of a unitary form of government." I pointed out that the Government did everything possible to resolve these differences but when all failed, the Secretary of State expressed his view that Independence could be achieved only by demonstrating to the world that we had had a full and free opportunity to consider our Constitution and to express our view on it in a General Election. "The Secretary of State," I went on, "then gave this pledge:

> 'If a General Election is held, Her Majesty's Government will be ready to accept a Motion calling for Independence within the Commonwealth passed by a reasonable majority in a newly elected Legislature and then to declare a firm date for attainment of their purpose.' "

The General Election had been held, the results known, and it was my view, I said, that there was nothing to prevent us now fulfilling the final conditions of the Secretary of State's statement. There was also no reason why the Secretary of State, in his turn, should feel any reluctance to fulfill his pledge.

I then dealt in detail with the Opposition's desire to partition the country into a number of small autonomous regions. "Such a prospect," I said, "in the conditions of the modern world, is too unreal to contemplate." In any event this case had been put to the country in the recent election and had been rejected.

"There is no shame in electoral defeat," I continued, "shame lies only in being a bad loser." And I added that to allow the minority to override the decision of the majority would be to make a farce of parliamentary government. I had always been ready to recognize, I went on—as had been put forward in the Government's Constitutional Proposals last May—that there should be a measure of devolution of powers from the Central Government to the Regions. I confirmed that the proposals contained in Sir Frederick Bourne's Report on the subject, as modified by the Achimota Conference, were generally acceptable to the Government. "But," I emphasized, "The Government considers that it would be impracticable, and indeed dangerous, for this country to try to proceed further than that along the road to federalism."

I went on to point out to the House the immense burden of administration that federalism would impose on our small country and to consider whether, with our present manifold problems, we could shoulder such an increased burden. "How are we to finance such a lavish structure of government?" I asked. "Are we to sacrifice the welfare of the masses of our people to multiple government for its own sake? Are our people—only now beginning to struggle painfully out of dismal want—to be pushed back to support an administrative structure so cumbersome and eating so heavily into our financial resources that there would be nothing left for it to administer?" I repeated what I had said in the House in August of the previous year, that my determination was that we should attain independence with as workable and as simple a system of government as we could devise.

In this way I came to the heart of the motion:

"What I am now formally asking the people of the Gold Coast, is to request from the United Kingdom Government the fulfillment of our national aspiration for independence. We are ready to assume the responsibility—the heavy responsibility—and the right to order our own affairs and to decide our own destiny as citizens of a sovereign and independent State. I hope, Mr. Speaker, that there is none here whose heart beats so faint that he will refuse to join in this grand purpose. Let me make this quite clear. It will require the help and hard work and loyalty of every man, woman and child in this country to make a success of our entry into independent nationhood. We should realize this, and having done so, let us realize also that we cannot afford to fail.

"We have the pledge of the Secretary of State that if a Motion calling for independence within the Commonwealth is passed by a reasonable majority in a newly-elected Legislature he will declare a firm date for the attainment of this purpose. Mr. Speaker, the newly-elected Legislature referred to by the Secretary of State in his pledge is now assembled here, and we are the Members. All we have to do this day is to pass by a reasonable majority the Motion before us and then the United Kingdom Government will declare a firm date for our independence. From the results of our recent General Election, responsible opinion throughout the world has affirmed that we already have this reasonable majority here and now in this Assembly; but we must declare our decision ourselves before all the world.

"Truly has it been said that 'once to every man and nation comes the moment to decide. . . .' The Gold Coast people, the British Government—nay, the whole world—are waiting this day to hear our decision. Which is it to be? For my part, my stand is clear. I am determined to serve my country to the end, and to give her the best service of which I am capable. I am determined in so doing to see that nothing stands between the people of this country and the attainment of independence. I am equally determined to ensure that a firm date for Independence is announced without delay. I vote for Independence. And I humbly ask Honorable Members to do the same. . . ."

The mighty cheer that arose from all parts of the House at the conclusion of my speech was, I felt, the authentic voice of the people—those who understood the triumphant nature of the occasion and whose hearts soared with happiness and pride as they realized that we were already crossing the threshold of victory.

It was a pity that the Opposition Members had not found it in their hearts to take part on such an historic occasion. But, still determined to try and throw cold water on our success, Dr. Busia and his supporters declared that the struggle for them was no longer centered in the Gold Coast, but in London. They at once set about preparing a delegation to go to England.

Dr. Busia, official Leader of the Opposition, announced that he was leaving the country to undertake a lecture tour in Europe, to which he had previously committed himself. He later led the Opposition delegation to the British Government. Even when the influential *Manchester Guardian* published an editorial warning him of the futility and irresponsibility of his mission, he failed to see the way the wind was blowing against him. The Conservative *Daily Telegraph* gave no less than thirteen inches of space to a statement he made appealing to the British Government not to grant independence because the country was not ready for parliamentary democracy. "We still need you (the British) in the Gold Coast," he stated. "Your experiment there is not yet complete. Sometimes I wonder why you seem in such a hurry to wash your hands of us."

The Secretary of State, when he met the Opposition leaders in London, felt that he had been able to persuade them to take a more reasonable view of the Gold Coast's constitutional problems. But it is unfortunate that there seemed to be a great difference between what was being said in London and what was declared publicly in the Gold Coast. Because at the same time that the Leader of the Opposition was praising the beneficial rule of the British in the Gold Coast in his agitation against the granting of independence, the other section of his followers in this country were calling for the removal of the Governor.

It is equally unfortunate that certain leading journals of opinion in the United Kingdom continued to support and encourage misunderstandings by publishing criticisms of my Government's conduct without fully understanding the implication of the political situation facing our country.

There can be few—if any—governments in the world who have exercised so much tolerance and devoted so much valuable time to considering the whims of such an un-cooperative minority, as my Government did during these years.

The Hour of Triumph

NOW THAT THE GENERAL ELECTION HAD BEEN HELD AND MY MOtion for Independence had been passed by "a reasonable majority in the newly elected Legislature," the conditions laid down by the Secretary of State in his statement to the House of Commons on the 11th of May had been complied with. The next and final step was to request the United Kingdom Government to declare a firm date for the attainment of Independence by the Gold Coast. On the 23rd of August, therefore, I made a formal request to the Governor to transmit my request for such a declaration to the Secretary of State.

For perhaps the first time in my life I discovered that there was a vast difference in waiting for something that you hoped for and in waiting for something that was a certainty. There was not the slightest doubt in my mind that the Secretary of State's pledge would be honored; it was just a matter of waiting.

It was the 17th of September. I had a full morning's work ahead of me and I was going over my diary of appointments. Suddenly there was a ring from the telephone that connected me direct with the Governor.

"Good morning, P.M.," said Sir Charles. "I just wanted to tell you that I had received some good news for you. I wondered if you could come up and see me for a few minutes when you are free."

"Yes, certainly, Sir Charles," I said, as I hurriedly scanned through my appointments. "I'm afraid this morning is pretty hectic —would three o'clock this afternoon be all right?"

I arrived at Government House promptly. If there had been any doubts in my mind as to the contents of the message that was awaiting me, the look of pleasure on Sir Charles' face as I entered his office swept it away at once. He shook me firmly and warmly by the hand and then handed me a dispatch from the Secretary of State. There were, as is often the case with dispatches, a number of long paragraphs. When I reached the fifth one, however, the tears of joy that I had difficulty in hiding blurred the rest of the document. After a few minutes I raised my eyes to meet those of the Governor. For some moments there was nothing either of us could say. Perhaps we were both looking back over the seven years of our association, beginning with doubts, suspicions and misunderstandings then acknowledging the growth of trust, sincerity and friendship, and now, finally, this moment of victory for us both, a moment beyond description and a moment that could never be entirely recaptured.

"Prime Minister," the Governor said, as he extended his hand to me. "This is a great day for you. It is the end of what you have struggled for."

"It is the end of what *we* have been struggling for, Sir Charles," I corrected him. "You have contributed a great deal towards this —in fact I might not have succeeded without your help and cooperation. This is a very happy day for us both!"

I arranged with the Governor that I would return the following morning and collect the dispatch from him and immediately afterwards read it to the Legislative Assembly.

"This has been a national struggle," I said, "and it is only right that when the date of Independence is announced, the whole nation knows it from my lips."

The Governor nodded agreement. "Before you go, P.M., I would like to express to you my own heartfelt congratulations on this great day," he said, "and also my best wishes for the future of you and your colleagues and the people of Ghana." As he walked to the door with me he added, "And you know, P.M., that so long as I remain here as Governor, I shall continue to do all I can to help."

"Thank you, Sir Charles," I said. "I have always been deeply grateful for your help."

Many and varied emotions have swelled in my breast during the countless times that I have descended those white stone steps leading from the Governor's office, but never until that day had I experienced the sensation of walking on air.

As the cloud that seemed to transport me gently lowered me on to the seat of my car and the mundane whirr of the self-starter brought me slowly to earth, I became aware of the anxious face of my driver awaiting my directions.

"Oh—take me home," I said.

I shall never forget that night. How I was going to keep that store of dynamite in my chest without it exploding, I just didn't know. People came as usual and they talked as usual, but not once could I forget that vital information.

Usually nothing can prevent me from sleeping—during the very worst crises of my life I have always managed to escape from realities by laying my head on a pillow and drifting into a deep sleep. But on this night I lay awake until after 3:00 A.M. before I managed to get any sleep. During those hours the whole story of my life passed before me like some kind of pageant. I saw myself as a boy in Nzima, as a proud scholar at Achimota, as a struggling student at Lincoln; I saw myself in London where my studies gave way to politics; my return to the Gold Coast; the struggles that ensued both from within and without; detention, positive action, imprisonment; my final acceptance as a politician—events which were only the beginning of bigger and bigger struggles and intrigues. Then, after almost ten long years of it all, those words that represented the end of the road, the end of what had sometimes seemed to be a never-ending struggle—just a few words on paper handed over to me quietly by the man who had both imprisoned and released me and who had since afforded me every encouragement in my arduous task. "The 6th March," I said to myself. "The 6th March. *The 6th March. . . .*"

The day following this news was my forty-seventh birthday. I woke early in spite of a sleepless night and stared at myself in the mirror. "Is it possible that all men feel as young as I do on their forty-seventh birthday?" I asked my reflection.

When I had dressed I went downstairs to greet my mother. Somehow I seemed to find less and less time to see her these days and, although she understood and never complained, the fact nevertheless worried me. She noticed that I was restless and keyed up but she made no comment.

"What an excellent wife she must have been!" I thought to myself. "No questions, no hints, no suspicion!"

I arrived at the office and then went down to the Assembly. At about 10:45 I left for Government House and the Governor handed over to me the Secretary of State's dispatch. My hands trembled as I took possession of it.

I looked at the Governor and my lips felt as if they moved but no sound came out. Sir Charles came to the rescue by saying that he knew that I would not want to waste any more time in announcing the good news to the people.

My intention was to make my announcement to the Assembly at midday, the same time that the news would be broadcast in the United Kingdom. I had previously arranged with the Speaker that I had an important announcement to make and that as soon as I stood up he would permit me to take the floor. I was so anxiously watching the minutes pass between eleven-thirty and midday, that I took no interest in the debate that was going on. I was so keyed up that I simply didn't know how I could contain myself.

As soon as the hands of the clock reached noon, I stood up. The Speaker interrupted the discussion. There was dead silence in the House and Members were obviously expecting me to raise some point of order or to contribute something to the matter being debated. Before I spoke I looked at my watch. It was three minutes past midday. I took a deep breath and prepared myself for the most triumphant moment of my life.

"Mr. Speaker," I said, "with your permission, I should like to make a statement. With effect from midday today, the publication of two dispatches of vital importance to the future of our country has been authorized." I paused for the cheers to die down. "They are," I continued, "the Dispatch from the Governor at the request of my Government to the Secretary of State asking him to declare a firm date for the attainment of Independence by the Gold Coast, and the Secretary of State's Dispatch in reply thereto. Copies of these two dispatches will be distributed to Honorable Members as soon as the House rises today."

I then proceeded to read the statement from the Secretary of State. In this dispatch the Secretary of State recalled his statement in the House of Commons on the 11th of May, noted that a General Election had been held, that the Convention People's Party had been returned to power with a majority of over two-thirds, and that the motion for Independence had been passed in the newly elected Assembly by 72 votes to none, the Opposition members having absented themselves from the debate.

"Since the motion calling for Independence within the Commonwealth has been passed in the newly elected Legislative Assembly by a majority which must clearly be regarded as reasonable," the dispatch went on, "I now have the honor to inform you that Her Majesty's Government will at the first available opportunity introduce into the United Kingdom Parliament a Bill to accord Independence to the Gold Coast and, subject to Parliamentary approval, Her Majesty's Government intends that full Independence should come about on the 6th of March, 1957."

The whole of the Assembly was for a few seconds dumbfounded. Then all at once the almost sacred silence was broken by an ear-splitting cheer, cheers that must have been unprecedented in the Assembly. Some were too deeply moved to control the tears, among them some of my closest associates, those who had really felt the brunt of the battle and who perhaps realized more forcibly the true meaning of the word "Victory."

I then continued and read to the House the Secretary of State's reference to the Trust Territory of Togoland and the plebiscite that was conducted there which had resulted in a clear majority vote in favor of union with an independent Gold Coast. "The Trusteeship Council of the United Nations passed a resolution in July noting that the will of the majority of the inhabitants was for union with an independent Gold Coast, and recommending that steps should be taken for the Trusteeship Agreement to be terminated upon the attainment of Independence by the Gold Coast. Provided that this resolution is endorsed by the General Assembly of the United Nations, appropriate action will be taken to include the territory of British Togoland within the independent Gold Coast."

Her Majesty's Government had noted our desire to rename the

country Ghana upon the attainment of Independence and the necessary legal steps would be taken to give effect to this desire.

The dispatch from the Secretary of State concluded by saying: "It is the earnest hope of Her Majesty's Government that, at this turning point in the history of the Gold Coast, all sections of the community will be able to work together for the general good. In the name of Her Majesty's Government I wish to convey to the Government and the people of the country our heartfelt wishes for its future success."

After prolonged cheering, I said that I had nothing to add to the Secretary of State's dispatch, in which he had rightly described that moment as the turning point in our history. It was, I said, an occasion for serious reflection and I hoped that when the House re-assembled the following day, I would be able to make a further statement.

Cheers greeted the Deputy Leader of the Opposition as he stood and welcomed the statement on behalf of the Opposition.

Then the whole Assembly went wild with excitement. I was suddenly whisked off my feet and carried shoulder-high into the streets where the masses were jubilantly singing and dancing to the strains of the Party song, "There is victory for us."

Congratulations poured in by telephone, telegram, cable and letter, to say nothing of the hundreds of personal callers. It was a wonderful feeling to know that thousands of people from all corners of the world were rejoicing in our victory.

I thought that it would be a nice gesture if I and my Ministers paid an informal visit to the Governor to share with him the victory that he had helped so much to secure. At five-thirty that afternoon, therefore, we all turned up at the Castle where the Governor was waiting to receive us. It was a most happy occasion.

The whole country was celebrating. That evening a friend of mine arrived from Kumasi and excitedly related to me how the news had been received there.

"Kwame," he said, "you should really have been there! As sure as I'm standing here, Kwame, the supporters of the N.L.M. were more wild with excitement than even the 'C.P.P.-ists.' Many of them, not content with a single 'Freedom' salute, raised both hands in the air as they yelled 'Freedom!' "

What a day it had been! How could anybody have wished for a more wonderful way of celebrating one's birthday?

On the following day, the 19th of September, I made a further statement to the House. I pointed out that with the promise of our Independence on March 6, 1957, the last phase of our struggle had been reached.

"We have reason, Mr. Speaker, to be proud as well as thankful that this historic declaration has at last been made," I said, "and I was happy to hear the assurance, given yesterday by the Deputy Leader of the Opposition, that the Opposition welcomed the Secretary of State's announcement."

On the one hundred and thirteenth anniversary of the Bond of 1844, which led to Britain's political domination of the Gold Coast, our country would be free. Since I had dedicated myself to bringing our struggle for Independence to an end when I returned home in 1947, I had been heartened by the loyal and unstinted support of the people and sustained by the steadfastness and unwavering courage of the Convention People's Party. We were, as the Secretary of State had said, at a "turning point in the history of the Gold Coast." I knew, I said, that the Assembly would wish to know what the Government's intentions were at this point.

"We are determined to play our part in drafting a constitution which will satisfy the genuine aspirations of every lover of freedom.

"The Government proposes that this Assembly shall have ample opportunity to debate and determine our constitution. To this end the Government will at the earliest practicable date publish a White Paper setting forth the detailed provisions of the proposed constitution. Subject to the ultimate responsibility of this Assembly, which cannot be abrogated, the Government will be willing to discuss constitutional questions with representatives of the Opposition, should they desire it, outside the House before the debate." This was greeted by loud cheers from both sides of the House.

"Mr. Speaker," I continued, "on this great occasion our hearts are full to overflowing. Our thoughts are turning to the splendid ceremonies and the festivities which will be held to mark our attainment of Independence. But let us pause for a moment. Let us think of the tasks that lie ahead and the new responsibilities we shall be called upon to shoulder when Ghana becomes a free, sovereign and independent state. Let us dedicate ourselves to serve this country of ours, this nation, with all the strength, knowledge and wisdom that God has given us. And let us pledge ourselves anew to serve our country selflessly, to protect her rights and interest and to play our part among the nations of the world in promoting peace, happiness and the progress of mankind."

The Opposition expressed their satisfaction at the opportunity offered for discussion of the constitution outside the Assembly and hoped that they would be able to come to some kind of an agreement.

I accordingly arranged that representatives of the Opposition in the Assembly should be invited to meet members of the Government in order to work through the proposed Constitution, article by article. When any change or addition was agreed upon, the Government undertook to adopt the change. I proposed that the Assembly should begin consideration of the Constitution in the first week of November when any differences that had not already been resolved could be decided after debate and vote in the Assembly. The Constitutional Proposals only included very general provisions with regard to the definition of Regions and the powers to be exercised by the Regional Assemblies and, because of the controversial nature of this particular matter, I felt that further time should be allowed for a detailed consideration of what was required, and decided not to introduce the necessary legislation, therefore, until early in the New Year.

On the 20th of September I had arranged to broadcast to the country. I suddenly had an idea and sent for Daniel Chapman.

"Dan," I said, "I want to throw a party for all the children of Accra before I do my broadcast tomorrow."

Chapman was unperturbed at the short notice and was as enthusiastic about the project as I was. The following afternoon, therefore, hundreds of children of every nationality arrived to enjoy a large tea party in the grounds outside my office. As soon as the Gold Coast Police Band started to play, the orderly assembly of somewhat overawed and seemingly well-behaved youngsters came to life and proceeded to do the things that were expected of them —filling themselves with lemonade, sandwiches, buns and cakes; bursting other children's balloons; screaming with excitement and generally entering unreservedly into the spirit of the thing. The Governor arrived at about five-thirty and spent an hour or more mixing with the children. But I think the highlight of the afternoon for most of them was when I announced that the following Monday would be a school holiday. I was thoroughly enjoying myself and was sorry to have to tear myself away to rush off to Broadcasting House.

In my message to the nation I said that the announcement of a firm date for Independence marked the end of one epoch and the beginning of another. It also brought to an end a period of political uncertainty. In preparing for our Independence celebrations, we should ensure that these were such as would be worthy of our country and of our new status among the nations of the world.

An overwhelming majority of the people, I said, had wisely voted for a unitary form of government. I was satisfied that within the framework of a unitary constitution it would be possible to insert safeguards which would meet legitimate regional aspirations. The finalizing of our Constitution necessitated speedy action and in order that no time should be wasted, I had cancelled the Cabinet Recess. The White Paper would, I promised, be published as early as was practicable. We were anxious to produce a constitution which would satisfy the genuine aspirations of the chiefs and people and we were approaching the task with the best interests of the nation at heart.

In spite of the joy that filled our hearts about the firm date of Independence, I said, we should think of the tasks that lay ahead. On receiving independence, my Government would become fully responsible for the foreign policy of Ghana, for defense, for the maintenance of law and order, and for the stability of our currency.

In the hour of triumph we should look back and give thanks to all the statesmen who down the years had worked and striven to make possible the attainment of our Independence, and to all those who had more recently played their part, both great and small, in bringing our struggle to its close.

"In this solemn hour," I concluded, "let us not merely rejoice because we have reached our goal. Let us not merely make merry because our dearest hope has been fulfilled. Let us think first and foremost of the best interests of our country. Let us put aside petty political controversy and intrigues and lay a firm and stable foundation for the political structure of Ghana. May your thoughts, your deeds and your prayers strengthen and sustain the statesmanship of the nation."

As I drove home, physically and mentally tired but indescribably happy and content, I reflected on the long and difficult road on which we had travelled towards the goal of Independence. African nationalism had now been established in the Gold Coast—the new Ghana. From now on it must be Pan-African nationalism, and the ideology of African political consciousness and African political emancipation must spread throughout the whole continent, into every nook and corner of it.

I have never regarded the struggle for the Independence of the Gold Coast as an isolated incident but always as a part of a general world historical pattern. The African in every territory of this vast continent has been awakened and the struggle for freedom will go on. It is our duty as the vanguard force to offer what assistance we can to those now engaged in the battles that we ourselves have fought and won. Our task is not done and our own safety is not assured until the last vestiges of colonialism have been swept from Africa.

As a ship that has been freshly launched, we face the hazards of the high seas alone. We must rely on our own men, on the captain and on his navigation. And, as I proudly stand on the bridge of that lone vessel as she confidently sets sail, I raise a hand to shade my eyes from the glaring African sun and scan the horizon. There is so much more beyond.

Appendix A

CONSTITUTION OF THE CONVENTION PEOPLE'S PARTY (C.P.P.)

Motto: Forward ever–Backward never

PART ONE

NAME

The name of the Party shall be the *Convention People's Party* (*C.P.P.*)

AIMS AND OBJECTS

NATIONAL

(i) To fight relentlessly to achieve and maintain independence for the people of Ghana (Gold Coast) and their chiefs.

(ii) To serve as the vigorous conscious political vanguard for removing all forms of oppression and for the establishment of a democratic government.

(iii) To secure and maintain the complete unity of the people of the Colony, Ashanti, Northern Territories and Trans-Volta/Togoland regions.

(iv) To work with and in the interest of the Trade Union Movement, and other kindred organizations, in joint political or other action in harmony with the Constitution and Standing Orders of the Party.

(v) To work for a speedy reconstruction of a better Ghana (Gold Coast) in which the people and their chiefs shall have the right to live and govern themselves as free people.

(vi) To promote the Political, Social and Economic emancipation of the people, more particularly of those who depend directly upon their own exertions by hand or by brain for the means of life.

INTERNATIONAL

(i) To work with other nationalist democratic and socialist movements in Africa and other continents, with a view to abolishing imperialism, colonialism, racialism, tribalism, and all forms of national and racial oppression and economic inequality among nations, races and peoples and to support all action for World Peace.

(ii) To support the demand for a West African Federation and of Pan-Africanism by promoting unity of action among the peoples of Africa and of African descent.

MEMBERSHIP

There shall be two classes of membership:

(I) Individual
(II) Affiliated

(I) *Individual Membership.* Any person who is of the age of 18 or above and who accepts the objects, policy, program and discipline of the Party shall be eligible for membership provided that:

(*a*) He or she does not support imperialism, colonialism, tribalism and racialism.
(*b*) He or she is not a member of any other political party or of any organization whose policy is inconsistent with that of the Party.
(*c*) He or she is not a member of a Trade Union, Farmers' Organization or other *bona fide* organization proscribed by the Party.

Application for individual membership normally shall be made on a duly prescribed form which shall be completed by the applicant and passed to a Branch Secretary for consideration by his committee as to acceptance or otherwise. On enrollment every member shall be supplied with a membership and dues card.

Admission Fee: Each individual member of the Party shall be requested to pay on enrollment an Admission Fee of two shillings.

Membership Dues. Each individual member of the Party shall pay membership dues of three shillings (3s.) a year to his Branch, or as otherwise determined by the Party at any particular time.

(II) *Affiliated Members* shall consist of the following:

(i) Trade Unions.
(ii) Ex-Servicemen's Union.
(iii) Farmers' Organizations.
(iv) Co-operative Societies, Unions, Associations.
(v) Organizations of professionals, artisans and technicians.
(vi) Youth and Sports Organizations.
(vii) Cultural Organizations.
(viii) Women's Organizations.
(ix) Other organizations approved by the National Executive of the Party.

(*a*) All such organizations must accept the aims and objects, policy and program of the Party.
(*b*) They must in the opinion of the National Executive be *bona fide* democratic organizations.
(*c*) An organization wishing to affiliate shall forward a resolution to that effect duly passed by that organization and signed by its President and Secretary, to the General Secretary of the Convention People's Party, who shall in turn bring it before the National Executive Committee of the Party for acceptance or otherwise.
(*d*) Each organization upon being accepted for affiliation shall pay an Affiliation Fee of one pound one shilling.

(*e*) Affiliated organizations shall pay an annual fee as determined by the Party.
Note. Affiliations are apt to cause divided loyalties; so as much as possible only individual membership should be encouraged, though the Party should be on the closest of terms with the various organizations.

Funds of the Party

The general funds of the Party shall be derived from proceeds of functions (dances, football matches, etc.), voluntary subscriptions, appeals, donations, bequests, sale of Party literature, badges, admission fees of individual members and organizations, membership dues and other sources approved by the Party.

Except in the case of authorized imprest accounts all funds shall be deposited in a Bank, and applications for withdrawals must be signed by the Chairman and either the Secretary or the Treasurer.

N.B. All remittances to National Headquarters should be sent to the Treasurer, National Headquarters, Convention People's Party, P.O. Box 821, Accra. Cheques, Postal and Money Orders should be made payable to the Convention People's Party and crossed.

Party Flag

The official colors of the Party shall be: RED, WHITE AND GREEN. The Party tricolor flag shall be in horizontal form with red at the top.

NATIONAL ANNUAL CONFERENCE

The National Annual Conference of the Party shall be convened annually in August at such date and place as may be fixed by the National Executive. A special emergency national conference may be convened by the National Executive whenever deemed necessary, provided that at least two weeks notice is given. As regards the former, notices must go out at least two months before the Conference.

Composition of Annual Conference

The National Annual Conference shall be constituted as follows:

(i) Six delegates duly elected by each constituency.
(ii) Six delegates elected by the C.P.P. Women's section.
(iii) Six delegates elected by the C.P.P. Youth League.
(iv) Delegates duly elected and mandated by each affiliated organization to the number of two delegates for each five thousand or part thereof.
(v) Ex officio Members. Ex officio members of the Party Conference shall be the following:
  (*a*) All National officers of the Party.
  (*b*) Members of the National Executive of the Party.
  (*c*) Members of the Central Committee.
  (*d*) Members of the Legislative Assembly.

Note. The ex officio delegates shall not be entitled to vote unless they are also duly elected as representatives by their constituencies, Women's Section, Youth League or an affiliated organization.

Election of Delegates to the Party Conference

Qualifications and disqualifications of delegates:

(i) Every delegate must individually accept and conform to the constitution, program, principles and policy of the Party.
(ii) Delegates must be *bona fide* members or officials of the organization electing them.
(iii) No person shall act as a delegate for more than one organization.
(iv) No person shall act as a delegate who has not paid his or her dues up to date, or who has not paid the political levy of his or her Trade Union or other affiliated organization.

Functions and Powers of the National Annual Delegates' Conference

The National Annual Delegates' Conference shall have the power:

(i) To lay down the broad basic policy and program of the Party for the ensuing year. The decisions of the Annual Delegates' Conference shall be binding on all members of the Party and affiliated organizations.
(ii) To consider the reports and audited accounts presented by National Officers on behalf of the National Executive Committee.
(iii) To deal with other matters affecting the Party and the Country.

Amendments to Constitution

The existing Constitution, or any part thereof, may be amended, rescinded, altered, additions made thereto by Resolution carried by a majority vote at an Annual Delegates' Conference.

Proposals regarding any amendment of the Constitution must be sent to the General Secretary at least two months before the Conference for inclusion in the Agenda. Notice of such Resolutions and the Conference Agenda shall be communicated in writing to all Constituencies at least one month before the Delegates' Conference.

Only Party organizations—Branch, Constituency, Regional or Affiliated Organizations—and *not individual members* shall send resolutions for determination at the Annual Delegates' Conference.

NATIONAL EXECUTIVE COMMITTEE

Composition: The National Executive Committee shall be composed of:

(i) Chairman.
(ii) National Officers.
(iii) Chairman of Standing, Finance and Staff Committee.
(iv) Secretary of Standing, Finance and Staff Committee.
(v) Members of Central Committee.
(vi) One Representative elected by each Constituency at the Annual Constituency Conference.

All members of the National Executive Committee have voting rights.

The Chairman (and in his absence the Deputy Chairman) shall preside at meetings of the National Executive Committee. In the absence of both a member shall be elected at the meeting to preside.

DUTIES OF THE NATIONAL EXECUTIVE COMMITTEE

(i) To carry out the policy and program of the Party as laid down by the Annual Delegates' Conference.
(ii) To help organize Regional Councils, Constituencies and Branches and to guide and supervise their work.
(iii) To enforce the Constitution, Rules, Regulations, Standing Orders and By-laws of the Party and to take any action it deems necessary for such purpose whether by way of disaffiliation of an affiliated organization, dissolution or suspension of a branch of the Party, suspension or expulsion of an individual member of the Party. Any such action taken by the National Executive Committee shall be reported to the next Annual Delegates' Conference of the Party, to which appeals shall lie from the organization, branches and members concerned.
(iv) To maintain Party Finance and submit a report and a statement of account to the Annual Delegates' Conference of the Party.
(v) To initiate and undertake all such activities as may further the aims and objects of the Party.
(vi) To approve candidates for Central and Local Government Elections from lists prepared and submitted by the regional and Constituency Executive Committees or other body duly empowered by the Committee.
(vii) The National Executive Committee shall delegate powers to the Central Committee to set up specialized departments and other advisory bodies at the National Secretariat to carry out the aims and objects of the Party.
(viii) Any vacancy occurring in the National Executive Committee during the course of the year shall be filled as provided in the Constitution.
(ix) The National Executive Committee shall be in plenary session at least once every six months to hear reports on the state of the Party and the work of the Central Committee.
(x) Emergency meetings of the National Executive Committee shall be convened as thought fit by the Life Chairman or on a resolution endorsed by twelve Constituency Executives.

Quorum. At least one-third of the Constituency Representatives must be present.

CENTRAL COMMITTEE OF THE NATIONAL EXECUTIVE

Composition

The Central Committee of the National Executive shall consist of:
(i) The Party Leader.
(ii) Eight other members selected by him and approved by the National Executive Committee.
(iii) Other special members also approved by the National Executive Committee.

Functions

(i) The Central Committee shall act as the 'Directorate' of the National Executive in seeing that the decisions and policies of the National Executive are duly executed.

(ii) To supervize the administrative machinery of the Party at all levels—national, regional and branch executives—and to take such measures as it deems necessary to enforce decisions and the program of the Party as laid down by the National Executive.

(iii) The members of the Central Committee shall normally reside in Accra the capital and shall meet in permanent session at least once a week or if emergency arises from day to day to review major trends, formulate tactics and strategy for the guidance of the National Executive, and in the event of emergency to assume full responsibility of safeguarding the basic program of the Party, its security and defense, and report to National Executive.

(iv) The Leader of the Party shall appoint from among the members of the Central Committee a Secretary who shall be held responsible for summoning the meetings of the Central Committee, keeping its records, and preparing necessary reports to the National Executive Committee.

(v) The Central Committee shall work in closest collaboration with all members of the Party in the National Legislative Assembly and see especially to the proper working of the Parliamentary Committee.

(vi) As the main 'Directorate' of the National Executive Committee, all actions taken by the Central Committee shall be reported to the next half-yearly meeting of the National Executive Committee in plenary session for ratification.

Discipline

There shall be a Tribunal of Justice consisting of three or more members appointed by the National Executive Committee.

Its decision shall be reported to the National Executive Committee at its next session for ratification or otherwise. Appeals lie to the Annual Delegates' Conference. Members of the Tribunal of Justice are appointed annually, but members can be re-appointed.

Only the National Executive Committee can expel a member and submit this to the Annual Delegates' Conference for ratification. Branches, Constituencies, Regions and the Central Committee can only suspend defaulting members and report to the National Executive Committee for action.

Any member acting as candidate or supporting a candidate in opposition to the Party's official candidate in any Central or Local Government Election as duly announced shall be expelled from the Party.

REGIONAL PARTY ORGANIZATION

Regional Conference

A Regional Conference shall be convened annually by the Regional Committee or on the instructions of the National Secretariat. A special Regional Conference shall be convened by the Regional Committee on the instructions of the National Executive Committee through the Secretariat at National Headquarters, Accra, or on the demand of at least one-third of the Constituencies of the Party in the Region. The Regional Conference shall consist of two representatives from each Constituency within the Region.

Regional Officers

The Regional Officers shall be as follows:

(i) Regional Chairman, elected at the Annual Conference.
(ii) Regional Vice-Chairman, elected at the Annual Conference.
(iii) Regional Treasurer, elected at the Annual Conference.
These officers are elected for one year, but can be re-elected.
(iv) Regional Propaganda Secretary.
(v) Regional Secretary.
(vi) Other Regional Officers.
These officers are appointed by the National Executive Committee as full-time officers.

The members of the National Executive from the Region concerned shall be ex officio delegates to the Regional Conference with full rights.

Powers of Regional Conference

The Regional Conference shall have the power:

(*a*) To lay down Regional policy and program for the ensuing year providing that such policies and programs are in conformity with the basic policy and program laid down by the Annual National Delegates' Conference.
(*b*) To consider the political and organizational reports and statements of account presented by the Regional Secretary on behalf of the Regional Organization.
(*c*) To do things calculated to promote the Party in the respective regions.

Composition of Regional Committees

The Regional Committee shall consist of the following:

(i) All the National Executive members in the Region.
(ii) All the Assemblymen in the Region.
(iii) Six members appointed by the National Executive Committee.
(iv) The Regional Secretary.
(v) The Regional Propaganda Secretary.
(vi) Other regional officers appointed from time to time by the National Executive Committee.
(vii) Regional Chairman, Vice-Chairman and Treasurer.

Duties of Regional Committees

The duties of the Regional Committees shall be:

(*a*) To help organize constituencies and branches in the cities, towns and villages within the Region and to coordinate their activities and work.
(*b*) To help carry out the policy and program of the Party and instructions and directives received from the National Headquarters Secretariat. The Regional Committees shall be entitled to make recommendations to the National Secretariat on matters of disaffiliation, dissolutions or expulsions of affiliated organizations, branches and members of the Party within the Region.
(*c*) To submit reports and statements of accounts to the Regional Conference, as well as to the National Secretariat for transmission to the National Executive Committee.

(*d*) To help manage, control and guide the work of the Party in Local Government affairs as well as the work in educational and cultural organizations under the general supervision of the National Headquarters Secretariat.

(*e*) To undertake all such activities as may further the work of the Party in the Regions concerned.

Regional Funds

Any funds for the region shall be properly kept as determined by the National Executive Committee.

CONSTITUENCY PARTY ORGANIZATION

Annual Conference

A Conference of the Constituency shall be held at least once a year to which every branch in the Constituency possessing a Charter shall send two delegates. The place of the Conference shall be determined by the Constituency Executive. Special Emergency Constituency Conferences shall be held at the discretion of the Constituency Executive Committee or at the instance of a resolution endorsed by one-third of the Branches in the Constituency.

Composition of Constituency Executives

The Constituency Executive Committee shall consist of:

Chairman
Vice-Chairman
Financial Secretary
Treasurer
Eight Committee Members elected at the Annual Delegates' Conference
Retiring members may be re-elected
Constituency Secretary
Constituency Propaganda Secretary appointed by the National Executive Committee

The Secretary and Propaganda Secretary for the Constituency shall be full-time officials appointed by the National Executive. Other paid officers may be appointed from time to time.

The Quorum for a meeting of the Constituency Executive Committee shall be eight.

Functions of the Constituency Executive Committee

The Constituency Executive Committee shall carry out the policy and decision of the Annual Constituency Conference which must be in keeping with the basic policy and program of the Party as laid down by the Annual Delegates' Conference and in the Constitution, Rules and Regulations of the Party.

BASIC PARTY ORGANIZATION

The Branch is the basic organization of the Party. The Party shall establish branches in all towns and villages. Each branch shall be governed by a Branch Executive Committee which shall be elected annually at a General Meeting of the Branch. The Branch may appoint full-time paid officers where funds permit.

In big towns which have been divided into wards for local elections, there shall be Party Wards corresponding with these wards. All Party Wards shall function within their respective branches in the towns, but each Party Ward shall have a Party Ward Executive, and representatives of the various wards shall be members of the Branch Executive. Where towns are considered too large they could be divided up into Wards as in the Municipalities.

Branches in the rural constituencies shall deal direct with their respective constituency Headquarters.

Kumasi, Accra, Sekondi/Takoradi, Cape Coast, being constituencies in themselves shall deal direct with National Headquarters.

BRANCH GENERAL MEETINGS

There shall be a general meeting of each branch once a month.

BRANCH EXECUTIVE COMMITTEE

There shall be a branch Executive Committee consisting of the following officers: Chairman, Vice-Chairman, Secretary, Assistant Secretary, Treasurer, Financial Secretary, Propaganda Secretary, 5 Executive Members.

DUTIES OF BRANCH EXECUTIVES

The duties of the Branch Executives shall be:

(i) To carry on propaganda and organizational work among the masses of the people in order to realize the stand point advocated by the Party.

(ii) To pay constant attention to the sentiments and remarks of the masses of the people, and report same to the National Headquarters Secretariat, Accra.

(iii) To pay heed to the political, economic and cultural life of the people and to take the lead to organize the people in the locality in which the branch operates in order to solve their own problems by encouraging the spirit of initiative among the masses.

(iv) To recruit new members, and to collect Party membership dues.

(v) To check and verify the record for Party membership and to report to the National Headquarters Secretariat, Accra, any act of indiscipline and other offences which might bring the Party into dishonor and disrepute.

(vi) To foster the political and general education of Party members and especially Party Cadres.

The Branch Executive Committee has no mandatory powers to expel any member. In cases of indiscipline, the Branch can suspend the members so concerned and report the matter to the General Secretary for action.

PARLIAMENTARY COMMITTEE OF THE PARTY

(i) The Parliamentary Committee of the Party shall consist of

(*a*) all Party members in the Legislative Assembly,

(*b*) members appointed by the National Executive Committee

(ii) The Parliamentary Committee shall be under the direct supervision and control of the Party Leader who will report to the National Executive and the Central Committee of the work, activities and general behavior of all members of the Party in the Assembly.

(iii) The Party Leader shall appoint the Chairman of the Parliamentary Committee. The Parliamentary Committee Chairman shall maintain daily contact with the Party Leader or his deputy.

Quorum. The quorum of every organization of the Party shall consist of one-third of the membership of Party Branch Executive, Constituency Executive, Regional Committee or the National Executive.

PART TWO

INNER PARTY ORGANIZATION

National Secretariat

(i) The Central Administrative machinery of the Party shall be known as The National Secretariat and shall consist of the Deputy Chairman, General Secretary, Assistant General Secretary, National Treasurer, and National Propaganda Secretary. They shall be appointed by the National Executive Committee. The National Executive Committee shall also have power to appoint such other officers as the work of the Party may necessitate.

(ii) The National Secretariat shall be under the direct supervision and control of the Central Committee of the National Executive Committee of the Party.

(iii) The Secretary of the Central Committee shall serve as a liaison between the National Secretariat and the National Executive Committee of the Party. He shall be responsible to report to the plenary meetings of the National Executive Committee on the work and activities of the Central Committee.

(iv) The chief function of the National Secretariat is to transmit decisions of the National Executive Committee and the Central Committee to the Regional Committees, Constituency Executives and the Party branches, and to perform such other duties connected with Party administration. The National Secretariat shall maintain close contact with Branch Secretaries as well as Constituency and Regional Secretaries.

C.P.P. Women's League

Individual women members of the Party shall be organized into women's sections. Women's sections may be organized on a Branch and Ward basis. A General Council of Women's Sections shall be established to co-ordinate the activities of the women in the Party. Leaders appointed by each Women's Branch or Ward shall be responsible for the co-ordination of work amongst women in the Branch or Ward.

There shall be no separate status of women in the Party. A woman who becomes an individual member of the Party becomes thereby a member of the Women's Section of her Branch. Women may join the Party through the Women's Sections.

The Women's Section shall hold rallies, dances, picnics and other social functions throughout the year. A special Ghana Women's Day shall be observed once a year at Easter.

Each Party Branch shall have a Women's Section to cater for the special interests of women, but the Women's Section shall be part and parcel of the Branch. There shall be only one Executive Committee for each Branch, including the Women's Section.

C.P.P. Youth League

The Youth of the country (aged 15 to 30 years) shall be organized into the C.P.P. Youth League. The Central Committee shall appoint a member to serve on the Party Youth League Executive, and each Branch of the Party shall also appoint a member of the Local Branch to serve on the Branch Youth League Executive.

Publications

The Party shall publish its own literature, periodicals, magazines, pamphlets, books, etc., as and when they shall be deemed desirable.

Party Manifesto

The National Executive Committee of the Party shall decide which items from the Party Program shall be included in the Manifesto which shall be issued by the National Executive committee prior to every General or Local Government Election.

Party National Holidays

1 Independence Day	January 8
2 Youth Day	February 21
3 Women's Day	Easter Sunday
4 Anti-Imperialist Day	May 24
5 Party Anniversary	June 12
6 Annual Conference	August Bank Holiday
7 Life Chairman's Birthday	September 18

Appendix B

THE DOCUMENT KNOWN AS "THE CIRCLE"

Name .. .. THE CIRCLE

Motto .. .. THE THREE S's { Service, Sacrifice, Suffering }

Aims .. .. 1. To maintain ourselves and the Circle as the Revolutionary Vanguard of the struggle for West African Unity and National Independence.

2. To support the idea and claims of the All West African National Congress in its struggle to create and maintain a Union of African Socialist Republics.

INTRODUCTION

Since no movement can endure unless there is a stable organization of trained, selected and trusted men to maintain continuity and carry its program forward to successful conclusion.

And since the more widely the masses of the African peoples are drawn into the struggle for freedom and national independence of their country, the more necessary it is to have an organization such as THE CIRCLE to establish stability and thereby making it impossible and difficult for demagogues, quislings, traitors, cowards and self-seekers to lead astray any section of the masses of the African peoples.

And since, in a country like West Africa with foreign, despotic and imperialist governments the more necessary it is to restrict THE CIRCLE to persons who are trained and engaged in political revolution as a profession, and who have also been trained in the art of combating all manner of political intrigues and persecutions thereby making it difficult for any one to disrupt the national liberation movement.

I therefore accept and abide by the laws of THE CIRCLE which are as follows:—

1. I will irrevocably obey and act upon the orders, commands, instructions and directions of the Grand Council of THE CIRCLE.
2. I will always serve, sacrifice and suffer anything for the cause for which THE

CIRCLE stands, and will at all times be ready to go on any mision that I may be called upon to perform.

3. I will always and in all circumstances help a member brother of THE CIRCLE in all things and in all difficulties.
4. I will, except as a last resort, avoid the use of violence.
5. I will make it my aim and duty to foster the cause for which THE CIRCLE stands in any organization that I may become a member.
6. I will on the 21st day of each month fast from sunrise to sunset and will meditate daily on the cause THE CIRCLE stands for.
7. I accept the Leadership of Kwame Nkrumah.

Oath of Allegiance

On my life, honor and fortunes, I solemnely pledge and swear that I shall always live up to the aims and aspirations of THE CIRCLE, and shall never under any circumstances divulge any secrets, plans or movements of THE CIRCLE, nor betray a member brother of the circle; and that if I dare to divulge any secrets, plans and movements of THE CIRCLE, or betray a member brother or the cause, or use the influence of THE CIRCLE for my own personal interests or advertisement, I do so at my own risk and peril.

Duties of Circle Members

Each circle member should join an organization and should adopt two methods of approach:

(*a*) Advocate and work for the demands and needs of that Organization.

(*b*) Infuse that Organization with the spirit of national unity and the national independence of West Africa, and the creation and maintenance of the Union of African Socialist Republics.

Circle Fund

Members of each branch of THE CIRCLE shall maintain a fund by voluntary contributions, such fund to be used for furthering the cause of THE CIRCLE only.

Circle Meetings

The Grand Council of THE CIRCLE shall meet at least once a year and shall decide general policy and give directions to territorial and local branches of THE CIRCLE. Members of each branch of THE CIRCLE shall meet on the 21st day of each month, and at such other times as members may deem advisable.

Circle Communication

A close liaison shall at all times be maintained between the Grand Council and the individual territorial and local branches of THE CIRCLE. As far as possible all communications should be done by personal contact, couriers and messengers. Letters, telegrams, telephones and cables should be used only for making appointments. Discussion of CIRCLE matters in public places is forbidden.

Circle Member Recognition

Ordinary handshake with thumb pressure.

Circle Goal

At such time as may be deemed advisable THE CIRCLE will come out openly as a political party embracing the whole of West Africa, whose policy then shall be to maintain the Union of African Socialist Republics.

Date Due

JUL 18 '61			
AUG 11 '61			
AUG 25 '61			
MAR 2 '62			
MAR 4 1968			
APR 1 1969			
NOV 4 1969			
DEC 3 1970			
APR 13 1971			
APR 29 1971			
FEB 22 1972			
DEC 8 1972			
JUN 8 1973			
JUN 19 1973			